STUDENT NATIONALISM
IN
CHINA
1924-1949

SUNY SERIES IN CHINESE PHILOSOPHY AND CULTURE
DAVID L. HALL AND ROGER T. AMES, EDITORS

STUDENT NATIONALISM IN CHINA, 1924-1949

Lincoln Li

State University of New York Press

Published by
State University of New York Press, Albany

© 1994 State University of New York

For information, address State University of New York
Press, State University Plaza, Albany, N.Y., 12246

Production by E. Moore
Marketing by Bernadette LaManna

Library of Congress Cataloging-in-Publication Data

Li, Lincoln, 1939-
    Student nationalism in China, 1924-1949 / Lincoln Li.
        p. cm. — (SUNY series in Chinese philosophy and culture)
    Includes bibliographical references and index.
    ISBN 0-7914-1749-2 (acid-free). — ISBN 0-7914-1750-6 (pbk. : acid
-free)
    1. Chung-kuo kuo min tang. Lu chün chün kuan hsüeh hsiao-
-Students—Political activity—History. 2. Chung-kuo jen min k' ang
Jih chün cheng ta hsüeh—Students—Political activity—History.
3. Hsi nan lien ho ta hsüeh (K' un-ming shih, China)—Students-
-Political activity—History. 4. Nationalism—China—History.
I. Title. II. Series.
U644.C36L1   1994
322.5—dc20   93–6639
                                                                          CIP

10 9 8 7 6 5 4 3 2 1

To my loving wife Linnei

Contents

Acknowledgments

This book developed from a study on the Resistance University at Yanan conducted at the Hoover Institution a number of years ago. The Curator-scholar of the East Asian collection, Dr. Ramon Myers, was generous with his time and raised many issues that helped to expand the scope to a comparative study on the Whampoa Military Academy and the Resistance University. I am also indebted to Professor Lloyd Eastman of the University of Illinois at Urbana-Champaign for a generous and thorough guide into the literature on the Lixingshe and the Whampoa alumni.

I should like to express my gratitude to Professor Wang Gung-wu for his incisive comments on various versions of the manuscript. I benefited immeasurably from his comments. For offering criticism of certain portions of the manuscript, for helping me to improve the expression of my ideas, for lending me or leading me to important source materials, or for giving me encouragement at critical junctures of my research, I wish to thank Professor Jack Gregory, Professor John D. Legge, Professor Graeme Davison, Professor Lee Ngog, Mr. T.L. Tsim, Professor James Wilson, Dr. John FitzGerald, Dr. Thomas Fisher, Dr. Michael Godley, Professor Lai Jehhang, Dr. Lau Yeecheong, Dr. Alice Ng-lun, Professor Chan Hoklam and, last but not least, Dr. Chan Sinwai.

For financial support I express my gratitude to the Australian Research Grants Committee, the Hoover Institution, Monash University, and the Chinese University of Hong Kong for their generosity and patience.

I offer my special thanks to the staff of the East Asian collection of the Hoover Institution, the Asian collection of the Menzies Library in Canberra, the Oriental section of the National Library of Australia, the Nanjing University Library, the Number Two Historical Archives at Nanjing, and the Inter-Library Loan Service of Monash University for their continuous support.

I owe much to my wife Linnei, who shared with me the anxiety, hardship, and joy of this intellectual venture in the midst of her own active career. In the final stages she even did a thorough editing in cleansing the manuscript of many a simple error which the writer himself had become blind to. My daughters Joyce and Rosanna I thank for the joyous moments they bring to sustain me during difficult times.

1 Culture and Politics

Before this disintegrative process was set in full motion, it seems reasonable to understand China as a system in which the state, society, and the arts were viewed as inseparable parts of a whole . . . the state and its attendant bureaucracy were expected to be not only sources of ultimate temporal authority but also the perpetuator of ethical and aesthetic norms. . . .[1]

Nationalism is not one universal system of thought. It is a complex system of values embedded in community self-perception evolved over time. Ben Anderson describes nations as "imagined communities."[2] When national communities experience rapid changes, national imaginations are transformed. Yet in their new national imaginations, the force of tradition, of inherited culture, remains tangible. We should bear this in mind when discussing Chinese nationalism.

In the 1910s the New Culture and May 4th movements articulated two tactical concerns in China—namely, cultural and political. Leaders of the New Culture Movement stressed the unity of culture and society, articulating the view that cultural renaissance was the a priori to political rebirth.[3] Their students, activists of the May 4th movement, did not reject the importance of culture, but changed the emphasis from cultural renaissance to political action.

The disintegrative process created a deepening sense of unease and uncertainty within the national community, an uncertainty created by the absence of a polity that traditionally defined overall ethical and aesthetic norms. How deep down did this sense of unease go, this feeling of the loss of a national identity? Western scholars of China present varying perceptions. In *Region and Nation*,[4] Dianne Lary explains the warlord phenomenon as one visible limit when the nation is broken into its regional parts. In *China Turned Rightside Up*[5]

Ralph Thaxton perceives that disintegration had reached the village level, arguing that the emergence of communist power in the country-side could be equated with the rebuilding of a moral order at the village level by a new political force that redefined communal norms. Is this not suggesting that social revolution in the Chinese village followed some recognizable, traditional patterns?

Some Chinese intellectuals, observes Schneider, were more optimistic in consciously distinguishing between the realms of politics and culture, refusing to accept that there was a parallel between the fragmentation of state and the fragmentation of culture. This optimism led them to the defense of "national essence," a notional term expressing the belief that Chinese culture transcended the life span of any one political structure.[6] In their view Chinese identity was essentially cultural. Leaders of the New Culture Movement shared the view that culture was the foundation of society. They argued for a cultural rebirth, a renaissance, to precede the birth of a new political structure.[7] To them there could be no new nation without a new culture.

Among fellow culturalists the terms of debate between conservatives and radicals were those of classical revival or of intellectual enlightenment, yet both saw the West as a source of intellectual inspiration. In spite of their professed preoccupation with cultural issues, these protagonists shared a common objective of revitalizing political China through cultural action. Cultural activism was decidedly a means to an end, a means to reestablish the traditionally pivotal role of intellectuals in defining ethical norms for state and society.

Cultural rebirth, in retrospect, was inseparable from the process of political reintegration. The liberal intellectuals of the New Culture Movement did not plan to introduce a party state, yet both the Chinese Communist Party (CCP) and the reorganized Guomindang (GMD) claimed inspirations from the New Culture and May 4th Movements. The political and cultural disintegration of traditional China, under the two-pronged attack of internal malaise and external encroachment, brought fragmentation to the intellectual scene. This intellectual crisis, however, generated a vibrant intellectual environment for debate and liberal thinking. Intellectual revitalization proceeded within the pervading atmosphere of a Chinese response. The new liberal environment became a means toward an end. Liberalism acquired a utilitarian purpose in the decade of the 1911 revolution; liberalism became a political strategy.

Liberal tendencies of the New Culture Movement were noticeably eclectic, as intellectuals experimented with new ideas. Advocates of cultural revolution, while championing the demise of old society, were dedicated to the creation of an alternative cultural political tradition. Their revolution was true to traditional form. The liberal intellectual approaches of the 1910s and the authoritarian ways of the GMD and the CCP were different facets of this selfsame process towards national reintegration. The liberal campuses in Beijing, the military academy at Whampoa[8], and the Resistance University at Yanan (Kangda) were engaged in the common enterprise of training a new national elite. These elite groups each claimed ultimate authority to redefine community norms.

This study on the political life of the Whampoa Military Academy, the Resistance University, and the Associated University of the Southwest (Lianda)[9] hopes to draw some of the disparate threads together to appreciate how such elitist groups competed in the process of rebuilding a system in which, as Schneider so aptly puts it, "the state and its attendant bureaucracy were expected to be not only sources of ultimate temporal authority but also the perpetuator of ethical and aesthetic norms."[10] Culture and politics were inseparable in the traditional order. Is this not also true of the alternatives on offer?

Education, as the means of perpetuating cultural norms, was primarily political; scholars were instructed in the virtues of public life.[11] Is this not true of the training of cadets at Whampoa and of cadres at Yanan? Dedication to active propagation of the virtues of public life was rewarded with the prospect, though not the certainty, of bureaucratic careers and political power. This tactic became a cornerstone of socio-political stability, but it also narrowed Chinese intellectual visions, and relegated intellectual and professional endeavors, other than those concerned with state and society, to secondary importance. Was liberal education at the Associated University providing an alternative?

By the late nineteenth century European expansion aroused a rude awakening among members of the ruling elite. They began to see that existing structures and contents of education, of officially defined culture, had become critical sources of Chinese weakness. Their own vested interest in the system led them to confine their advocacy of reform to the concept of "Chinese knowledge as foundation, Western knowledge for use." They were still hesitant to admit that Chinese values were not universal and could no longer be asserted as such without doing serious damage to China.

While different slogans were offered,[12] this restrictive formula of cultural defense transcended political differences. The self-strengtheners and the constitutional reformers of the nineteenth century, the nationalists, the communists, and the liberal intellectuals of the twentieth century, all shared in this traditional commitment of making political preoccupation a prime objective for education. Each faithfully continued the traditional strategy of rewarding the loyal with prospects of official positions and political power. The establishment of the University of Beijing in 1898, of the Whampoa Military Academy in 1925, and of the Resistance University in 1936 were representative of this mainstream continuity in the maintenance of a political elite core, by training a new elite to fill the void left by the departure of the Confucian elite. Each in turn created a relatively exclusive socio-political leadership group. The Whampoa Military Academy, the Resistance University, and the universities of Beijing and Tianjin became centers of organized political activity through which student nationalism could gain expression as an organized political force.

Student Nationalism

The qualities of nationalism, if they were to be given some concrete description, need to be associated with specific time and place. During the 1924 to 1949 period, the rise of the GMD and of the CCP were related to their success in capturing the national mood and in organizing a new elite core. This short study on student nationalism and student work in China aims to highlight the process and the setting within which the GMD and the CCP captured the political mood of young students and organized them into tangible political forces in the guise of commissioned officers and political cadres. This organizational effort was described as student work.

China is large and a comprehensive treatment of the subject of student nationalism would be unwieldy, even if possible. By selecting the Whampoa Military Academy, the Resistance University, and the Associated University, this book aims to illustrate, with the student work of the GMD and of the CCP, how the two parties attempted to turn explosive and ephemeral national feelings into an organized political force between 1924 and 1949. Two of the campuses are selected to contrast the different styles of the two parties. The third is selected to show how a liberal campus community responded to the efforts of the two parties to influence and control it.

The 1924 to 1949 period saw the rise and fall of GMD power. During this period of study the GMD occupied the center stage of Chinese politics, hence fuller treatment is given to Whampoa. An analysis of CCP practices at Yanan is included to highlight competition and to sketch an alternative and parallel approach in student work. The practices of both parties exhibited serious shortcomings, but they did succeed in capturing the energies of student nationalism momentarily, and this success was vital to the fortunes of both political parties.

Within the compound term of student nationalism, what does student stand for? Strictly speaking it identifies those actively pursuing a formal education in a school, a university, or some such formal institution. Yet such a strict definition would inhibit our understanding of student nationalism as it developed within the broader social and political context of twentieth-century China. The young men and women politicized while they were students often gave up their formal education to begin an active political life. Is their political activism beyond the confines of formal education no longer appropriately identified as student nationalism? Is there a clear demarcation line between being a student nationalist and a graduate nationalist?

Such a distinction should exist, but how is that distinction to be made? Is the distinction a question of different age groups? Should student be treated as synonymous with youth? A quantifiable approach is appropriate, as student life does come to an end eventually. According to figures cited by John Israel, in 1932 some 69 percent of Chinese college students were in the 21–25 age bracket.[13] But this quantitative approach needs to be qualified. Should the political activism originating from a student group be regarded as having outgrown student nationalism once its practitioners were neither students nor youths? This is not a hypothetical problem, for we are faced with the reality of distinctly identifiable high points in the development of student nationalism as the "student tides" of May 4th, May 30th, December 9th, and June 4th come readily to mind. Those who left school for political action graduated from being student nationalist, but the distinguishing qualities of each "student tide" represented qualities of a specific phase of nationalism that would continue to influence those who left school. Leaders politicized by nationalism in student days may be more aware of the potential energies of student nationalism, and hence ready to organize that energy for effective political expression. Those who lead need not be students themselves, but they need to understand how nationalism motivates students.

One device adopted in this study is to identify student nationalism with specific institutions: the Whampoa Military Academy, the Resistance University, and the Southwestern Associated University. In the case of Whampoa the "student" label is extended to include its alumni as they became the focus of a nationalist pressure group in the 1930s.

Apart from selecting representative institutions, it is also important to identify the qualitative features of specific "student tides" to trace the changing qualities of student nationalism from one phase to another, from one "generation" to the next. Although the influence of student nationalism may spill over some status and age limits, it cannot transcend the larger social political reality within which student nationalism was born. It is therefore possible to identify student nationalism of the May 4th, of the May 30th, and of the December 9th phases.

It is possible to identify a point of initiation for student nationalists. But once initiated, can the influence of student nationalism be confined by age and status? Some young leaders who grew old, Mao Zedong and Jiang Jieshi, were initiators, and continued to be leaders, of new "generations" of student nationalism as each attempted to transform the nationalist feelings of students into an organized force. So student nationalism may be defined as the nationalist feelings of students and the institutions established to turn those nationalist feelings into a tangible political force.

Student nationalism may be interpreted as a distinctive aspect of nationalism in China. It is expressive of the continuing tradition that the political elite is a politically educated elite. Student nationalism expresses a "youth" phenomenon within this elite social stratum. This is a phenomenon often observable in societies undergoing deepening crisis. As the older generation fails to solve crisis situations, the impatience of the young to try their hands at the helms of power gathers momentum.

Student nationalism in China also reflects the lingering tradition of scholar-gentry rule. Chinese student nationalism, in spite of its radical image, represents a prominent feature of continuity in Chinese socio-political culture. Direct action by student groups reasserts the claim of the politically educated that they are the real political elite.

Student nationalism is a by-product of political instability. Crises constantly put pressure upon those in authority to consolidate their support base by appealing to the younger generation, even to the point of sharing power. Their failure to solve crisis situations aggravated the scene, as the younger generation took direct action to claim power. Twentieth-century China was continually in crisis and the young were prominent in active political involvement. The scholar gentry of traditional China was now substituted by students in modern attire parading in the streets and shouting slogans. This early entry into politics by student activists was lasting. Student nationalists did not fade from the political scene once they were no longer students. They remained highly aware of the student body as the source from which leadership material was drawn, and that it was essential for a growing political movement to maintain its momentum by retaining appeal among the young educated. Student nationalism encompassed a scene much broader than just campus and youth, though its nurturing ground was campus and youth. Its qualitative features also changed over time, and discussants need to be aware of the specific qualities of each particular "generation."

One consistent feature of student nationalists was the aim to become a *ganbu* or active functionary, more often translated as party functionary. For Sun Yatsen and Mao Zedong, the *ganbu* was ideally a professional revolutionary, one who was politically educated and who dedicated his/her life totally to a political cause. As Confucian scholars aspired to gain entry into officialdom, so modern students aspired to become active political agents, to act or *gan* in serving the national and revolutionary causes. What the activists, the *ganbu*, wish to act on was very much conditioned by the qualitative features of the particular "generation" of student nationalism into which they had been initiated. The Whampoa Military Academy and the Resistance University promoted different kinds of political strategy, their graduates were trained and organized to implement very different socio-political programs. In this way the energies of student nationalism were being harnessed to serve the interests of a party that defined socio-political norms. One of the objectives of this study is to compare and contrast the styles of the GMD and the CCP in this student work.

Why focus upon competing efforts at re-creating a political elite core? Why put stress upon the strength of tradition, of continuity, when the dominant note of China in the nineteenth and twentieth centuries is that of revolution, of discontinuity? The strength of tradition places limitations upon the pace and quality of change. Revolution is still an ongoing process, yet it is by looking at "the limits of change"[14] that qualitative features of contemporary China may become more readily understood. Change and continuity are interrelated, and student nationalism, with its varying qualities over time, reflects the nature of socio-political transformation. Student nationalism is part of nationalism in general, the part that is representative of nationalist feelings of the young, politically educated, elite.

For a society as deeply rooted in cultural pretensions as China, the principal area of the interplay of tradition and change was among the cultural elite. And in times of continuing crisis the burden of responsibility fell increasingly upon the shoulders of the upcoming generation. Student nationalism was an expression of this "youth phenomenon" within the political elite; it does not mean that only students were nationalists. The political debate was conditioned by the assumption that China was a cultural entity, that Chinese culture was more fundamental to the survival of a Chinese political identity than the trappings of traditional political forms. Conservatives and radicals alike saw cultural revival as fundamental to the rebirth of China. Conservatives looked for a classical revival, sought to defend the national essence, and accommodated change through identifying similarities in classical European and Chinese values.[15] Radicals in the new culture movement sought total rejection of the past, attempted their mode of East-West synthesis through adoption of contemporary Western values of "science and democracy" and of indigenous popular cultures. Such diametrically opposed views permeated a wide spectrum, for eclecticism became the order of the day for both radical and conservative persuasions. The 1898 reformers, for example, restated what they thought were the true values of Confucianism to justify constitutional reforms; advocates of national essence were active in promoting popular anti-Manchu feelings; and revolutionaries, who brought the dynastic order down, embraced a leadership that held a cross section of such divergent views.

While the course of cultural revitalization remained uncertain, the emergence of a new political structure stood in clear contrast. The reunification of China in 1927 and 1949 were severe shocks to the outside world, causing the Japanese to define their "lifeline" and the Americans to bemoan "the loss of China." Such expressions merely gave recognition to the resurgence of Chinese political vitality, to the rebirth of political China. The pivot of this newfound vitality, the nucleus of the rebirth of China as a political force, was its young educated elite. The younger generation of the 1920s was influenced by the cultural and ideological debates around them, they were actively immersed in the tradition of a political environment in which such debates were deemed to be central. Yet it was the pressure of deepening crisis and the impatience of the young for immediate action that set the political tone of the 1920s. In sharp contrast to the cultural debates of the 1910s, student nationalists of the 1920s were action oriented. It was not their mouthing of anti-imperialist slogans that set the scene for the decade, it was rather their activism on the streets of Shanghai, in the military campaigns of the "student army" from Whampoa, and in the organization of strike action in Hong Kong. Such actions attested the newfound political vitality of China.

While one can broadly discuss the educated elite as a distinct interest group, in political action they needed institutional bases from which to exercise their potential and influence on the national stage. With the demise of the dynastic order, the influence of the elite devolved from the bureaucracy to the surviving educational institutions: Beijing University, Qinghua University, Nankai University, and so on. These institutions, through activist groups advocating conservative and radical solutions, sought to revitalize Chinese culture and polity. These institutions provided the base from which the oncoming "student nationalists" were to appear center stage with the full status of faculty. Students such as Chen Duxiu and Lu Xun, who terminated their studies in Japan for patriotic reasons, soon became prominent professors and spearheaded the New Culture Movement. Just as they were demolishing traditional cultural values, they were sharing the belief of their protagonists that cultural revival was more fundamental than the survival of moribund political forms.

Traditionally academic institutions assisted the state in perpetuating political authority as well as ethical and aesthetic norms. The reintegration of political China and the reintegration of the Chinese cultural world, however, are of immense difference in magnitude. The May 4th "generation" took on the task of cultural revival, a task too grand for their energies to attain amid deepening crisis. Their lack of immediate success left the task of political action in the hands of the May 30th "generation," where radical talk continued, but it was political *action* that brought the fruits of reunification. The Whampoa Military Academy embodied the new trend of action-oriented student nationalism and initiated the process of political reunification through the northern expedition. Turning the gun against their communist allies at Shanghai further attested to the ascendancy of an action-oriented mood over ideological scruples. If gunning down an ally was thought to be essential to national revival, then it was to be done quickly, efficiently, and with the minimum of fuss. The December 9th Movement in Beijing continued this action-oriented trend into the 1930s. When the GMD government failed to make a credible response to Japanese incursions in north China, many students promptly trekked to Yanan to join the opposition. They trekked to Yanan not because of the attractions of communism, but in the hope of capturing the CCP for the anti-Japanese cause.

While both the nationalists and the communists succeeded in reuniting China with help from the educated young, the process of cultural revitalization championed by the May 4h "generation" remained incomplete. The New Life Movement and the Great Proletarian Cultural Revolution, among other efforts, were notable failures. Political and ideological intolerance, which were used to reinforce political authority, had to tolerate cultural eclecticism if a cultural rebirth was to be delivered. Both Jiang and Mao practiced eclectic choice on their road to power, with varying degrees of success. The May 4th use of intellectual freedom as a means to revitalize China was tolerated in areas where the state, whether communist or nationalist, accepted liberalism as essential for modernization, though such residual intellectual freedom was carefully reined in by the threat of force and a nurturing of self-motivated conformity through education. The rectification process instituted by Mao in the early 1940s reinstated ideological control with hardly a whisper of dissent. Intellectual liberalism was a tool rather than an end in itself, and hence dispensable.

This work is focused on the Whampoa Military Academy, its graduates, and the political movements they associated with. The Resistance University and the Associated University of the Southwest are drawn in as active participants on the political stage, as representative of parallel and contrasting strands, paralleling and interacting with the mainstream influence of the Whampoa group between 1924 and 1949. They were participants on the same political stage and during the same historical span. Each of their seemingly different stories was part of a larger canvas interrelated one to the other. Insofar as each was concerned with reviving a strong political system and in so far as it was principally the Whampoa group that dominated the stage in the period under study, it is only fitting to put Whampoa center stage.

The Framework

In a sketch of student nationalism, the selection of samples becomes critical. The action-oriented trend of the 1920s is best appreciated by narrating the experiences of the Whampoa Military Academy, of how it was formed and how it captured the mood of the May 30th period. Chapter 2 traces how the academy was planned, and how the conscious effort of the GMD to emphasize ideological instruction failed. Chapter 3 traces the early beginning and how the cadet force galvanized under the leadership of Jiang Jieshi and how this newly organized force came to champion and symbolize the May 30th Movement. Having established the point that it was action that distinguished the Whampoa force, the story of how the National Revolutionary Army (NRA) delivered the substance of national power to the GMD in the northern expedition is not pursued, for it has been treated ably elsewhere.[16] Chapter 4 is a brief background chapter on how the Whampoa model, that of militarizing student nationalists, was introduced onto the campuses at Beijing. The adoption of the militarizing approach by Qinghua University in particular is used to indicate the initial momentum of the Whampoa experience among the educated in general, even in areas as yet beyond the reach of GMD military power. The momentum of militarizing the young as a means of expanding GMD influence was halted by Japanese military actions in Manchuria and north China.

Chapters 5 and 6 on the young officers movement return the focus to the Whampoa alumni, to how they believed that they could provide the leadership, the organization, and the appropriate actions to stop the Japanese and to consolidate national unification. The young officers took the initiative into their own hands in establishing an underground political network without gaining prior support from either the GMD or their teacher and patron Jiang Jieshi. Their boldness for action without prior support from Jiang was a partial cause for his maneuverings to create and nurture factional rivalry within the young officers movement. The activities of the young officers movement sustained the credibility of GMD leadership in resisting Japanese pressure, consolidated support from the regional military, and suppressed internal military-political challenges. The young officers movement did have a notable failure: it failed to spread GMD power and influence to north China in the face of Japanese pressure. The Whampoa political organization could not resolve the crisis in north China.

During the Xian incident the Whampoa political organization marshaled troops to lay seige to Xian without heeding the cautions of the GMD government. When Jiang returned to Nanjing, he was determined to weaken the structural framework of the young officers movement because that organization chose to put loyalty to the nation above loyalty to the generalissimo. The Lixingshe and the Fuxingshe were dissolved, thus depriving the young officers' movement of its central coordinating body and front organization. These actions weakened the organizational effectiveness of the Whampoa alumni grouping and split the young officers movement into a number of factional interests clustered around the GMD youth corps, the secret service headed by Dai Li, and a number of military commands. The momentum to consolidate Whampoa influence as the foundation of GMD national power was halted.

In north China Japanese pressure also induced a new surge of nationalist energies among the educated young. A significant number of them trekked to Yanan in the hope of capturing the opponents of the GMD for the anti-Japanese cause. It is at this stage that this study briefly detours from a strict chronological flow, and Chapter 7 discusses how the GMD retained some campus support in north China nonetheless. This latent support reemerged with the outbreak of the Sino-Japanese war. Promptly campuses moved personnel and equipment southward to join the GMD-led resistance. The GMD, however, remained guarded about these once critical campuses and politely evacuated them to distant Kunming where distance would keep them safe from the Japanese and render them relatively ineffective in passing comments on the Chongqing government. In spite of this structured distance, the refugee campus at Kunming remained loyal supporters of the GMD government throughout the war years.

Chapter 8 resumes the chronological flow to discuss how the CCP coped with the influx of patriotic students into Yanan. The experiences at Yanan were remarkably similar to those of the early days at Whampoa. In spite of ideological reservations, the CCP did what it could to harness these new supporters. The Resistance University and the public school of northern Shaanxi province were the principal agents through which the CCP hastily turned its newfound supporters into an army of cadres. The CCP turned the flow of students to Yanan into an annual cadre production line of about eighteen thousand, and this force breathed a new political vitality into the decimated leadership ranks of the CCP. In contrast those who trekked south to join the GMD were placed at distant Kunming where, in the eight long years of the war, only twenty-five hundred graduates were produced out of an annual enrollment of three thousand. The attrition rate of close to 90 percent at Kunming, when contrasted with the massive flow of cadres from Yanan, told a telling tale about lost political opportunities for the GMD.

Chapter 9 is a cautionary discussion, cautioning against the assumption that the influx of students into Yanan could easily have transformed the Chinese communists into a de facto nationalist party. Mao devised the rectification campaign to institutionalize party ideological authority over the educated, legitimized by the very need for discipline and organization in the resistance war. Potentials for critical comments against the party was transformed by the political rituals of the rectification process into positive praise for the party. This partly explains why students and intellectuals in communist-held areas did not criticize or protest against communist policies.

Chapter 10 brings the narrative to a chronological conclusion. The campus community at Kunming was subjected to unnecessary high-handed action from GMD military commanders, former Whampoa cadets, because they suspected potential criticism from the campus community. Intimidation in the form of violence and assasinations turned the one-time loyal GMD supporters into sullen dissenters. If the campus community was not an enemy, it was no longer an enthusiatic friend. When the campus community was repatriated back to Beijing, distant from GMD power bases in central China, the suppressed anger of the campus community only waited for the occasion to give open expression.

2   Preparations

What is the lesson we have learned from the Russian Revolution?
It is that their Party vanguards created a revolutionary army to
support them, enabling them to make a success of their revolu-
tionary work in a short time.

—Sun Yatsen[1]

When the Whampoa Military Academy was established, the events of May 4th 1919, were some six years removed. There was no apparent connection between May 4th and Whampoa, while the next surge of national feelings on May 30th was yet to come. The Academy aimed to facilitate the building of a politically reliable army for the GMD, to provide a professional officers corps, which was appropriately indoctrinated. The institution was not designed to attract campus support or specifically to organize student nationalism into a political force. It was coincidental that Whampoa became a magnet for the nationalist emotions of the young educated.

In the 1910s anti-Japanese feelings created opportunities that Sun and the GMD were not well placed to benefit. The New Culture Movement focused attention upon campus communities and educational reforms rather than functioning as an organized political group.[2] Indeed the known connections between the GMD and its Japanese well wishers of right-wing persuasions, developed since the founding of the Revolutionary Alliance in Tokyo, made the GMD less attractive. When ousted from Canton in August 1918, Sun sought refuge in Shanghai rather than Japan, partly to distance himself and the GMD from taints of Japanese affiliations and partly to keep a closer pulse of events in China.[3]

Plagued by repeated failures to consolidate a territorial base and tossed in and out of Canton by the shifting support of regional militarists, Sun cast his eyes for new sources of support and was very much impressed by the October revolution of 1917.[4] The Karakhan manifesto of July 1919, renouncing Russian treaty privileges in China,[5] generated a new wave of popular goodwill for Russia and raised hopes of Soviet support in radical circles. For the GMD, hopes for Russian assistance began to shape when Comintern agent Maring came to see Sun in 1921. Together they mapped out some broad tactical approaches in developing political strength for the GMD.[6] The Soviet revolutionary model became an active source of inspiration for action and reform. Among these were a thorough reorganization of the GMD Party structure to tighten the lines of command and internal cohesion, as well as the establishment of a military academy to train a loyal officers corps to prepare for the founding of a party army.[7] Whampoa was not intended as a focus of student nationalism.

The military academy was modeled on recent Russian experiences in training a large number of officers through short-term courses. Through a system of command schools founded in February 1918, a total of 39,914 commanders graduated from three- to four-month intensive training courses between 1918 and 1920.[8] The Whampoa Military Academy was a vehicle through which Russians helped train a large number of officers in the shortest possible time. There was no articulated connections with student nationalism in the enterprise.

In August 1923 Sun Yatsen sent young officer Jiang Jieshi to observe red army organization and training facilities firsthand. Jiang learned that political control over the red army rested on the commissar or party representative at the regimental level. The commissar was consulted on all major decisions and military orders were subjected to his validation. In this way the red army was put under effective party control.[9] The Russian model provided a clear distinction between political commissars and commissioned military officers. On his return journey, Jiang also met the famous Russian commander Vasily K. Bluecher at Vladivostok. Bluecher, who used his nom de guerre Galen, later became the chief Russian military advisor to the GMD.[10] The personal rapport between Jiang and Bluecher was vital to the success of training programs at Whampoa.

While cultivating good personal relationships with the Russians, the private diary entries of Jiang at the time showed strong suspicion of Russian and Comintern motives. Jiang was uncertain of the reliability of Russia as an ally.[11] This was not surprising, since Sun made a point of indicating publicly that communism was not suited to Chinese conditions when releasing the Sun-Joffe joint declaration of 1923.[12] Both Chinese leaders expressed reservations about the Russian model.

Whatever private thoughts Sun and Jiang might have shared regarding Soviet intentions, Sun was emphatically pro-Russian in public. Addressing GMD members in March 1924, Sun praised the Russian model in no uncertain terms:

> Our revolution predates the Russian revolution, yet within a short space of six years the Russians have toppled their deep-rooted ruling class, triumphed over the evils of surrounding imperialists, and even extended a helping hand to the oppressed peoples of the world. In the thirteen years since the 1911 revolution, our party stands helpless against the misrule of warlord and bureaucratic cliques, and the increasing pressures from imperialism and capitalism. When we observe the Russian scene, we are amazed with our lack of success. The Russian model is a worthy example, and we should try to have Russia as a friend.[13]

This conscious effort to model upon Russian experience indicated that Sun was thinking of a Russian-style commissar, not a Chinese legacy of scholar-politicians. This emphasis on a Russian model ran parallel to reservations entertained by Jiang Jieshi.

Privately Jiang Jieshi was guarded about Russian intentions, yet such thoughts remained private because his political future at the time was beholden to the patronage of a vocally pro-Russian Sun Yat-sen. In 1924 the political futures of both leaders rested upon securing Russian aid for the GMD. First as chairman of the preparatory committee and later as the commandant of Whampoa, Jiang was himself an active agent in consolidating a working relationship with the Russians in Canton. Irrespective of suspicion about Russian motives, Soviet Russia was then a much needed ally.

At the beginning of 1924 Jiang was relatively junior in the party, certainly not senior enough to participate in policy-making. Nonetheless, confident that he was an indispensable professional soldier enjoying the personal trust of Sun, Jiang responded to Sun's appeal for service with deliberate reluctance. It was not until Jiang had received three telegrams from Liao Zhongkai, offering him chairmanship of the preparatory committee, that he finally indicated acceptance.[14] He took up the position at Canton in January 1924 and found that none of the eight committee members were prominent in the party.[15] Conspicuous by their absence from the preparatory committee were party luminaries Sun Yatsen, Liao Zhongkai, Hu Hanmin, and Wang Jingwei. The preparatory committee was merely an executive secretariat looking after details such as drafting regulations, repairing neglected premises on Whampoa Island, formalizing staff appointments, conducting entrance examinations, and other day-to-day administrative duties.[16] Even within the preparatory committee, Jiang protested against too much Russian influence over curriculum and administration.[17] Unwilling to accept a minor role and wary of Russian domination, Jiang tendered his resignation on February 21 and left for Shanghai on February 27.[18] He even instructed the few members of staff he had recruited to collect severance pay and leave entitlements.[19] In a letter to Liao Zhongkai dated March 12, Jiang indicated his strong suspicion of Russian motives, demanding a larger say than the Russian advisors if he were to return to Canton.[20]

Ironically the resignation elevated the political standing of the preparatory committee when Liao Zhongkai acted as chairman,[21] a senior party leader now led the academy staff. Liao, however, needed the professional military know-how of Jiang, and, after repeated urgings, Jiang rejoined the committee on April 26.[22] This early tussle between the party leadership and Jiang set the precedent and the projected party army was unlikely to be merely an obedient instrument of the party.

In May 1924 the preparatory committee of eight was replaced by a select committee of three, consisting of Sun Yatsen, Liao Zhongkai, and Jiang Jieshi.[23] All were ex officio members: Sun as the chief executive of the party, Liao as party representative at the academy, and Jiang as commandant. This gave Jiang formal access to the two leading party figures on matters affecting the army party. The status and influence of Jiang was assured, and the professional soldier Jiang established a claim to participate in policy matters affecting the academy.

Jiang added tension to the working relationship between party and military academy. One specific area of tension was over admittance procedure and policy. Two basic principles were adopted by the preparatory committee—namely, that of equitable regional distribution and a demonstrable commitment to the political programs of the GMD. A tentative enrollment target of 324 was decided as the initial intake, made up of a provincial quota of between twelve to fifteen places, and fifty places for the region of Manchuria.[24] Initially the party attempted to administer admission directly. In January 1924 the first national GMD congress, then in session in Canton, entrusted cadet recruitment to provincial delegates.[25]

The effectiveness of the various provincial delegates varied. Most were operating in areas outside GMD control and the many

provincial military regimes were predictably hostile to the recruitment of cadets intended for an army that would eventually be
deployed against them.[26] Some of the provincial delegates administering admission were communists.[27] But most of these recruiting agents
could fill only a third of the quota assigned to them, while only one
candidate was nominated from Manchuria.[28] This initial procedure of
direct party nomination did not work well. Its failure reflected a lack
of national appeal on the part of the GMD as late as 1924. Party control over the academy was weakening early.

The demand for places at Whampoa, however, was not lacking.
The prospect of a new military establishment controlled by and loyal
to the GMD touched the raw nerves of various military interest
groups then professing varying degrees of support for the GMD at
Canton. Hoping to introduce their influence into the future party
army, these friendly units conducted their own preliminary selection
tests and nominated candidates for admittance.[29] In response to such
overt pressures, the Academy issued a public statement on April 7,
1924, denouncing such nominations.[30] Control over admission was
essential if the academy was to be protected from infiltration by vested interests friendly or otherwise to the GMD. The public statement
of April 7 may be regarded as the effective date on which the academy reclaimed authority over admission. Wresting control over admission from the GMD party structure also increased the autonomy of
the military academy. One early confirmation of this autonomy was
that the academy would not accept candidates nominated by party
delegates without subjecting them to a final screening test, adminis-
tered at Shanghai and Canton.[31]

Although the establishment of the Whampoa Military Academy
was intriguing, in 1924 neither the GMD nor its military academy
enjoyed much national attention. Their political promises still
belonged to the future. Richard B. Landis observed that although the
concept of short-term training courses at Whampoa was based on that
of the command schools started in Russia in February 1918, the Russians dispersed their training to 151 command schools, while the
GMD concentrated its parallel efforts within one single military
academy[32]. In 1924 the GMD simply did not have the broad social
support and wide territorial control that the Bolsheviks enjoyed in
Russia in 1918. Dispersing its cadet recruitment program to GMD
national congress delegates proved inadequate. Dispersing training
for a politically reliable officers corp to the units of politically unreli-
able military allies was certainly out of the question. Concentrating

cadet training in one organization made it doubly difficult for the party to exercise effective control over its military wing.

The assertiveness of the commandant established Jiang as the effective leader of the teaching faculty. Assisting Jiang was a Russian advisory group of twenty-four, led by General Galen.[33] The Chinese faculty included graduates of the Japanese Military Academy, the Baoding Military Academy, and the Yunnan Military Academy.[34] Jiang, assisted by Galen, headed what was principally a faculty of professional soldiers. The team was dedicated to the training of a large number of junior officers in as short a time as possible.

In spite of the stated importance of political training, the GMD party representative, Liao Zhongkai, was not able to devote the time and effort himself after delivering a few lectures.[35] Headship of the Political Department soon fell into the hands of a communist leader, Zhou Enlai.[36] The GMD failed to institute effective political control over the academy from the start. The transplant of the Russian model, that of a party-controlled army, did not materialize.

Cadets were selected by open competitive examinations, though candidates could be recommended by party members. About twelve hundred candidates sat for the first entrance examinations. Three hundred fifty were admitted into the first class in April 1924, and this was boosted to about five hundred by approving twenty special admissions for sons of party martyrs and selecting another hundred from examined candidates.[37] At this stage the cadets were student nationalists only in the general sense that they were students individually opting to support the GMD. That anti-imperialism formed a prominent part of the GMD party platform. The military academy was providing organization, but the cadet force was yet to be identifiable with a particular upsurge of nationalist feelings. Considering the size of the Chinese population, the numbers attracted to Whampoa were very modest.

The Communist Factor

Although established to train politically loyal officers for the GMD, the known presence of communists within both faculty and student body created instant tension. The CCP was both a partner in revolution and a competitor for power. The price exacted by Sun Yatsen in granting a working relationship was that communists would be admitted into the GMD as GMD members, but at the same time they would be permitted to retain their CCP membership. In this arrangement those who worked within the GMD were expected to declare their communist affiliation. This was, however, often honored in the breach. For example, the Canton party branch of the CCP decided to send three to four members to sit for the entrance examination for Whampoa without declaring their communist affiliation.[38] This was infiltration pure and simple, thus further weakening prospects of effective political control by the GMD party structure.

According to Guo Yiyu, he was instructed by the Hunanese communist leader He Shuheng to apply for entry into the military academy and his affiliation with the CCP was deliberately concealed.[39] Prior to sitting the screening test, Mao Zedong, as one of the examiners, forewarned Communist infiltrators to prepare well for the examination, otherwise Mao could not ensure their success.[40]

Infiltration was extensive, though Guo Yiyu could identify only four other communists in the unit he was assigned to.[41] Recalling his experiences at Whampoa, Zhou Enlai estimated that between fifty to sixty cadets of the first class were members of the CCP.[42] That is to say, over 10 percent of the first class were communist infiltrators. In addition other communists, such as Zhou Enlai and Ye Jianying, had declared their party affiliation and were holding faculty positions.[43] The CCP maintained a secret party branch at Whampoa to coordinate its underground operations within the academy.[44]

Chinese communist activities were directly undermining the efforts of the academy to train an officers corp with unquestioning loyalty to the GMD. Jiang was in the unenviable position of working openly with communists such as Zhou Enlai and Ye Jianying, and being alert to their secret activities at the same time. This led Jiang to develop intelligence networks within the academy so as to keep communist activities under surveillance, first under Deng Wenyi and later under Dai Li.[45] In the open known communists were closely watched by those Jiang trusted. Zhou Enlai recalled how his activities were continually under the watchful eyes of He Yingqin and Wang Boling.[46] The commandant was developing autonomous political surveyance networks within the academy, further weakending GMD party control.

In spite of such watchfulness by Jiang, the Chinese communists were able to cultivate considerable influence. In February 1925 the communists established the Young Soldiers' Association in Whampoa as a front organization to develop Marxist sympathies among the cadet populace. This prompted the formation of the Sun Wenism Study Society by Dai Jitao to develop support for the political principles of the GMD.[47]

The two front organizations, with their competing claims for ideological commitment, were threatening to split the cadet populace openly. Jiang tried to prevent this with an executive decision, ordering the two front organizations to disband to minimize open factional divisions.[48] Executive action, rather than ideological resolutions, became the principal instrument in enforcing unity and discipline over a cadet force, which was fundamentally split over competing political loyalties. Ideological unity was not an attainable design of training at the Whampoa Military Academy from the outset. The Russian model was thus effectively modified in practice, enhancing military rather than political command. Within this command structure, political loyalties were split. At Whampoa the experiment to produce officers exclusively loyal to the party had limited success.

3 The Whampoa
    Military Academy

The Whampoa Military Academy was established in 1924, at a time when the GMD had a precarious hold over Canton. Even as a priority project, it was difficult for the party to finance and equip the academy. The declared purpose of training a loyal officers corp to facilitate the founding of a party army was received as a serious threat by militarist allies Yang Ximin and Liu Zhunhuan. Their forces were then stationed in and had physical control over Canton. Yang Ximin and Liu Zhunhuan were determined to stifle the project and attempted to starve the academy of funds and equipment. Zhang Zhizhong, then a faculty member, spoke of how the party representative Liao Zhongkai patiently secured funds from these hostile militarists by the stratagem to keep the academy going:

> Liao, the first party representative, took up financial responsibilities. However, tax collection in Guangdong was firmly controlled by the warlords and Liao was often close to tears as he told us his difficulties in securing funds [for the academy]. When the academy ran out of provisions, he would seek solutions everywhere. Failing to raise the needed funds by evening, he headed for the residence of these warlords. They were often lying on couches smoking opium. As a revolutionary Liao felt uneasy at such surroundings. But, for the sake of keeping five hundred young revolutionaries alive, he sacrificed his dignity. Sensing the warlords were in a good mood, he would then mention some urgent need for funds, not daring to mention the academy.[1]

Apart from blocking financial support, the two militarists were equally determined in denying the academy of access to weaponry. Sun Yatsen requested three hundred rifles from the local arsenal, but only thirty rifles were actually delivered by the time the academy started. Thirty rifles were barely enough to arm the sentries. [2]

Thus starved of funds and equipment locally, external sources of assistance became critical for the military academy in its early days. The arrival of Michael Borodin at Canton in October 1923 signaled the beginning of serious Russian interest. With Borodin came political and military advice, financial assistance, and arms shipments.[3] The establishment of the military academy proceeded soon after Borodin's arrival, and many of the physical necessities—in terms of personnel, finance, and arms—came from this newfound ally. It should be noted, however, that the scale of Russian aid was small, only three million rubles were reported.[4] But the timing of such aid was critical.

The first Russian arms shipment brought "8000 rifles and all equiped with bayonets and 500 rounds of ammunition."[5] With Russian aid the academy was able to develop a fighting force in spite of the hostilities of regional units and the threat of preemtive strikes from them.

The modest scale of foreign aid could not sustain the national pretensions of the GMD. It was imperative for the party to enlarge its territorial and revenue base. There was a feverish need to expand the military academy, and a dire need to transform the cadets into an effective fighting force in the shortest possible time. Hard pressed for both funds and staffing, the academy started its second class with 449 new cadets in August 1924,[6] and the third class with a further twelve hundred in December, the same year.[7] But rapid expansion led the military academy to become less selective in choosing cadets, and the intake into the third class was reported to be of very uneven educational standard. The educated young were not yet rushing to enlist at the academy by the end of 1924, and those who came faced extremely austere conditions:

> What were the living conditions of cadets at the time? They wore one suit of gray cotton civilian clothes, had no socks, and had a pair of straw sandals on their feet. Their living quarters were even more primitive; at the time only some cadets lived in borrowed dormitories formerly used by primary school students. The rest lived in improvised tents made up of bamboo mats, and the beds they slept on were made of woven bamboo. And speaking of the pressures the cadets were under, they studied in the day and kept sentry duties at night to ensure the safety of Whampoa. During their entire training period, they attended classes and fought battles. In the first six months, there were

many crises which the first class had to face. . . . The most
important of which was that of the challenge from the Canton
merchants' militia[8]

The pressure of events made the distinction between training
and active military duties difficult. The urgency in producing a military arm for the party in the shortest possible time led to the expediency of giving the first class no more than six months' training. Still
the pressure of events did not allow the first class to concentrate on
training during this short period. When discussing the formal training of the cadets at Whampoa, one should take their hurried battle
experiences and the various political crises they were involved in as
an integral part of that training. Actual military and political experience were the more important parts of their training. Formal professional training could only be basic.

The Challenge of the Merchants' Militia

The cadet force was steeled under the pressure of events with the first
serious challenge coming from the merchants' militia. In 1924 the
GMD government was relatively unpopular with the mercantile community in Canton. Unstable political conditions since 1911 saw successive military groups vying for control of Guangdong province.
Canton was the prize of these rival factions, making the local mercantile community weary of the continual financial demands made by
one authority or another. The GMD survived in Canton by lending a
mantle of legitimacy to some of these militarists, and so received
much of the ire of public complaint. Nor was the GMD blameless, for
its own urgent need for funds to finance diverse political activities
aggravated the situation. The national ambitions of the party was a
burden on limited local resources.

While tax collectors were happy to collect, they were not effective in maintaining law and order. Policing functions were supple-
mented by local communities through the erection of road blocks and
stockades, manned by volunteers and mercenaries. In 1924 the
strength of these merchants' militia groups in Guangdong was estimated between thirty thousand and forty thousand strong.[9] Though
impressive in aggregate numbers, the merchants' militia was a collection of ill-armed and ill-trained independent units. As such they were
no serious political threat to the GMD or regional military units, yet
their existence expressed the depth of communal distrust. The poten-

tial of turning the militia into a coordinated force and improve the leverage of the mercantile community was there to be tapped.

The efforts of the GMD to establish its own armed force were paralleled by those of the mercantile community to reorganize and improve the militia units. When the Whampoa Military Academy started in May 1924, a merchants' militia congress was also convened at Canton. The convenor was Chen Bolin, comprador of the Canton branch of the Hong Kong and Shanghai Banking Corporation. This militia congress decided to form a province-wide alliance to bring the scattered groups of private security guards into one centralized coordinated structure.[10]

Emboldened by the prospect of having a military arm of its own, the mercantile community refused to accept a newly imposed road tax.[11] In such hip-pocket issues, the mercantile community was certain of public sympathy in Canton. In this way the merchants' militia emerged as a major political challenge to the GMD locally. Sun Yatsen tried desperately to persuade the merchants' militia to declare political support for the GMD, hoping to turn this new military force into an ally. The approaches were soundly rebuffed, however, on the ground that the merchants' militia saw itself as being politically neutral.[12]

Chen Bolin also planned to improve the fire power of the militia. He secured agreement for the militia units to pay one hundred silver dollars for each new rifle delivered. Arms were then bought in Europe, with finance provided by the Hong Kong and Shanghai Banking Corporation.[13] Chen also negotiated with Sun for a license to import arms after paying a fee of fifty thousand silver dollars.[14]

In early August, Sun expressed his unease about the political implications of a well armed merchants' militia and issued orders to Jiang Jieshi to have its shipment of arms seized.[15] This was easier said than done, for the Whampoa Military Academy could only muster around a thousand men, made up of five hundred cadets of the first class whose training started in June, and four hundred fifty cadets of the second class who enrolled in August. This cadet force was very lightly armed, so Jiang was being given what appeared to be an impossible task.

With the element of surprise on their side, the cadets hurriedly manned a few discussed batteries left on the campus site by the late Qing authorities. The Norwegian freighter carrying the arms shipment was forced to berth at Whampoa. Nine thousand rifles and three million rounds of ammunition were unloaded.[16] This was the very first taste of success by the cadet force, giving it access to a significant number of weapons.

This bold act, however, isolated the GMD politically. The merchants promptly declared nontrading days throughout Guangdong, directly reducing revenue income. This hurt the hip-pocket nerves of the militarists in Canton, and they in turn exerted political pressure on Sun Yatsen.[17] Sun reluctantly agreed to a compromise formula in which the Canton government was to receive $200,000 in voluntary contributions in exchange for the release of five thousand rifles to the militia.[18]

The prestige of the GMD was given a further blow by the British, who threatened to use their gunboats to protect the Canton merchants should Sun venture to use force.[19] This was an unnecessary affront, for the merchant community was visibly more than able to fend for itself. What was more under threat was the political survival of Sun Yatsen and the GMD government in Canton. This political setback so disheartened Sun Yatsen that he left Canton for the small township of Shaoguan in northern Guangdong. There he boldly announced another "northern expedition" and gave formal instructions to Jiang to lead his cadet force from Whampoa to join him.[20]

Jiang ignored the instructions and stayed on at Whampoa. He took the political setback at the hands of the merchants' militia in his stride, and honored the agreement by releasing five thousand rifles to the merchants' militia.[21] In the midst of this crisis, Jiang expanded enrollment for the second class to twelve hundred men in September.[22] With this enlarged cadet force of less than two thousand, equiped with some of the arms seized from the merchants' militia, Jiang was soon to confront the much larger and better armed merchants' militia.

The choice of October 10, the anniversary for the 1911 revolution, to return five thousand rifles to the militia was a deliberate and bold political gamble. Arms were unloaded at the wharf located close to the central business district. The merchants' militiamen were jubilant and success went to their heads. GMD supporters parading in the streets celebrating the 1911 revolution were provoked with insults. The atmosphere was electric and shots were fired into the ranks of cadets and GMD sympathizers, killing some twenty people in the process.[23]

Violence turned public opinion in the city against the militia. Their actual possession of five thousand rifles also alarmed the regional militarists in Canton. Having thus politically isolated the merchants' militia, Jiang moved his cadet force into the city. The principal leaders of the merchants' militia were surrounded at the affluent western suburbs of Canton by the joint forces of the cadets and the regional militarists. The merchant community was unwilling to face the prospect of street fighting in which their very comfortable homes would be under fire. Jiang moved in his cadet force quickly to disarm the militia, recapturing the arms which he had returned only days before.[24] The cadet force triumphed over the Canton merchant community and gained popular urban support at the same time.

The combined political and military strategies of Jiang worked miracle for Sun and the GMD. It was Jiang's decisive actions that solved a major political crisis, and, in the process, regained community support for the GMD and attested the effectiveness of the military arm of the party in action. The cadet units became a real political force in Canton by October 1924, barely three months after the formal establishment of the Whampoa Military Academy. Further, the cool and decisive leadership qualities of Jiang turned the commandant into a heroic figure in the eyes of his cadets. Jiang's abilities to stand the test of political fire, at a time when Sun had practically given up Canton, showed that he was a political figure to watch.

The Whampoa cadet force was also popularly referred to as the "student army," for the terms "cadet" and "student" were both addressed as *xuesheng* in Chinese. The public recognition gained by this "student army," just prior to the May 30th incident of 1925 was perfectly timed, for this "student army" soon became the focal point upon which the energies of the next surge of student nationalism were to converge.

Toward Forming a Party Army

The successful demobilization of the merchants' militia in October 1924 brought no respite. The newly acquired credibility of the cadet force stimulated various regional militarists to action. These included the forces of Chen Qiongming, then operating along the eastern coast of Guangdong province, and the "friendly" forces of Yang Ximin and Liu Zhunhuan stationed in Canton.

At Whampoa hurried plans were made to recruit soldiers for two drill regiments. Sun proposed that the academy recruit soldiers locally from the workers and peasants of Guangdong province, and that recruitment from outside Guangdong was to be a supplementary effort.[25] Given the financial constraints of the GMD and of the military academy, the proposal was in tune with the need to economize.

Recruiting locally, however, did involve the risk of creating yet another regional force, one identifiably Cantonese in composition. The suggestion from Sun was inconsistent with the intention expressed at the first national congress of the GMD that a cadet force of mixed provincial origins be recruited. Jiang ignored Sun's suggestion and proceeded to entrust a personal confidant, Chen Guofu, then a businessman in Shanghai, with the task of recruiting men from outside Guangdong.[26]

The use of Chen Guofu's services began in September 1924, amid the merchants' militia crisis. Jiang found out that prices for horses, mules, uniforms, and other sundry items needed by the military academy was about one-fifth cheaper in Shanghai than in Canton. Chen was asked to act as procurement agent for the military academy at Shanghai.[27] At the end of 1924 Chen was given the additional task of recruiting soldiers for the academy. According to Chen Guofu the formal request came from Sun, indicating that by December 1924 Jiang had won his leader over to this arrangement. But the use of Shanghai as the principal base for procurement and recruitment also extended the personal authority of Jiang and his confidant Chen Guofu. Later seven trusted cadets were dispatched to Shanghai to assist Chen Guofu.[28]

Initially little emphasis was placed on the political background of the recruits. Sun Yatsen, for example, wrote to the militarist Lu Yongxiang, then operating in the lower Yangtse area, soliciting his assistance. Lu impeded the recruiting drive instead.[29] In total the Shanghai office delivered over four thousand recruits to Canton between December 1924 and April 1925 at an estimated cost of C$21 per head. The principal costs were transportation expenses and bribes demanded by customs officials and wharf laborers at Shanghai when they found out that certain groups of travelers were really new recruits for a GMD party army.[30] Such were the beginnings of the first drill regiment, formed to give the cadet officers some training in combat command. The cadets and the drill regiment combined to form the nucleus of the party army.

Instead of waiting to have the drill regiment trained and equiped, Jiang initiated action against Chen Qiongming immediately. Leading a force of three thousand, Jiang initiated the first eastern expedition early in 1925. At the time Chen Qiongming massed a force of thirty thousand strong in the Swatow-Huizhou area. In spite of the unfavorable odds of ten to one, the cadet force stood their grounds and scored a tactical victory by capturing the township of Tansui on

February 15, 1925.[31] Chen was forced to regroup and valuable time was gained for Jiang to prepare his cadets and drill regiments.

The consolidation and growth of an effective fighting force at Whampoa led to increasing tension between the party army and two nominally pro-GMD militarists stationed at Canton. The support of Yang Ximin and Liu Zhunhuan for the GMD had been tenuous at the best of times and they were unwilling to sit idly by while the GMD forged a military force that would be used against them in due course. By May 1925 the military academy was fearful of a preemptive strike. A state of alert was declared on May 21.[32] With characteristic decisiveness, Jiang led his cadet force, now expanded to about ten thousand, into Canton between June 12 and 14. There the forces of Yang Ximin and Liu Zhunhuan were surprised, surrounded, and disarmed.[33] Only then did the GMD gain effective control over Canton. By that time Sun Yatsen was no longer alive and the initiative for action came mainly from Jiang Jieshi rather than from party leadership. The growing party army was visibly more effective in action than the GMD party leadership just as the political succession issue came onto the agenda.

Gaining effective control over Canton in June 1925 soon proved critical for the political future of the GMD. In 1925 the May 30th antiimperialist movement, started at Shanghai, was rousing a new surge of nationalist feelings among the educated young throughout China. It was important that the GMD be seen to be actively engaged in support of the anti- imperialist activities if it was to tap the political support of the educated young. On June 23 the GMD organized a mass demonstration on the streets of Canton, just days after gaining control over the city,[34] in a calculated effort to capture the momentum of the May 30th movement.

Party leaders Hu Hanmin, Wang Jingwei, and Liao Zhongkai addressed a gathering estimated at fifty thousand strong. There they were joined by the "student army" from Whampoa. Cadets helped to organize the demonstrators into neat formations, and marched them through the streets of Canton waving banners and shouting antiimperialist slogans.[35] The Whampoa cadets proved themselves equally at home in battle as in mass political rallies.

The foreign community of Canton at the Shaji concession area was understandably alarmed. Local police faced the demonstrators with loaded weapons, while British gunboats provided support from the river. The Shaji concession was separated from the main Chinese section of the city by a narrow moat, a mere stones throw distant. The demonstrators were menacing in gesture and in words, but otherwise unarmed. The British, however, chose to be provoked and fired at random into the demonstrators. The Whampoa cadets who led the demonstration remained in control, moving the demonstrators to a safe distance, while suffering casualties themselves.[36] The discipline and restraint shown by the Whampoa cadets contrasted strongly with the overreaction of the British, and the Shaji incident put the GMD and the Whampoa Military Academy into the forefront of the May 30th movement. *Cadets in military uniform*, instead of students in civilian attire, now became the new leaders of mass demonstrations. This was the first instance of a regimented mass demonstration sponsored by the GMD and led by a "student army."

The organization and discipline of Whampoa cadets, together with their readiness for sacrifice on June 23, 1925, turned Canton into the fulcrum of the May 30th movement. The political gains for the GMD were incalculable as it recaptured national attention and support. Canton was offering more than protest; it was offering organization, training and action. While the anti-imperialist cause in Shanghai and elsewhere had to go underground in the face of stern repression, the same cause in Canton operated in the open. And the Whampoa Military Academy was seen as the core of this newfound activism. But the "student army" was not yet ready to challenge the might of the British Empire. Moving quietly away from the limelight, Jiang translated political attention into a flood of volunteers. The focus of his attention now turned toward the forging of a unified military command in preparation for launching a northern expedition. Jiang was moving for a *military* solution.

Meanwhile the limelight of political protest was taken over by the labor movement when a general strike was called in Hong Kong as a direct retaliatory action against the British. During the strike, workers were marched back to Canton, a trade embargo was imposed on Hong Kong, and an armed picket force was formed to enforce strike action and trade embargo.[37] Thus developed the rivalry between the labor movement and the "student army" on both the political and military planes in the course of the May 30th movement.

Beyond the drama of street demonstrations, martyrdom, strikes, and boycotts, the GMD proceeded firmly with a structural reorganization of its military support base. The military and political reputation of the Whampoa cadet force became the foundation upon which the GMD was to develop a more centralized military structure. On April 13, 1925, the Whampoa units were formally designated as the Party Army.[38] In September 1925 the party established a Military Affairs Commission, the first centralised coordinating body for the various military elements in support of the GMD.[39] In January 1926 the party announced the formal establishment of the National Revolutionary Army (NRA).[40] Formally all military elements were reorganized as one army. Wang Jing-wei, serving as chairman of the Military Affairs Commission and party representative at the Whampoa Military Academy, claimed that the formation of the NRA should erase the regional identity of its component units, and thus better prepare the military arm in serving a national cause.[41]

Wang's claim expressed more of a future prospect than an immediate reality. At the time the NRA was made up of a number of army corps each clearly identifiable with a specific regional force. The second army was formerly the Hunanese units of Deng Yangai. The third army consisted of the Cantonese units of Zhu Beide. The fourth army was identifiably the Cantonese units of Li Jishen. The fifth army was formerly the Fujian units of Li Fulin. Only the Party Army, now designated as the first army, was strictly not a regional force. Additional army corps were created when more regional units sought to affiliate with the GMD cause of national reunification. By the beginning of the northern expedition the NRA had eight army corps, made up of the Party Army and seven other regional military groupings. The reorganization, however, was not entirely nominal, for in joining the NRA the regional units had to hand over all cadet training functions to the Whampoa Military Academy and to accept Whampoa graduates into their respective command structure.[43] In this way the educated young could aspire to actual military command by first enrolling in the Whampoa Military Academy. The emphasis of the reorganization was eventual domination of the NRA by graduates of the Whampoa Military Academy.

The consolidation of centralized party control in the NRA was dependent upon the immediate ability of the Party Army to assert its authority over the former regional units and on the eventual deployment of Whampoa graduates throughout the NRA. The task of imposing discipline upon the party's military arm fell squarely upon the shoulders of Jiang Jieshi and his Whampoa cadets. The military academy became an institution through which young nationalists could join and control the military.

Increasing political support for the GMD resulted as the party successfully projected itself as the champion of the May 30th movement. This in turn made the tasks of expanding the party army and consolidating control over the NRA feasible. The Whampoa Military Academy intensified its recruitment efforts and was able to establish underground offices in Beijing, Kaifeng, Hankow, and Shanghai.

Entrance requirement was set at secondary-school graduate level, a fairly high requirement in a land where educational opportunities were limited. And recruiting was unquestionably targeted at the student populace, enabling those youths who were motivated by patriotic feelings to seek military enlistment as a concrete expression of political commitment. During the recruitment drive, the ability of local party branches to fund the costs of sending candidates to Canton reflected increased nationwide support for the GMD. The four underground recruitment centers had little difficulty in filling the quota of five hundred recruits each.

The main difficulty was to avoid detection by the various hostile regimes in whose territories these recruitment centers were located. The Hankow office, for example, was detected by Wu Peifu and the recruited candidates were dispersed by Wu. The political attraction of Whampoa was so strong that most of them found their own way to Canton nonetheless.[43] Indeed there were more qualified applicants than the military academy could admit, even though the enrollment figure for the fourth and fifth classes were expanded to twenty-five hundred each. The excess number was not turned away, but enlisted in a preentrance class where they were trained as foot soldiers in the drill regiments of the academy. Since the May 30th movement students poured into both the cadet classes and into the drill regiments of the Whampoa Military Academy. Enlistment was an accepted alternative to other forms of political involvement and enlistment meant principally joining the military training programs sponsored by the GMD. This ensured that the Whampoa cadets, as well as soldiers in the drill regiments formed after May 30, 1925, were from a select social group.[44]

The growing nationwide support for the GMD was reflected in the pattern of regional origins of the cadets. Before May 30, 1925, cadets of Guangdong origins accounted for about a quarter of the total. By the fourth class this dropped to 9.61 percent and recovered to 13.73 percent in the fifth class. In contrast there was a marked increase of recruits from central China: accounting for close to half in the fourth class and increasing further to about two-thirds in the fifth class[45].

While the nationwide anti-imperialist mood of the May 30th Movement generated a steady flow of recruits to Whampoa, it remained for the military academy to translate the ephemeral emotions of the new recruits into firmer commitments to the political ideals and programs of the GMD. What stood for GMD ideals, however, appeared to be less than clear in 1925. Acceptance of Russian aid and tolerance of Chinese communist cooperation within the GMD did not sit well with Sun's statement that communism was not suitable for China. Such apparent inconsistencies raised the political question as to whether the doctrines of Sun Yatsen and those of Marxism were compatible. Evasions and delays in resolving the issue necessarily compromised the ideological authority of the GMD. At the same time the emotions generated by the May 30th movement and the volatile political balance of power within the GMD since the death of Sun in March 1925 necessitated a high degree of flexibility. Dogmatism on matters of political doctrine could prove damaging to the fortunes of the party.

The ideological indecision of the party was reflected in the military academy. In one of the entrance examination papers, for example, candidates were given the impression that the Chinese national revolution and the socialist "world revolution" were inseparable elements one from the other. They were asked rhetorical questions such as "Can the National Revolutionary Movement gain a victory without the participation of the peasantry and why?" and "Can the National Revolutionary Movement gain victory without being supported by the world revolution?[46] Without resolving these issues at the top leadership and party congress levels, the GMD and the military academy were unlikely to be able to give firm ideological directions to cadets. Indecisive political instruction provided leverage for the CCP to preach its preferred doctrinal positions. It thus preempted much of the GMD intention of cultivating ideological commitment and loyalty for the GMD from among cadets.

The lack of ideological clarity was paralleled by inadequate provisions for political training, even though a stated purpose of the Whampoa Military Academy was to train a politically loyal officers corps. Political lectures were often canceled because the guest lecturers such as Hu Hanmin, Wang Jingwei, Dai Jitao, and others did not turn up. The political leadership of the party failed to create an image of active involvement and did not play its expected role of explaining party doctrines to cadets. Was this because key party leaders could not agree on what the major party doctrines were? Or was this because they simply did not think it was important enough for them to devote time to cadets at Whampoa? Both Wang Jingwei and Hu Hanmin later paid the price of their neglect of this key support base of the party.

In the first six months the provisions for political training at the military academy were more apparent than real principally because of neglect by key GMD leaders. By default, the task of giving political lectures fell on the shoulders of professional instructors such as Jiang and his lieutenant He Yingqin. Taking on such tasks at short notice, addresses by the commandant became familiar moral exhortations.[47] In contrast Zhou Enlai and his communist comrades in the secret Communist Party branch at Whampoa were devoting their attention to the propagation of Marxist ideas. Ideological tension rather than cohesion was developing within Whampoa. With general neglect and unpreparedness on the part of the GMD, Zhou Enlai skillfully increased communist influence at the Political Department, as the following quote would suggest:

> Dai Jitao was the first head of the Political Department. Soon after taking office he had disputes with Zhang Ji and Xie Yang regarding the acceptance of CCP members into the GMD, and he left for Shanghai in anger. Therefore the Political Department had no one in charge for a few months. At the time the department had two secretaries, and even without a departmental head, [they] managed to have some lectures organized. When Shao Yuanzhong took office there were no appreciable changes except for the convening of two political discussions. Then Shao accompanied the chief executive [Sun] to go north. With the evolving merchants' militia crisis, Jiang, Liao, Wang, and Hu were pressed by events, so the frequency of lectures also decreased. In November 1924, Zhou Enlai was appointed head of the Political Department."[48]

Confronted with insufficient funds, inadequate accommodation, and almost devoid of equipment of any description at the start, infantry drills were the principal trainings provided for the first class.[49] Final examination for the first class consisted of one mock battle in the surrounding countryside.[50] Military training was rather basic for those in the first class.

Training for the second class was relatively more complex, for the weapons captured from the merchants' militia and those supplied by the Russians made the planning for some degree of technical diversification desirable. Accordingly the second class was divided into five groups, each with a specialized training program: infantry, artillery, engineering, transport, and military police.[51] Military training, however, continued to be unsatisfactory because of the very short training period of six months and because the trainees were sent into battle right in the midst of this short period. The second class was enrolled at the time of the merchants' militia crisis, and, before graduating, the class formed part of the battle force in the first eastern expedition. Training was not completely interrupted, for a temporary campus was set up at Swatow during the lull of the battle. This improvised training was also terminated after less than a month, for the cadets were moved back to Canton for military action against the units of Yang Ximin and Liu Zhunhuan.[52]

In the early days of Whampoa neither political nor military training was of noted quality. What then welded the force together? What qualities enabled this small force to handle numerically superior regional forces?

Firstly, during the first twelve months the force at Whampoa was small. Starting with the five hundred members of the first class, the Whampoa force grew to about ten thousand by June 1925 before the May 30th movement. Approximately half of the first ten thousand were made up of cadets, and the other half of foot soldiers recruited from central China. The percentage of educated young was extraordinarily high, and their patriotic motivation instilled a correspondingly high morale into this small force. Besides, keeping a small force tightly organized was relatively easy.

Second the provincial origins of the Whampoa force were predominantly nonlocal. For most of the cadets and soldiers, Guangdong province was almost "foreign" and hence there was a natural tendency for them to band closely together in an alien land.

Third, the Whampoa Military Academy was surrounded by hostile military and political elements. The siege mentality that the situation encouraged made those at Whampoa respond well to the leadership of Jiang Jieshi in handling one crisis after another.

Fourth a stern code of military discipline was imposed. This was known as a system of linked responsibility, imposing summary execution on the commanding officers, from the corporal to the commanding officer of an army corps, should their respective units retreat in battle on their own initiative. The regulations were issued in January 1925 and served Jiang well in his customary approach of "no retreats" in military action. [53]

Finally, the leadership qualities of Jiang Jieshi were significant. His judgment proved correct in handling the merchants' militia, in dealing with Chen Qiongming, in eliminating Yang Ximin and Liu Zhunhuan in Canton, and in the tactics of provoking the British to overreact in the demonstrations of June 23, 1925. A leader who performed again and again in critical moments rightly earned the trust of his following.

One significant factor in favor of Whampoa was the element of surprise. The small force, ruled by stern discipline, and operating in a hostile environment, surprised its opponents with its sheer ability to stand the test of fire. The regional forces commanded by Chen Qiongming and the Yunnanese militarists Yang Ximin and Liu Zhunhuan had been used to the more leisurely march and countermarches where losers were prepared to concede territories with the minimum of casualties. But the small force from Whampoa defied such logic, and opted to fight to the last, irrespective of odds. This determination to die for the patriotic cause triumphed over weaker willed opposing forces. The fragility of opposing militarist units can be attested in the low casualty figures for the Whampoa force. In the six-month long first eastern expedition, the Whampoa force suffered less than twenty casualties.[54] This is an incredibly low figure for what was a major military campaign in which the Whampoa force was outnumbered ten to one.

Nothing succeeds like success. The performance of Jiang earned him trust and obedience from the cadets, so much so that they were prepared to die as martyrs if commanded to do so. The absolute effectiveness of such unquestioned obedience can be seen during the Shaji incident on June 23, 1925, when no less than twenty-seven Whampoa cadets perished at the hands of the British without returning a single shot.[55] On that day Jiang demonstrated that he had a very well-disciplined force under his command, while the sacrifices of the cadets also propelled the GMD to national focus in claiming leadership of the May 30th movement.

Increased political support made the task of expanding the Party Army easy as volunteers poured into Canton. This rapid expansion of the military support base for the GMD created both opportunities and pitfalls for Jiang and his cadets. In general the post-May 30th recruits were well-educated and politically motivated. Whampoa, however, did not have a firm ideological platform of its own. Ideological tensions between the GMD and the CCP within the military academy made the development of internal cohesion based on ideological concensus unlikely, if not impossible. The establishment of the NRA was another instance of the mix between opportunity and compromise. The NRA institutionalized the ascendancy of the Party Army over other regional forces working with the GMD, but the various regional armies remained largely intact in practice. The Party Army, now renamed the first army, became an instrument in enforcing loyalty from these regional units. The GMD fell short of a thorough reorganization of its mixed military support base into a truly centralized national army. Instead, Jiang was given the task of gradually expanding Whampoa influence into the regional units by being given the exclusive right of training future cadets for all army corps and the opportunity of appointing his cadets as officers at various regional units.[56] Tension and rivalry were sustained within the military under this gradual takeover approach, but how else could patriotic students be enlisted, given training, and used to expand GMD control over the various regional units?

For other supporting regional armies, the ascendancy of the Whampoa group was a fact that they had to live with comfortably or otherwise. The establishment of the NRA, however, did give them the opportunity to share the political popularity of the GMD at the time. Giving up the right to train officers of their own of course diminished their autonomy, but there was the immediate trade-off of expanding the size of their units in the common effort of preparing for a northern expedition, a reunification of China through military means, under the leadership of Jiang and the Whampoa cadets. By focusing on a military solution, the military as a whole was enjoying political ascendancy. Besides the ascendancy of Jiang and the Party Army could be weakened in the simultaneous expansion of all army corps within the NRA. The argument for an evenhanded treatment in terms of funding, equipment, and rate of expansion was essentially one of asserting that the Party Army should not be given a privileged position. The regional components of the NRA continued to lobby for a less centralized military structure. It can then be argued that politics in the GMD military remained unstable in spite of the ascendancy of the Party Army and the formation of the NRA. If cadets trained at Whampoa could stay as a cohesive group irrespective of which army corps they were assigned to, then the cadet would become key elements in forging a relatively more united command over the military.

How cohesive were the Whampoa graduates as a political force? Could cohesion among the cadets be retained when they were not directly under Jiang's command?

One way of providing a tentative indication is by looking at the record of the branch campuses. These were often temporary campuses set up to provide training for cadets in the midst of military campaigns. The first branch campus was at Swatow established during the first eastern expedition. Cadets receiving training at Swatow were those of the second class. While the Swatow campus was in operation, a further eight-hundred cadets were recruited from among the rank and file.[57] Of these eight-hundred, only 345 graduated in June 1925 and they were all retained by the Party Army.[58] Though they started their training with the second class, they graduated as part of the third class. In June 1925 another fifty cadets were selected from the rank and file, and they too were enrolled at Swatow.[59] Opportunities for the rank and file to enroll as cadets were principally limited to these two occasions. The camp training at Swatow was under the direct control of Jiang. When the first eastern expedition concluded, the Swatow campus was also closed, and the cadets returned to the main campus at Whampoa. There were no other branch campuses being established prior to the northern expedition. The question of developing central control over a network of dispersed campuses was not tackled by Jiang.

During the northern expedition branch campuses were established at Changsha, Wuhan, and Nanjing.[60] Jiang could not be at all fronts at the same time, and difficulties of retaining effective central control emerged. Jiang tackled the issue by delegating control to trusted lieutenants. The Whampoa home campus was entrusted to Fang Dingyi, who soon suggested that the main campus be moved to either Changsha or Wuhan, so that proximity to the front would enable the academy to provide fresh supplies of officers with greater ease.[61]

Jiang acted on the advice in November 1926. He ordered another trusted lieutenant, Deng Yanda, to make the necessary preparations to relocate the Whampoa Academy at Wuhan. In December three brigades of cadets were transferred from Whampoa to Wuhan, and a further twelve hundred were recruited directly by the Wuhan campus. With a total of between five thousand to six thousand cadets, the Wuhan campus replaced Whampoa as the main campus of the military academy by the end of 1926.[62]

The Wuhan campus, however, was affected by the infightings between the GMD and the CCP in the united front. Deng Yanda proved disloyal to the authority of Jiang.[63] Jiang promptly established another campus at Nanjing, closer to his command headquarters at Nanchang, and there he exercised direct control as the commandant of the military academy.[64]

Jiang was unable to delegate the duties of the commandant without the risk of losing effective control. The organizational cohesion of the military academy seemed to be inseparable from the leadership of Jiang in this early phase prior to the emergence of the Whampoa alumni and the young officers movement. The Whampoa interest group could not stay together without the direct personal authority of Jiang.The NRA could not be knitted together without the influence and authority of the Whampoa cadets, the first army, and Jiang himself. When Jiang left Canton to lead the NRA on the northern expedition, the military academy had to be moved to wherever Jiang's command was.

General Observations

One stated function of the Whampoa Military Academy was to train a politically loyal officers corps for the GMD. The emphasis on political training was modeled on the Russian red army and consistent with Chinese political tradition. In practice, however, both the pressure of events and the ideological tension between the GMD and the CCP made the implementation of political training more apparent than real.

The presence of the CCP within the Whampoa campus also undermined the political cohesion of the academy. Contrary to formal declarations of loyally serving the GMD, the CCP established its own secret party network within the military academy. Irrespective of ideological merits or otherwise of Marxism, the competing ideological appeals of the two parties proved divisive. CCP activities directly undermined both the ideological and organizational cohesion of the Whampoa Military Academy.

The open and secret organizational techniques of the CCP also provided a model for Jiang and cadets loyal to the GMD. Later Whampoa alumni groups also employed the techniques of maintaining front organizations and secret networks in controlling the leadership of the military arm.

The appointment of Zhou Enlai as head of the Political Department gave the Chinese communists undue influence on political education. This was the consequence of GMD neglect in political education. Communist infiltration made the task of training a politically loyal officers corps for the GMD doubly difficult.

Rivalry between the GMD and the CCP led to open splits among the cadet populace. The Young Soldiers Association and the Sun Wenism Study Group were front organizations reflecting this undercurrent of party rivalry. Patriotic students who enlisted at Whampoa were divided by party loyalties.

Political division was countered by cohesive devices of a non-political nature. A strict disciplinary code and the personal authority of Jiang Jieshi were the principal unifying influences. And since this unity was threatened by underground activities of the CCP, the counter infiltration efforts led to the development of a secret intelligence network.

The formal training at Whampoa emphasized military drills and battle experience, the quality of which was limited by time and resources. Limited professional training, however, did not prevent the emergence of the Whampoa force as the most effective unit in Guangdong. Morale and political commitment compensated for the relative weakness in formal military training. In retrospect one has to conclude that Whampoa provided what training it could, and that its organizational efforts were vindicated by military and political successes. With the limited resources allotted to Whampoa, its achievements were impressive indeed.

Internal cohesion was dependent on a command structure and the force of personality of Jiang Jieshi. The intended political commitment to the GMD, to the ideological authority of the party, remained unattainable. Obedience to the commander and personal loyalty to Jiang Jieshi became the key cohesive qualities in practice. When the GMD military operated in more than one front during the northern expedition, it became difficult to maintain an effective central command structure. The personal authority of Jiang did show signs of inadequacy as the influence and power of the Whampoa cadets expanded. Instead of devising a more sophisticated institutional structure, the course taken to remedy the defect was to try to maximize the influence of Jiang over future academy graduates by transferring the main campus closer to the command headquarters of Jiang.

The GMD failed to develop effective control over the academy, its cadets, and the armed units they commanded. The party failed to control the gun. This failure resulted in the personal ascendancy of Jiang at Whampoa, making Jiang rather than the formal party hierarchy the focus of loyalty for the Whampoa cadets and the military forces they commanded. Jiang's influence over the Whampoa cadets produced a particular type of internal cohesion, one that made GMD access to its own military force contingent upon the goodwill and support of Jiang.

The Whampoa Military Academy was established as a first step in the building of a party army for the GMD. This basic objective was attained. In addition it served as a channel for patriotic students to enlist and be trained. It opened up the road for the young educated elite to gain control over the military. But the political cohesiveness of Whampoa cadets was compromised by ideological differences within the academy. There was no ideological cohesion and discipline was maintained by a command structure, a strict military code, and an intelligence network.

4 Militarizing the Educated Young

Led by cadets trained at the Whampoa Military Academy, the National Revolutionary Army spearheaded a drive for national reunification in 1927. Militarizing a student elite and trusting them with military command were important factors underpinning the success of the northern expedition. Nonetheless, Chinese reunification remained incomplete when a new national government was established at Nanjing in 1928.

Could practices at Whampoa be extended to student populations beyond one military academy? Could the fervor and discipline of Whampoa, could the spirit of Whampoa, be instilled into the educated young of a nation and have an entire generation transformed into a disciplined force dedicated to the cause of national reunification? Could the model of Whampoa be a guide to the education policy of the new national government?

Political priorities of the Nanjing government influenced its early practices in higher education at Beijing. The city contained some of the nation's most prestigious campuses, with their cultural and political vitality attested by the New Culture movement and May 4th movements. In the 1910s campus activism rejuvenated China. The northern campuses were seen as focuses of national energy. It was essential for the nationalist government to capture the active support of these campuses if only to preempt the possibility of organized dissent or the development of an alternative focus for national leadership:

> The abolition of the Confucian examination system in 1905 undermined the position of the traditional literati. Their successors lived in the dormitories of several dozen colleges and universities in the principal cities and immersed themselves not in

Confucian classics, but in chemistry, sociology, and foreign literature. They wrote in colloquial *pai hua*, not in classical *wen yen*;
they spoke not of serving their country, but of saving it. Upon
graduation some entered the professions; many became teachers, writers, and businessmen; others entered Kuomintang
[Guomindang] government service after 1925; a radical minority
joined the Communists. Many found no employment. By comparison with the scholarly gentry of earlier times, nearly all
were, psychologically and socially, displaced persons.[1]

John Israel may be underestimating the immediate impact of
GMD rule upon the campuses of north China. Were students who
lived in dormitories and immersed in chemistry, sociology, and foreign literature so different from their literati forebears? It is comfortable to see a familiar Western campus setting, but then why were
these Chinese students seen as being "psychologically and socially,
displaced persons"?

In spite of appearances, that the students of Confucian and
republican China studied different subject matters, their continued
search for personal identity in political action and debate was unmis-
takable. The distinction between "serving" and "saving" China was
one of circumstance, not of intent. That Israel can perceive the generations between 1905 and 1949 as "psychologically and socially displaced" is because for most of this period the educated young were
searching for a state to serve. Their drive against authority, as Israel
puts it, was a drive in search of new loyalties. The establishment of
the Nanjing government offered them a tangible and viable focus for
their loyalties to converge:

> The nature of student commitment was radically altered
> between 1919 and 1049. The May Fourth generation was in
> revolt against all authority: family, school, and state alike
> seemed decadent, venal, and hopelessly encrusted with worn
> out ways of thought. From about 1915 through the early 1920's,
> the accent was on liberating the individual from the old order.
> Anti-Confucianism, the family revolution, and the "literary
> renaissance" were foremost in students' minds. But though the
> family revolution continued, after the May Fourth demonstra-
> tion the battleground began to shift from the home to society
> and the nation. The new student generation acquired new loyal-
> ties[2]

The drive against authority was integral to the search for an alternative authority. In retrospect the writings of Lu Xun typified the iconoclastic spirit of the New Culture and May 4th movement. Yet even this bold spirit was motivated by political feelings to give up his medical studies to pursue a literary life. The change of career was a change in the means, not in the end. Medicine and literature were alternative means to *save* the nation, to *save* the literate elite from being "psychologically and socially displaced persons." Traditional society was attacked not just because it was "decadent, venal, and hopelessly encrusted with worn out ways of thought"; it was attacked because the state, and the very existence of a national social elite, could not survive upon rotten foundations. There was an inherent conservatism in the radical thoughts of intellectuals such as Lu Xun, Chen Duxiu, Li Dachao, Ku Jiegang, and Hu Shi—leading lights of the May 4th generation. "There is method in his madness" can be lifted from the pages of Hamlet for these Chinese radicals. How were intellectuals and students to receive the Nanjing government and how would they respond to the efforts of Nanjing in militarizing the educated young?

A literate community which was psychologically and socially displaced, as the students of the 1920s were, was ready to be led, "to serve" *if* in the process the authority of the state, the source of their own elite identity, could be revived, restored, or regenerated. For most the search was for a *new* China, a new centralized political structure, not for intellectual freedom or the stimulation of new thought. New ideas were to be sought if they served the cause of national rejuvenation, but this search was subordinated to national purpose. Both the GMD and the CCP were alive to such possibilities and both endeavored to improve their technique in the enterprise. The anti-British demonstrations at Canton on June 23, 1925, signaled the coming of age of the GMD in tapping the force of student nationalism. Subsequent political success of the GMD further attracted support from these "psychologically and socially" displaced persons. The educated could see hope for their own future in the rise of the Nanjing government. There were reservations among some, for the break up of the first united front and the jockeying for power between different GMD factions reflected serious divisions. Some intellectuals who had acquired their reputations as critics of society also found it difficult to accept the new authority overnight. Those who opposed and those who criticized the new government were of relatively minor import in 1928, unless the new government failed to live up to expectations.

Could the GMD accomplish its own grandiose vision of national reunification and, in doing so, fulfill the expectations of the educated young? Could the educated young be harnessed to assist in this enterprise? Could the GMD succeed in merging party interests with those of the educated young and so earn their support?

The northern expedition brought about what was in fact an incomplete national reunification. The aura of success was qualified by the harsh realities of a divided country. Autonomous regimes might or might not fly the new national flag of blue, white, and red. Beijing was so far away from the power base of the new national government in central China. The northern expedition created expectations in Beijing which the GMD could not fulfill at the time. But the reunification enterprise was common to both the Nanjing central government and university students at Beijing. Could support from the educated young be harnessed to consolidate the authority of the Nanjing regime in north China?

In spite of the liberal intellectual traditions of the New Culture movement and May 4th movement, intellectuals from the Beijing-Tianjin area responded favorably toward government attempts to introduce authoritarianism into the campus scene. The new government assumed financial responsibility for many tertiary institutions and claimed the right to nominate top administrators. The new president of Qinghua University, Luo Jialun, for example, was a GMD party appointee.[3]

When Luo Jialun assumed office on September 18, 1928, a blatant militaristic image was displayed. Luo put on the uniform of a lieutenant general for the occasion.[4] To make the message doubly clear, the keynote address was given by another military figure, General Bai Chongxi, with this clear message: "To have President Luo at the head of Qinghua is to give Qinghua hope: the hope to identify Qinghua with the Party, and the hope to turn you gentlemen into loyal comrades of the Party."[5] Were such words and gestures out of tune with the iconoclastic intellectual traditions in Beijing?

The mood of Beijing in the mid-1920s was militantly anti-imperialist. The highhanded actions of the British and the Japanese at Shanghai provoked the May 30th movement and students in Beijing organized mass street protests on June 3 and June 10, 1925. An estimated two hundred thousand joined the demonstrators.[6] The anti-imperialist moves taken at Canton and Hong Kong under GMD leadership were in tune with the militant mood of students and teachers in Beijing. There was a convergence of mood in Beijing and Canton well before GMD authority reached the north.

Campus populations in Beijing in 1928 were not against governmental control, but against a weak national government. When the Nanjing government sent a telegram to the dean of students, Dr. Mei Yiji, on June 11, 1926, appointing him to be the acting head of Qinghua,[7] the authority of the central government was accepted without a murmur. Dr. Mei remained steadfastly loyal to a GMD government to the end of his life. But before the Nanjing government assumed control over Qinghua, the foreign ministry and the tertiary education Yuan disputed as to which agency should have authority over Qinghua University.[8] Only then did the student union pass a resolution, objecting to be taken over until dispute over jurisdiction was resolved in Nanjing.[9] This was framed in terms affirming the authority of the national government. The students were openly in favor of GMD control.

The newly appointed university president wore a military uniform and issued stern calls for discipline, providing a welcomed authoritarian image. A military lifestyle was introduced into the Qinghua campus: regular drills, morning and afternoon roll calls, and the threat of expulsion after nine recorded absences. Party ideology became a compulsory subject, and, by December 1928, a GMD party branch was established.[10] There were also the expected police and military actions for rooting out communist elements from campus. Staff response to such actions was one of quiet acceptance, and Mei Yiji explained to his colleagues:

> I think it is impossible to stop them [the military authorities] from coming. We can only try to minimize the unease afterwards. . . . I [was admitted] to see Song Zheyuan yesterday. He said the [name] list has not been finalized because the central [Government] has not yet sent him the final version. As to when they would come [to campus], and how many would come will be decided after receiving the final name list from the central [Government]. There is no doubt that they will come[11]

There was hardly a murmur against political suppression directed by the GMD. The desire to protect a liberal academic tradition was not as powerful as the desire for a strong and effective central government. The argument that a liberal academic institution such as Qinghua should preserve a politically nonpartisan position was simply not made.

The political compliance of staff and students to GMD control and anticommunist efforts enabled Luo Jialun, the university president, to be given a special commendation by Jiang Jieshi in March 1931: "President Luo has an excellent record at Qinghua. He has improved the administration of Qinghua according to Party ideals [and] government policies [and, in doing so], has rectified scholarship trends [in the direction of] the unification of thought"[12] In six months time, as the Japanese launched their occupation of Manchuria, this pliant campus mood was to change radically. Nationalism was the primary political force on campus, and patriotic students would turn against those who failed to defend national interests.

Qinghua University did not suffer at the hands of an authoritarian central government. Indeed Qinghua benefited, for a strong government was able to increase university funding, making rapid expansion feasible. The annual student intake was increased from three hundred to five hundred in 1928. Qinghua could even boast of a major social reform as female students were admitted for the first time that year, reflecting a more liberal social attitude consonant with the demands for a stronger nation. With increased capital grants, more new buildings were constructed. Under GMD leadership, Qinghua University was to continue as a center of excellence in study and research.[13] Qinghua and other tertiary institutions could assist a strong authoritarian GMD government in modernizing China.

For three years the political influence of the GMD went from strength to strength. Japanese intervention at Jinan in 1928 failed to prevent a formal reunification as militarist regimes declared their allegiance to Nanjing one by one. Only pockets of Chinese communist resistance remained outside Nanjing authority. National unity, however, was seriously compromised by the continued existence of autonomous military regimes, even though they too shared in the mood of nationalist fervor. Most of them welcomed the establishment of GMD party branches within their territories at the risk of compromising their regional autonomy. Nationalist sentiments and GMD leadership seemed likely to combine to make China strong again.

This prospect threatened the well being of the Japanese Empire, for a significant part of its strength was derived from special privileges, concessions, and territorial holdings in China. The China question was a controversial issue in Japan throughout the 1920s. In September 1931 radical military elements pressed for a military solution to protect what they called Japan's "lifeline" and launched the invasion of Manchuria.[14] The invasion dealt a serious blow to GMD prestige, seriously straining rapport between Nanjing and campus populations. Criticism against Nanjing was directed mainly at its lack of success in national defense. By the end of September 1931 student protest turned violent inside Nanjing itself where the foreign ministry was broken into and the foreign minister physically assaulted.[15]

The distance between Manchuria and the Lower Yangtze Valley, which formed the principal territorial base for the Party Army, made it difficult for Jiang to check the invasion with force from Nanjing. Jiang made a fatal political judgment, however, when he did not give clear instructions to the regional forces under Zhang Xueliang to resist. While Manchuria was lost with hardly a shot fired, the Nanjing government placed its hopes on some form of international intervention through the League of Nations.[16] It can be argued that Jiang and the Nanjing government, realizing the limitations of their own military capabilities, were simply being pragmatic. To take the Japanese on frontally could lead to military disaster and bring the Nanjing political edifice to an early ruin. To a government in power, one that claimed to have achieved reunification, the ideal of a reunified China became inseparable from its own survival. To the educated young, political and territorial integrity, particularly when it involved a piece of territory the size of Manchuria, was beyond negotiation. Political pragmatism was writing China small and in the process Nanjing was shown to be weak when it could not, would not, and dared not live up to the defense responsibilities of a national government.

To be fair to the Nanjing government, the national responsibilities it claimed in north China and Manchuria were not matched by the substance of political power it enjoyed in those areas. The political influence of the GMD in these areas rested heavily on the support of regional militarists and the educated young. The former supported the GMD because they wanted to avoid a frontal clash with the party military in which they might lose. Their support was partially based on fear. At the same time they also hoped that affiliation with Nanjing would lend them some support in resisting Japanese pressure. The educated young supported the GMD because it represented the best promise for achieving national unity at the time. Staff and students at an institution such as Qinghua were proud of their formal links with Nanjing, proud to be a Guoli or "nationally sponsored" university. There was also a keen awareness of how weak GMD presence in north China and Manchuria was. When students in the Shanghai and Nanjing areas organized mass demonstrations and petitions, pressuring Jiang for a firm stand against the Japanese invasion of Manchuria, campuses at Beijing and Tianjin were remarkably quiet. The jubilant mood, which came with the establishment of the Nanjing government in 1928, was replaced by sullen disappointment in 1931. The Manchurian incident thus ended the honeymoon period between the educated young in North China and the GMD.

At Nanjing the scale of student-led popular anti-Japanese demonstrations escalated between September and December 1931. The demonstration on September 24 mustered a mere two thousand, those in October were estimated at five thousand to six thousand, and by December the demonstrators numbered over thirty thousand.[17] In the heartland of GMD power there was a much stronger popular perception that the nationalist government actually had the means with which to combat Japanese incursion. Such popular emotions might not express levelheaded pragmatism, but it was precisely such nationalist feelings that had propelled the GMD to power. Jiang's reliance on international intervention and his appeal to the students to return to the classroom and "study with peace of mind"[18] were cooling the emotions of the educated young. What was much more ominous was the need to call out troops to disperse demonstrators by December, for this was an open admission that the GMD was no longer able to manipulate the political mood of students and the urban populace to its own advantage. Under the strain of Japanese incursion, the fragile link between the GMD and the educated young was seriously strained.

The rising tide of anti-Japanese feelings in central China led the Japanese navy to launch a punitive attack. On January 28, 1932, marines were landed at Shanghai to teach the Chinese a lesson.[19] Although the Chinese 19th route army put up a brave resistance, it became apparent that central China, the most important territorial base of the GMD government, was vulnerable to direct Japanese attack. Both popular demonstrations and Japanese military actions served to expose the weakness of the GMD.

The period between January 1932 and December 1936 was one of growing disenchantment with the GMD leadership. As Jerome Grieder so aptly observed: "In the course of the 1930s, under the deepening threat of Japanese aggression, and harassed by a government which seemed more concerned to silence its critics within than to confront the enemy without, many Chinese students, and many of the country's most persuasive and popular literary talents drifted towards the Left."[20] If the government had performed better in containing the Japanese threat in Manchuria and north China, there would have been much less need for silencing critics.

Japanese pressure was also directly weakening the GMD's capability in silencing its critics. In north China the Japanese made sure that the formal structures of GMD party apparatus could not develop. Under direct military threats, the Japanese signed the He-Umezu agreement with Nanjing in which the GMD agreed to withdraw all party branches from north China.[21]

Between 1928 and September 1931 students and intellectuals in north China firmly supported Jiang and the Nanjing government, for they seemed to be delivering the substance of national revival. Direct GMD efforts to regiment campus life were welcomed as a formula for strengthening internal cohesion. With the signing of the He-Umezu agreement, the GMD signed away its own right to organize and lead the students. The ensuing disenchantment with the GMD was a logical consequence of the party's failure in defending north China against Japanese incursions.

In 1928 a liberal institution such as Qinghua surrendered its liberalism willingly to GMD regimentation. In 1932 the GMD was compelled to give up such formal and organized control under duress. It was not the lack of a liberal intellectual environment that bred disenchantment with the GMD. A liberal, a relatively more autonomous, environment was a reflection of internal political weakness. Liberal environment was associated with weak organization and ineffectual political action. "Saving the nation" continued to be the principal catch cry of student groups irrespective of whether the environment was regimented or liberal. With the formal departure of GMD party presence, it became more difficult, if not impossible, for the GMD to lead the students in north China "to save the nation."

To those in power the integrity of the state was synonymous with the substance of power in hand. To the students in Beijing and Tianjin, it meant the immediate and effective protection of north China from Japanese ambitions. They saw the plight of homeless students from Manchuria, and they despaired at the continuing rounds of compromises with the Japanese, compromises that made even the existence of GMD party branches in north China illegal and made government suppression of anti-Japanese protests mandatory. Hopes for national leadership from the GMD were slowly turned into disappointment. Those who remained hopeful of the GMD organized mass petitions and traveled to Nanjing to beg for action. They succeeded in trying the patience of those in authority and were forcibly escorted back to the railway stations and told to go home. Instead of pleading with Nanjing, others organized propaganda teams to appeal to the rural populace in the countryside.

Disillusion came not with the lack of socio-economic justice. It came with the inability of the GMD government in making a firmer stand against the Japanese between September 1931 and July 1937. Students in Beijing were rarely interested in the welfare of workers and peasants, they were driven to seek support from, rather than to give assistance to, these social groups.

The December 9th movement of 1935 marked the climax of student disillusion with the GMD. In Beijing students took matters into their own hands by staging demonstrations in protest against Japanese designs to turn north China into another autonomous state. The prospect of allowing the Japanese to duplicate the Manzhouguo experiment in north China was unacceptable. Whatever sympathy the Nanjing government might have for the students, it did not and could not come out in open support of this new wave of student nationalism for fear of antagonizing Japan. Instead, the militarist allies of Nanjing tried to keep the students in check with force. But such actions only deepened disillusion. They put the very legitimacy of a government in doubt. The issues of nationalism and political suppression were merged in emotional condemnations of Nanjing:

> Since the founding of the capital [at Nanjing] the press has reported the slaughter of almost three hundred thousand youths. Disappearances and imprisonments are beyond estimate. The September 18th incident led to the loss of ten thousand *lis* of territory in three days. Are our people not aware who is responsible? But in the face of an external peril, [the people] are not willing to take issues with their own government. The government, however, has taken advantage [of the people], using the pretext of a united national stand to justify [silencing dissent]. Previously the pretext was "red subversion," now the crime is "endangering foreign relations." Every action taken by the people is a potential crime. Discussions on anti-imperialism organized by Beida students, and discussions on current affairs organized by Qinghua students are all legally permitted activities. But the government [suppresses them] with arrests. Entertaining patriotic feelings is a crime. Whosoever cries for national salvation will be persecuted.[22]

Suppression, however determined, could not discipline the patriotism of the educated young. Suppression alienated them from the GMD because that party had come to symbolize ineffectual government. Many opted for the opponents of the GMD, trekking to Yanan to join the Chinese communists in search of alternative leadership for "national salvation." It would be difficult to sustain the argument that these students were trekking to Yanan in search of a more liberal environment. Many who decided to stay in the Beijing area joined regional military units. The defiant stand taken by Chinese soldiers at Lugouqiao, in direct contrast to the compromising mood of those in higher authority, was partly the result of the presence of patriotic youths among the rank and file of the regional military. Student nationalism continued to be very potent and became increasingly volatile. The "voice of dissent" was not in search of political or intellectual freedom. It was in search of effective leadership in the national cause.

The nationalist government came to power by harnessing nationalist feelings; it could not afford to have its commitment to nationalism questioned. The Nanjing government regarded the right to interpret nationalism as its own prerogative and responded to student protests by standing on its own dignity. Such political tactics simply alienated the government from its own foundations of sociopolitical support.

To the students their show of love for their country was beyond reproach. They were facing the issue in terms of moral example, the students themselves providing the moral example of direct political action. They too thought they could do no wrong, since their moral purpose was pure. They demanded that the government heed their moral strength or risk becoming politically defunct. The December 9th movement threatened to put the nationalist party and students on opposite camps by mid-1930s.

5   Origins of the Young Officers' Movement

The Whampoa model for militarizing campuses in the late 1920swas replaced by the slogan "Trading Space for Time" in the 30s, explaining repeated territorial losses to Japan. Losses eroded hard-won political momentum. Mounting campus unease, in both north and central china, was one symptom of this loss of momentum.

Former cadets from Whampoa were naturally sensitive to the new trend. These Whampoa graduates formed an important power base for the Nanjing government. During the period 1928 to 1937, they were mainly serving as mid-level army officers, at the captain to major general range, commanding units of the National Revolutionary Army (NRA).[1] Realizing that their military training at Whampoa was quite basic, many joined training programs at home, while the select few went overseas for further studies. This officer cum student group organized a clandestine revival movement (*Fuxing Yundong*) to halt further erosion of the political credibility of the nationalists.

Many Whampoa alumni identified the national cause with the leadership of Jiang Jieshi and blamed national frustrations on other party and government leaders. Holding command of key units of the NRA, their military muscle created and sustained the Nanjing government. They were the cornerstone of the Nanjing regime and they were uneasy with the weak diplomatic stance of that regime. The revival movement was formed to organize pressure from inside and outside the Nanjing government to press for more determined stands against Japanese incursion.

Whampoa alumni did not form a homogeneous group in terms of age and educational background. Beneath the surface of national purpose and unity of command, existed strong factional tendencies.

At least three factions were involved in organizing the revival movement. These were identified as the Teng Jie, Liu Jianqun, and Dai Li Factions.

The Teng Jie Faction

Teng Jie led the mainstream faction formed by young protégés of Jiang Jieshi. Between 1928 and 1930, thirty Whampoa graduates were selected by Jiang for further studies in Japan.[2] They were the cream of the Whampoa alumni, which consisted mainly of young men in their early twenties.[3] These select few could expect good positions on their return. Their career prospects were tied to those of their patron Jiang Jieshi and the well-being of the Nanjing government.

Being intensely nationalistic, these young soldiers found it difficult to endure Japanese arrogance and felt disturbed that their own government was not more forceful in dealings with Japan. In 1930 the Japanese deliberately fanned up racial antagonism between Korean and Chinese settlers along the Korean-Manchurian border. This served as a catalyst in stirring the young cadets in Japan to political action. In July over twenty alumni then studying in Japan met on two occasions to discuss what they could do to influence Chinese policy.[4] They elected Teng Jie and Xiao Zhanyu to present their views to government leaders back home.[5] Back in Nanjing the two young men were simply ignored, for they had no recognised standing to express political views. Frustrated in their mission, the two went their separate ways to visit friends and relatives.

While visiting relatives Teng Jie drafted some plans for reform,[6] the full contents of which have not yet been officially released to date. In the plans Teng Jie proposed to set up an extensive underground network to "revive" China,[7]—that is, to engage in politically sensitive activities underground. Later the revival society, or *Fuxingshe,* was formed as a popular front organization, hence the term "the revival movement." It was an organized political pressure group led by Whampoa alumni intent on influencing government policy and popular opinion so that China would take a more determined stand against Japan. Though the full contents of the Teng draft remains unknown, some of its main points can be deduced from a few public statements made by Teng, from contemporary observations of Teng, and from what we know of his background.

Teng Jie had a classical education at home from the age of seven to twelve. After that he enrolled at a technical school run by American missionaries. In 1924 Teng was active in anti-imperialist demonstrations and his actions resulted in the closure of the technical school. Then, at the age of eighteen, he enrolled at Shanghai University, a favorite recruiting ground for the CCP.[8] In 1972 Teng claimed that he was attracted to Sun-wenism since his technical school days, but this cannot be verified by collaborating evidence from the 1920s.[9] His leadership in anti-imperialist demonstration did show that he was intensely patriotic, and his subsequent enrolment at Shanghai University would suggest that he was attracted to leftist radical circles.[10] With Chu Qiubai as a leading figure at the university, students were well exposed to Russian literature and Marxist writings.[11] Teng Jie was exposed to socialist ideas at Shanghai University.

Although the university was a favorite ground for the Chinese communists to recruit,[12] and Teng Jie, with his proven ability in organizing student protests, was a likely recruiting target, he remained uncommitted to the radical left. On leaving Shanghai University Teng Jie enrolled at the Whampoa Military Academy (4th class).[13] It was only during the heated rivalry between the Young Soldiers Association and the Sun-wenism Study Society that Teng exposed anti-communist inclinations in public. In spite of strong anticommunist views[14] he was not a member of the Sun-Wenism Study Society. This seems to indicate that the Sun-Wenism society did not see fit to accept a former graduate of Shanghai University into their midst.

The first time that Teng is known to have published anticommunist views was in early 1926. Upon graduation he was assigned to the 21st division where his anticommunist views expressed in the divisional broadsheet attracted a formal complaint from the CCP.[15] GMD party policy then was to ally with Soviet Russia and to cooperate with the Chinese communists. The CCP was acting within its rights in complaining against Teng Jie. The divisional commander referred the matter to Jiang who, after a personal interview with the young man, made Teng one of his protégés. Teng served on the personal staff of Jiang before being sent to Japan for further studies.[16]

Arriving in Tokyo he enrolled at Meiji University to study political economy. Teng was of intellectual bent, interested in new ideas and strongly anticommunist. We do not know whether he was influenced by the ideas and tactics of radicals in the Japanese military, those of Kita Ikki and the Sakurakai, for example. Nor do we know whether he was open to fascist influence at this time. Later observations of how he wore Nazi-style military uniform cannot be used to substantiate the allegation that in 1930 he was a convert to Nazism.[17] Nor can his later visits to Germany and Italy be used to suggest that his draft proposal of 1930 was influenced by fascism.[18] Only indirect evidence suggests that Teng and his associates entertained fascist ideas—for example, their attempts to address Jiang as the leader or duce. Teng boldly tried to pursuade Jiang to accept the new title even though Jiang protested that it was inappropriate.[19] Another suggestive evidence is that Teng was unsure how Jiang would receive his reform proposals initially and launched his effort to organize a political arm among his fellow alumni without first informing Jiang. [20] Were the political ideas expressed in the reform proposal known to be unacceptable to Jiang, such as radical communist or fascist ideas? A frequent admonition of Jiang Jieshi at the time was "When speaking of leftist ideas, do not model them on Communism. When speaking of rightist ideas, do not model them on Facism."[21]

The Liu Jianqun Faction

In 1930 Liu Jianqun was a senior staff officer at the Nanchang headquarters of General He Yingqin. Liu was not a professional soldier, he was rather a political adviser to He Yingqin, holding military rank.[22] Liu was at the center of military and political initiatives aimed at eliminating the Chinese communists from their rural soviet bases in central China. Liu was part of a small brain trust, endowed with leisure and pleasant surroundings, to analyze the current scene and propose solutions.[23]

In late 1931 Liu completed a written proposal for political action entitled "Zhongguo Guomindang Lanyishe" or "The Blue-Shirt Society of the Chinese Nationalist Party," The opening words of the document were:

> At the present this Party has more than a million members, including warlords, corrupt officials, local bullies and unscrupulous elders. This mixed political color renders it difficult to distinguish between the genuine from the false, there is no way of rectifying [this confusion], nor is it possible to re-order the [Party] register. The existence of the Party is more apparent than real. The best [reform] method is to begin afresh from the foundations. But [accepting] historical reality and upholding [existing] legal frameworks, we are unwilling to cause serious dissension. [Instead] we propose to keep the outer shell of the Party and [proceed] to establish a Lanyi Tuan [Blue Shirt Brigade] to give substance to the Party and to serve as the soul of the Party.[24]

In the document Liu was proposing to establish an inner core to take over control of the GMD through a "block within" strategy. Who were to be members of this inner core? This was defined in the five criteria required of members of the proposed blue shirt society. These were:

(1) Total commitment to the three principles of the people
(2) Total observance of group discipline
(3) Imbued with the spirit of public service
(4) Be objective and avoid making emotional decisions
(5) Mutual respect among members, putting comradely relationship above all else.[25]

The most important are the first two—that is, unquestioned ideological commitment and group discipline. It was a structure designed to distinguish between "true" and "false" GMD members. The "true" believers would be recruited into the inner core, and the "false" elements to be jostled out of real positions of power and influence.

The proposed title of this body of "true" believers, the blueshirt society, has lent itself to suggestions of fascist influence. This is unfortunate. The blue shirt uniform was proposed because blue was the dominant color on the GMD party flag and because blue dress was the designated commoners' attire in traditional China, and so representative of the masses. Blue-shirt and fascism are not directly related.

A factional organization developed in the course of soliciting support for the ideas of Liu Jianqun. Initially there were only a handful of suppporters, all colleagues of Liu at the Nanchang headquarters.[26] The difficulty in gathering support among the Whampoa alumni was the fact that Liu himself was not a Whampoa graduate and it was essential to have Whampoa alumni as members of the inner core. Political advisers such as Liu and his immediate supporters did not possess the substance of military power upon which the Nanjing government rested.

First, Liu sought to present his views to the GMD. In the winter of 1931 Liu Jianqun and Xuan Jiexi attempted to submit a written proposal to Chen Lifu at Nanjing.[27] Chen Lifu was the younger brother of Chen Guofu; both were close advisers of the generalissimo. At the time Chen Lifu was head of the organization department of the GMD. While at Nanjing, Liu was denied access on the ground that Chen Lifu was away at Hangzhou on official business at the time.[28] A serious political submission composed by key advisers of He Yingqin deserved better reception. But the fact that Liu first approached Chen

Lifu indicates that Liu did not entertain the thought of lobbying directly for political support among the young officers. He had a plan for party reform and he tried to interest a key party leader in those plans.

With their access to Chen Lifu blocked, the proposers retired to Zhen Jiang for a day of sightseeing, and there they were joined by three other supporters. Together they decided (1) to seek the patronage of Jiang Jieshi directly, (2) to solicit support from younger people among Whampoa graduates and college students, and (3) to subscribe to a publication fund of five thousand for distributing a shortened popular version of the blue shirt society proposal among potential supporters.[29] Liu and two supporters stayed on in Nanjing to lobby for support.[30]

By February 1932 Liu had completed an abbreviated version of the proposal, entitled "Contributing a Few Opinions on Party Reforms," and was distributing it to interested parties.[31] The principal points emphasized in this version were:

(1) step up preparations for resisting Japanese pressure
(2) tighten party organization, enforce discipline, and regain popular support
(3) implement these proposals by a core group to be known as the blue shirts.[32]

By May 1932—that is, just over a month *after* the establishment of the *Lixingshe*,[33]—the Liu Jianqun faction expanded its core group from five to seventeen.[34]

In 1932 the Liu Jianqun faction was identifiable by his views on political reform, supported by a small lobby group. Its political impact became significant when information on the group reached the hands of Jiang some time in early March 1932.[35]

The Dai Li Faction

Apart from the Teng Jie and Liu Jianqun factions, there was a third organized element in the Revival Movement, led by Dai Li. Though enrolled relatively late at the Whampoa Military Academy, Dai Li was older than his fellow cadets. At the age of thirty Dai seemed to be a "generation" apart from his contemporaries. Enrolling late in the sixth class also meant that this older man was junior to most of the other cadets.[36] He was an odd man out, unable to form extensive social ties, or be involved in the political debates between the Young

Soldiers Association and the Sun-wenism Study Society. As such Dai was hardly noticed except by a couple of close friends who were similarly older and isolated.[37] A loner was unpromising material as leader of a faction.

His relative isolation at Whampoa gave Dai Li the opportunity to observe. When Jiang needed reliable intelligence during the purge, Dai was able to submit detailed reports, which facilitated the purge at Whampoa.[38] Although Dai proved he had the ability to be a good intelligence gatherer, recognition went to his immediate superior, Wu Jingan. Wu was assigned by Jiang to head a small intelligence unit and Dai was merely a recruit. To reward him for his meritorious service, Wu was sent to Germany in January 1928 for further studies.[39] Wu did recommend Dai as his replacement, but Dai himself did not have an established working relationship with Jiang. Consequently the unit itself was neglected and Dai became practically the only member of staff left.[40]

Intelligence work was the jealously guarded preserve of the select circle of protégés around Jiang. The apppointment of Dai to perform intelligence work in January 1928 was viewed by the chief of Jiang's personal staff as an unwelcomed intrusion. His personal intervention made it difficult for Dai to submit reports or to seek appointments to see Jiang.[41] Dai thus found himself to be a victim of the Whampoa alumni hierarchy, being both junior and an outsider.

Dai Li, however, was confident of the professional quality of his reports. He risked his own life in submitting reports unannounced as Jiang was getting in or out of his limousine. Such exploits brought threats of court martial from fellow officers until Jiang recognized the quality of his reports and gave Dai Li special access to see him.[42] By 1928 Dai had found himself a career in special intelligence, though somewhat isolated from fellow alumni. His future depended on the usefulness of his intelligence skills to one person, Jiang Jieshi. Dai was "the eyes and ears of the leader."[43] His ambition was to build an intelligence organization. Dai Li was formally introduced to join the Teng Jie faction by He Zhonghan.[44] This enabled Dai Li to infiltrate the Teng Jie faction just as it was setting up a secret organization to underpin the revival movement. At this early stage Teng Jie was already suspicious of Dai's motives and cautioned him against reporting the activities of the movement to the generalissimo.

The Lixingshe Organization

The Lixingshe developed in close to two years of behind-the-scenes political maneuvrings by the Teng Jie faction, with the Liu Jianqun and Dai Li factions being brought in by Jiang Jieshi to act as checks and balances within the organization.

Having drafted his plan for "national revival,"[46] Teng Jie solicited support for action. Teng counted on the loyalty and friendship of former cadets and approached several of them for comment. First he showed the draft to Chen Jiyu, the brother of his fiancée and a fellow student who recently returned from Japan. Chen politely praised his prose, but thought the ideas impractical.[47] Then Teng thought of Hu Buri, an alumnus of the fourth class who had been vocally anticommunist in early Whampoa days. Hu was serving in the Jiangsu provincial government and his office was located in Zhen Jiang. Teng sought Hu out personally. After reading the draft Hu stated bluntly that he thought the author was lacking in understanding of Chinese society.[48] Back in Nanjing, Teng solicited comments from He Zhonghan and was told that the ideas were unacceptable to Jiang.[49]

In spite of repeated rebuffs, Teng continued to lobby for support from Whampoa alumni then holding key positions. The next person he approached was Zang Kangqing, a graduate of the first class, secretary of the military department at GMD party headquarters, and onetime commanding officer over Teng.[50] There the draft was received with enthusiasm and Zang Kangqing agreed to be involved in organizing a support group.[51]

With the assistance of Zang Kangqing the revival movement was finally launched in secret. The core members were recruited in three successive dinner parties hosted by Zang. At the first meeting Teng drew up a guest list of ten, among whom were Kang Ze and Deng Wenyi.[52] At the time Deng Wenyi was serving as Jiang's secretary and entrusted with intelligence responsibilities.[53]

This initial group of twelve unanimously supported Teng Jie's plans, and each agreed to bring along a potential recruit to the next dinner.[54] During the following meeting the gathering was again unanimous. This enlarged group of twenty-four repeated the exercise of finding an additional recruit for the next party. So by the third meeting there were forty-eight core members, including He Zhonghan,[55] who had earlier dismissed Teng Jie's plan.[56] He Zhonghan personally introduced the admission of Dai Li soon after the third dinner party, so Dai Li was the forty-ninth member of the inner circle.[57] Knowing that Dai Li had been active in gathering intelligence for Jiang, Teng Jie spoke to Dai Li personally, asking Dai not to report the activities of the group.[58] The career record of Dai Li before and after suggests that he deliberately infiltrated the group. With him in the Teng Jie faction Jiang would soon be informed of the plans of the young officers in launching a revival movement.

At the third dinner party He Zhonghan pursuaded the group to establish a nationwide network of secret cells.[59] Deng Wenyi then promised to allocate $300 from the proceeds of a GMD bookshop under his control as seeding fund for the movement.[60] Premises were immediately rented to set up a preparatory bureau.[61] Teng Jie was nominated secretary—that is, formally recognized as leader.[62] Teng acted prompty and secret cells were established in Shanghai, Hangzhou, Anjing, Nanchang, Wuhan, Jinan, Beijing, and Manchuria.[63] The exact timing of all these developments is not known, but they did occur between Teng Jie's return to China shortly after July 1930 and prior to the Mukden incident of September 1931.

Early in 1932 the existence of the group was known to Jiang Jieshi. At the time the generalissimo was unpopular, because of his handling of the Manchurian crisis. The anti-Japanese orientation of the Teng Jie faction was indicative of general unease within the military power base. As an organized pressure group strategically placed, these young officers could exert considerable pressure.

It was advisable for Jiang to gain control over this secret group if his authority over the military was not to be weakened. At this juncture Teng Jie also instructed Deng Wenyi to submit a full report on the organization to Jiang, ostensibly to forestall a threat to expose the group from Li Yimin, another Whampoa alumnus.[64] Li Yimin later joined the Teng Jie faction, and this suggests that his threat to expose the secret organization could have been feigned.[65] The timing of the report did not suit Jiang. At the time he was in temporary "retirement" in his provincial home. Was the timing of the Deng Wenyi report one of maximizing pressure on Jiang Jieshi? On receiving the report Jiang did not show surprise and even expressed mild approval: "Very well But you are inexperienced and may not perform well."[66]

The "confession" of the Teng Jie faction, composed by Deng Wenyi, reached Jiang either late in December 1931 or early in January 1932.[67] It was not until January 22 that Jiang summoned the ring leaders to see him. That is to say, Jiang chose to defer his response until he was back in the saddle of power. On January 21, 1932, Jiang Jieshi returned to Nanjing. The very next day three of the leading figures of the Teng Jie faction were summoned to see him. The three were Teng Jie, He Zhonghan, and Kang Ze.[68] On seeing them Jiang simply could not contain himself as he said: "You are deficient in experience. Your performance I am afraid is not good enough. I shall lead you."[69]

Teng ignored the reprimand and tried to pressure Jiang to accept the secret organization by addressing him as the leader. The generalissimo unexpectedly found his match in Teng Jie and did not take the next move until late February 1932. He knew he had the potentials of a major crisis on his hands.

It was some time after this initial confrontation on January 22, possibly a full month later, that Jiang delivered a message to Teng Jie through Deng Wenyi, instructing Teng to assemble all the major figures of his faction for extended discussions from March 4.[71] Teng acted on the message, informed twenty-eight of his associates in person, noted that Hu Zongnan, Zang Kangqing, and Ye Wei could not be informed in time as they were away from Nanjing on official duties.[72]

On the night Jiang arrived without any body guard, accompanied by Deng Wenyi his secretary. He first assigned Dai Li to keep watch. Then the former cadets were asked to speak in turn, the order being arranged according to class seniority and then age.[73] The first to speak was He Zhonghan because he was the oldest from the First Class. The most lengthy speech was from Gui Yungqing, because he had just returned from an extended tour of Europe and was providing a briefing on the views of various European governments. Throughout the evening Jiang did not make any comments, listened attentively, and jotted down some key points now and then. After four hours Jiang indicated that the proceedings would resume the following evening.[75]

The proceedings on March 5 were similar except for an unexpected interruption from Gui Yungqing. Gui had taken the longest time to speak the evening before, so his request to speak was unexpected. Nonetheless Jiang approved by nodding, whereupon Gui introduced an article written by Liu Jianqun and proposed that Liu be invited to join the gathering.[76] This move enabled Jiang to decide whether to invite Liu Jianqun or not.

At the end of the third evening, March 6, Teng Jie spoke. He was neither the youngest nor the most junior, but deliberately chose to speak last so that he could act as the representative voice of the whole group.[77] Only part of his summing up is public knowledge, the part that dealt with the Japanese threat:

When we fight the Japanese, it is a case of the weak fighting the strong. Japanese national policy puts the conquest of China as a first priority. War cannot be avoided if China is to survive. Even though we are the weak fighting the strong, we can only seek salvation by risking all. Our actions will determine our survival. Therefore it is urgent to organize our manpower and material resources to improve fighting effectiveness, for final victory is often decided by manpower and material resources. We have five times the manpower of Japan, thirty times the material resources of Japan, if we only have strong organization and leadership...final victory will be ours.[78]

So at the end of three long evenings of articulation of political views by members of the Teng Jie faction, its representative figure launched a broadside on the Japan policy of Jiang, demanding a more resolute stand. The challenge from these Whampoa cadets could no longer be ignored and in a well-prepared speech Jiang signaled his agreement in principle and pleaded for time: "I do hope you would really understand my intentions. From now on, for the task of defending the liberty and independence of the nation, for the sake of achieving a revolutionary national reconstruction . . . we must . . . try to gain every minute, every second . . . for we know that one more minute of preparation is one less minute of sacrifice."[79]

The young officers won their point and successfully pressured Jiang Jieshi to agree that the most urgent issue was to prepare China for a war with Japan. But their success raised an immediate issue: Were they dictating policy to Jiang or were they loyal followers of their former teacher?

The continuing saga of this long confrontation resumed on March 7 at a different location and took on a different setting. At eight in the morning Teng Jie led his faction to the officers club at Nanjing, there they were met by Dai Li who showed them into a rectangular room arranged into a classroom setting. On the east wall was a picture of Sun Yatsen, underneath was a small blackboard in front were a wooden desk, a chair, and a box of chalk.[80] As Jiang entered the room, Teng Jie shouted drill commands, as if he was the duty officer.[81] Jiang gently put down a couple of books, eyed his audience, picked up a piece of chalk, turned around, and wrote an often quoted saying of Sun Yatsen: "To understand is difficult, but to act is easy. Knowledge is inseparable from action."[83] That was his lecture topic for the day. And after speaking for over an hour, Jiang wrote two essay topics on the blackboard. The gathering was told that each was to choose a topic, write an essay, and submit it when they were to meet again the following day.[83]

This ritual of distinguishing between teacher and student, between superior and inferior, continued the next day (March 8). Jiang was wearing a long blue silk gown, black leather shoes, and slacks. He waited for Teng Jie to do a roll call, told the gathering to sit down, then put on his reading glasses and proceeded to read the essays his students submitted that morning.[84] Everyone was given a high grade, except one.[85] Was Teng Jie the odd one out? The gathering was then asked whether it agreed with the teacher's comments and grading.[86] It was a ritual to reestablish the teacher-student hierarchy between Jiang and the Teng Jie faction.

The final ritual was the formal establishment of the Lixingshe and the election of office bearers. The term *Lixing* was a quotation from Sun Yatsen used in Jiang's lecture, so the naming represented a formal claim that the secret organization was legitimized by the ideas of Sun as interpreted by Jiang Jieshi. Then Teng Jie issued ballot papers, authenticated by his seal. Election of office-bearers was by secret ballot. Each voter was entitled to circle three names out of a list of twenty-eight. Teng was to collect the votes, Gui Yungqing to read each ballot aloud, He Zhonghan to act as scrutineer, and Deng Wenyi to record the results.[78] Jiang's name was not on the list; he was the leader, *not* an office-bearer. After all the efforts, Jiang failed to capture control of the Teng Jie faction, formally organized as the Lixingshe on March 8, 1932.

The Counterattack

When Liu Jianqun's article reached Jiang's hands in early March, Jiang was in dire need of ideas and organization to counterbalance Teng Jie and his supporters. Liu Jianqun was summoned for consultation with Jiang throughout March 1932, so Jiang was listening to the proposed courses of action of both the Teng Jie and Liu Jianqun factions without first bringing the two organized groups together.[88] To have identified another independent secret lobby group around Liu seemed almost tailor-made to Jiang's needs. The fact that the Liu group lacked access to the young officers of Whampoa origin became an added recommendation.

How was Jiang the leader, a leader denied executive authority within the Lixingshe organization, to introduce Liu Jianqun and his supporters into the Lixingshe? The first step was taken by Gui

Yungqing during the second meeting between Jiang and the Teng Jie faction. Gui interrupted the proceedings to mention the reform proposals of Liu Jianqun and to suggest that he be admitted to the group.[89] This move from one of Teng Jie's key supporters enabled Jiang to press for the admission of Liu Jianqun into the Lixingshe.[90] Teng Jie was resistent, and he did not recruit Liu until the end of April. Even then Liu was only accorded membership in a front organization of the Lixingshe, the revolutionary youth, and not into Lixingshe proper.[91] That is to say, Teng Jie resisted the admission of Liu into the inner circle of the young officers movement. The moment Teng Jie grudgingly admitted Liu, the reality of factional rivalry within the movement could no longer be avoided.

The junior status of Liu within Lixingshe was compensated for by extensive patronage from Jiang. Liu was appointed head of political training in the Central Military Academy and in the Military Affairs Commission. Both of these positions were likely to be high-sounding titles which carried little power or influence. Jiang, however, established an effective power base for Liu in May 1932 with the establishment of a cadre training unit (Zhengxun ban), entrusted to train six hundred cadres.[92]

Over three thousand candidates, composed of Whampoa graduates and college students, sat for the entrance test of the cadre training unit. Teng Jie was confronted with this large-scale open effort to compete for followers from among Whampoa graduates. It became politically unwise for him to deny Liu full membership in the Lixingshe. Teng even joined Liu's training staff to ensure that he would have some influence over this cadre force.[93] From October 1935 to September 1937 Liu occupied the highest executive office within the Lixingshe[94], so Teng Jie did lose full control over the Lixingshe. It is claimed that factional rivalry very much limited the effectiveness of Liu during his period of office.[95] Whatever the frustrations of Liu Jianqun and Teng Jie within the Lixingshe, Jiang had succeeded in weakening the internal cohesion of that organization.

Both Teng Jie and Liu Jianqun were in agreement on the urgency of a more determined stand against the Japanese. What they differed on was tactics. The Teng Jie faction emphasized *military* preparation, while the Liu Jianqun faction emphasized *political* organization. Teng Jie focused his attention in bringing Whampoa alumni into a tightly disciplined political pressure group. Liu Jianqun focused his attention on the training of political cadres to be deployed to spread GMD influence beyond territories directly controlled by GMD military units. Neither faction put loyalty to Jiang Jieshi above its policy and tactical preferences.

The Dai Li faction provided a third position as it placed loyalty to Jiang Jieshi above other considerations. It has been noted earlier that Dai Li joined the Teng Jie faction as the forty-ninth man, introduced by He Zhonghan.[96] His success in infiltrating the Teng Jie faction was not necessarily directed by Jiang, but his presence within the Lixingshe could be of immense service to Jiang.

When the Lixingshe was established on March 8 and office-bearers were elected, the organization incorporated an intelligence section. The Head of that Section was Gui Yungqing.[97] According to Gan Guoxun, Gui was selected because he had been a German student in the inner core of the Lixing She.[98] Gui was assigned a staff of over twenty and the entire unit given thirty days training in intelligence work conducted by a German adviser.[99]

Gui, however, was holding a key position in the army, which demanded his full attention. He resigned from the intelligence section just after one week.[100] The key position Gui held was the head of officers' supplementary training class of the Central Military Academy, a special scheme in which seventeen hundred commission officers of the rank of colonel and below were being given the latest German military training by three German advisers.[101] This German-trained officer corps was to be the core of an eighty-thousand strong elite military force, popularly known as the president's own.[102] But it must be noted that before Gui's resignation from the intelligence section, the Teng Jie faction already had over twenty of its members staffing that section. The departure of Gui did not threaten the faction's control over the intelligence section.

Jiang Jieshi took the opportunity of Gui's resignation to recommend to Teng Jie that Dai Li, because of his proven skills in intelligence work, could head the section *on probation*.[103] Jiang was not an office-bearer of the Lixingshe, so he could not appoint Dai to Lixing She positions. But as the leader—that is, a titular head—he could at least recommend Dai. Given the fact that Teng already had his men in place in the intelligence section, it was not difficult for Teng to accede to the leader's wish.[104] And so it was that Dai Li was appointed by Teng Jie to succeed Gui Yungqing as head of the intelligence section of the Lixingshe.

Members of the Lixingshe were sworn to obey the organization, and this gave Dai access to motivated people. He quickly expanded his staff complement to 145, mostly composed of Whampoa alumni.[105] The initial pattern of expansion was to establish an intelligence unit attached to each of the Lixingshe secret cells.[106] In this way Dai acquired full knowledge of the entire Lixingshe operation. Organizational details could no longer be withheld from Jiang Jieshi.

The implications of Dai Li's loyalty to the Lixingshe was clear to Teng Jie. According to Qiao Jiacai, Dai Li was approached by an unnamed alumnus who informed Dai that control over finance and personnel for the intelligence section was not entrusted to Dai. At this point Dai is said to have tendered his resignation to Jiang the next day, but was told by Jiang to stay. Jiang also assured Dai that his worries could be taken care of.[107] These claims are likely to be true in context, but not in detail. That Teng Jie might have tried to assert himself over Dai Li was to be expected. So the alumnus alleged by Qiao could be Teng, or someone else acting for Teng. It could also be true that Dai "submitted his resignation" to Jiang the next day, but since Dai was not appointed by Jiang, this "resignation" was a means to press for tangible patronage. If Dai Li were to act as a counterforce to Teng Jie, Dai had to be provided with the ways and means to do so. In return Dai could offer service, but by an organization that Dai was going to build. It was to have its secret elements that neither the Lixingshe nor Jiang could have full knowledge of; otherwise that secret service could not become effective.

That tangible patronage that Dai was seeking came in September 1932. In addition to his position as head of the intelligence section of the Lixingshe, Dai was appointed chief of the second section of the research and statistical bureau of the Military Affairs Commission, popularly known as the Juntong.[108] From September 1932 onward Dai Li submitted detailed requests to Jiang for personnel and funding, while at the same time holding on to his previous appointment with the Lixingshe. Dai thus acted with the full financial backing of Jiang, the full authority accorded to an office-bearer of the Lixingshe, and could choose whether his loyalty should be to the leader or the secretary of Lixingshe. The Juntong became an independent organization by balancing the rival interests of Jiang Jieshi and the Lixingshe.

The Juntong was an organization born of divided loyalty, and thrived on divided loyalty. Its principal duty was to serve as "the eyes and ears of the leader," but in order to enhance this service it was also beneficial to the Juntong to maintain the demand for that service. The growth and development of the Lixingshe organization created the Juntong and enhanced the continued growth of the Juntong. It was a complicated game of political shadow boxing in which Jiang, Teng Jie, and Dai Li could each perceive himself as the ultimate manipulator. The revival movement became faction-ridden from the outset.

6 The Young Officers' Movement

The three competing factions of the Lixingshe each had a different focus. The Teng Jie faction emphasized political cohesion of the officers corp, aiming to turn the alumni of the military academy into an organized political force amenable to command by the Lixingshe. The Liu Jianqun faction emphasized propaganda and the training of political cadres, using them to expand GMD influence in lieu of direct military action. The Dai Li faction focused on loyalty to Jiang Jieshi and the use of a secret police instrument to enforce that loyalty.

The Lixingshe was a secret organization with some of its activities conducted in the open through front organizations. These included newspapers such as the *Jiuguo Ribao* (*National Salvation Daily*) and the *Zhongguo Ribao* (*China Daily*).[1]

The *National Salvation Daily* was established by Gong Tebo in late 1931 or early 1932. Gong was stridently anti-Japanese and was deported from Japan for organizing demonstrations to protest against the Manchurian incident. The *National Salvation Daily* expressed the strong anti-Japanese views of fellow Whampoa alumni. Prior to the establishment of the Lixingshe, Teng Jie and his supporters used the *National Salvation Daily* as a cover for their political activities. [2]

The *China Daily* was established by the Whampoa alumni association. Initially Deng Wenyi was entrusted with the task of launching the newspaper. However, Deng could not be relieved from his post as the personal secretary to Jiang Jieshi. Kang Ze was entrusted with the task.[3] An existing paper known as the *Jian Ye Ribao* was taken over and became the *China Daily*.[4]

Both the *National Salvation Daily* and the *China Daily* were popular because of their anti-Japanese views.[5] Publication for the *China Daily* started in January 1932 and it soon became the principal media outlet for the Lixingshe.[6] But such traceable connections between the Lixingshe and its front organizations were few.

The organizational structure of the Lixingshe was kept secret so that its political enemies would have difficulty in identifying the organization and its diverse operations. Although extensive records were kept by the Lixingshe, these were unfortunately burned in the final stages of the civil war. Much of the information we have on the Lixingshe today is derived from subsequent recollections of its leaders and their advisers.[7]

At the establishment ceremony on March 8, 1932, there were twenty-nine founding members, including Jiang Jieshi. Even then the actual membership was at least fifty, and secret cells were already in place.[8] At its height the Lixingshe core group was around three hundred, and they were the only ones with some knowledge of the overall operations.[9] Even at this level activities were compartmentalized to enhance security and secrecy. The organizational design was set to minimize lateral connections between operating units.

The Lixingshe recruited by invitation. Target recruits were selected for their known public views and for strategic positions in government, in the military, in business, in the labor unions, and so on.[10] Members were therefore a highly select group of influential people. The stress was on quality, not quantity. The core leadership of three hundred were predominantly of Whampoa origin.

Beyond this small and tightly knit core of the Lixingshe were two outer rings of junior membership. These members did not know of the existence of the Lixingshe. They were members of either the Geming Qingnianhui (revolutionary youth) or the Fuxingshe (revival society).[11] These bodies were directly controlled by the Lixingshe; they had no separate organizational existence. These junior members did not know their connections with the Lixingshe. Entry was also by invitation.[12] The initiative for recruitment came from the tightly knit center of the Lixingshe, making infiltration almost impossible. Also defection by outer ring members could not yield much information to the enemy.

This secret structure with its emphasis on multiple parallels of vertical relationship and minimal horizontal connections was an ingenious design. Once recruited, members were expected to be totally at the service of the organization.[13] Disobedience invited disciplinary measures from the Lixingshe and executed by its own intelligence section, headed by Dai Li.[14] The organization was a patriotic body, it recruited members for their known views, but failure to live up to the demands of the organization brought reprisals. In this way patriotic commitment was reinforced by the sternest of discipline. The use of terror was legitimized in terms of ethical bonds and love of country.

The terror instrument was not restricted by legal scruples, but its use was deliberate and not indiscriminate. The total select membership of the organization amounted to one hundred thousand, with about thirty thousand in the revolutionary youth category, three hundred in the Lixingshe core, and the majority belonging to the most junior category of being members of the revival society.[15]

The Japanese were soon alerted, for the very nature of its work in organizing influence in secret often led to rumors and innuendos. Suggestions and editorial denials abounded in the popular press. [16] Most likely the Japanese had access to Liu Jianqun's article "Contributing a Few Opinions to Party Reform," which was distributed to solicit support. Denied a fuller picture by the tightly knit Lixingshe, the Japanese accused Nanjing of having established a secret terrorist organization known as the blue shirt society.[17] This was the likely origins of the popular name given to the entire clandestine operations of the Lixingshe.

Japanese desperation for information led to extreme acts. Suspecting that the north China propaganda brigade was part of Lixingshe operations, the Japanese military police arrested two of Liu Jianqun's lieutenants in broad daylight in the streets of Beijing.[18] This was most irregular and is an example of how the Japanese military ignored due legal process and diplomatic protocols in China. One of the two arrested was Xuan Jiexi who was a close adviser to Liu Jianqun.[19] Xuan was tortured and information extracted from him.[20] How much was given away was not known, but members of the Liu Jianqun faction, such as Xuan, probably did not know the full range of activities of the Lixingshe. The Japanese failed to break through the veil of secrecy by force.

According to the available record, only forty-eight persons were shown the original draft of Teng Jie.[21] Even Dai Li, as the forty-ninth person who joined, might not know the full planning details of the secret organization, at least not at the beginning.

Being a clandestine society conducting its activities in secret, the public image of the Lixingshe was principally built upon rumors and innuendos. Its power and influence were exaggerated, and in turn this exaggeration fed its power and influence. The anti-Japanese stance of the organization and the public exaggeration of its power helped sustain the credibility of the Nanjing government, even when it was being subjected to a series of intense Japanese military and diplomatic pressures. One such rumor was that the blue-shirt society was behind the spirited resistance of Cai Tinggai's 19th route army in Shanghai in 1932. There were elements of circumstantial evidence to support such a rumor, for Whampoa alumni were vocally expressing anti-Japanese views in their newspapers. Why should the spirited defense by a regional military group not be linked to a wider movement? Nor would the Lixingshe deny involvement, for being a secret society it could not do so in public. Besides, since this ambiguity might actually enhance its image, there was no reason for the Lixingshe to clear it up either. Although the central army units did not directly assist the spirited resistance offered by the 19th route army, two divisions did take up reserve positions in case the 19th route army failed to hold the line.[22] Such troop movements added to the ambiguity at the time and sustained controversy after the event.

One of the most effective means for the Lixingshe to build up its image was ambiguity. Its legendary power and influence became the food of Chinese popular opinion when the populace was desperately hoping that something could be done to stop blatant Japanese aggression. The effect of what might be called a "spiritual rallying," as a result of Lixingshe operations, cannot be overestimated.

There is no direct way of measuring the success of the Lixingshe. Its secret maneuverings circumvented the need for Nanjing to articulate anti-Japanese views directly. The Lixingshe thus enabled the Chinese to respond to Japanese provocation without formal government involvement. In this way the GMD government retained significant credibility in spite of repeated concessions made to Japan.

Liu Jianqun's Experiment

Liu Jianqun advocated a combination of secret and open activities to counter the Japanese.[23] In July 1932 Liu received authorization from Jiang to establish a postgraduate training course in propaganda work.[24] Recruitment was by open competitive examination, and about three thousands candidates sat for the entrance examination. They were either graduates of tertiary institutions or of military academies, and six hundred of them were enrolled.[25] Jiang took a personal interest, scrutinized the teaching materials and staffing arrangements, and selected maxims in his calligraphy to decorate the classrooms.[26] Teng Jie also took a personal interest and most of the teaching staff were members of his faction.[27] When the trainees completed the course in 1933, the majority of them were assigned to the newly created north China propaganda brigade.

Liu Jianqun and this brigade of six hundred were dispatched to north China in March 1933.[28] This represented a major effort of the

Lixingshe in staging a political presence for the GMD in north China. The brigade was attached to the north China office of the military affairs commission, with He Yingqin as the officer-in-charge.[29] In practice He was in charge of diplomatic negotiations with the Japanese military, and Liu was responsible for strengthening political support for the central government from among the regional militarists and their troops. Both He and Liu were in north China to reassure the regional militarists that the central government was not going to abandon them to the Japanese. It was an open activity of the central government carried out by members of the Lixingshe.

How did the north China propaganda brigade perform? First it received relatively warm welcome from the regional militarists as central government presence represented visible backing. By the summer of 1933—that is, within three months of his arrival—Liu found his cadres being installed as head of propaganda departments by nine regional militarists.[30]

This reviving political presence of the central government prodded the Japanese Kwantung command to intensify military and political pressure, leading to the signing of the Tangu truce and the He-Umetzu agreement. In the agreement He agreed to withdraw the propaganda brigade.[31] Liu Jianqun left two deputies in Beijing to continue the work in secret, but they were arrested by the Japanese military police in broad daylight, beaten up, tortured, and then sent packing back to Nanjing.[32] The entire operation was a fiasco and the Japanese attempt to establish an autonomous state in north China succeeded in all but name with the founding of the north China political council.[33]

Lixingshe and the December 9th Movement

In north China the Lixingshe was unable to revive the political credibility of the Nanjing government through open or secret activities. The regional militarists were convinced that they did not have the means themselves to curb Japanese expansion. The despondent mood of the Chinese bred a new wave of mass student demonstrations in the streets. This was the December 9th movement, which by itself could not stop Japanese aggression either. The exodus of students from the Beijing and Tianjin area to trek in the direction of Yanan marked a new low in student support for the Nanjing government.

By December 1935 the Lixingshe had been in existence for almost four years. How was the Lixingshe to prevent this trend of student disillusion from affecting central China? How were the damages of the December 9th movement to be minimized? In what ways could the Lixingshe contribute to stabilize a volatile political mood?

According to Liu Jianqun, the key location for brewing student discontent was Fudan University in Shanghai. Liu argued that Beijing was too distant to be of importance, and in Nanjing there was not much room for critical voices, but Shanghai was different because of the crisscross of international interests.[34] The presence of many missionary-sponsored schools, colleges, and universities made heavy handed government actions impracticable.

Once the trouble spot was identified, Liu obtained permission from the Fudan University administration to address the entire student body himself. On the day Liu found only three hundred students gathering to hear him speak. On confirming that the campus population was one thousand, Liu refused to speak unless the full student body was assembled. The university president warned of potential physical violence, but agreed to make the necessary arrangements provided Liu agreed to shoulder all responsibilities.[35]

At the public address Liu reiterated the government's position. His full speech is not available, but Liu claimed that he was not only well received, but that his agents inside Fudan University were able to organize a society for national salvation through anti-Japanese action (Kangri Jiuguo Shijianshe) and that up to 60 percent of the student body volunteered to join this pro-government body.[36]

Whether the figures were really 60 percent or not is beyond verification now. What can be verified is that Liu did speak publicly to the students, that he was not shouted down or worse, and that he continued the effort on other campuses.[37] With Liu's open effort, coupled with the undercover activities of his agents inside the campuses, the GMD was at least able to hold its own in maintaining substantial campus support. Given the potential for widespread emotional outbursts against the GMD at the time, this was no mean achievement.

Was the Lixingshe a Fascist Organization?

Rightly or wrongly the Lixingshe gained a fascist image. This is a separate issue from that of whether it was a fascist organization or not. The image was promoted by a number of circumstantial evidence. A German military advisory corps was in China,[38] and assisted in building a modern army of eighty thousand.[39] The Italians too contributed to the building of a modern air force.[40] Chinese delegations had been frequently visiting Germany and Italy since 1932. [41] Whampoa alumni, such as Teng Jie, added to the image by dressing in uniforms modeled on those of Hitler.[42] Leather and black boots made an impressive figure, but image is not necessarily a reflection of reality.

Were there fascist elements in the GMD since the ascendancy of Jiang Jieshi in the mid 1920s? Japanese Intelligence alleged that the anti-Japanese blue-shirt society was fascist.[43] This was a partisan accusation. The CCP echoed by accusing the anticommunist qualities of the Lixingshe as fascist. These was also a partisan accusation. The term fascist is often used to label oppressive militarist regimes. The whole tenor of such a "debate" is mired in accusation and counter accusations.

The issue of whether there were fascist elements in the GMD since the ascendancy of Jiang Jieshi in the mid 1920s has attracted serious scholarly concern. Do intense nationalist feelings not share something in common with fascism? Lloyd Eastman mentioned the fascist connection in his first major work on the nationalist period, *The Abortive Revolution*,[44] and this brought forth serious rejoinders across the continents. "No," said Maria Chang, the GMD regime was not fascist.[45] "Yes" claimed Michael Godley in his rather colorful piece on "the Italian connection."[46] The debate may become another dimension of the "who lost China" interchange, arguing whether the GMD were the "good guys" or "bad guys." Yet once the issue is raised, it should be addressed.

First let me quote an authoritative source on the interpretation of fascism—namely, Mussolini: "Fascism was not the nursling of a doctrine worked out before hand with detailed elaboration; it was born of the need for action and it was itself from the beginning practical rather than theoretical."[47] There is certainly this central emphasis on *action* by the Lixingshe. Indeed *action* may be an appropriate translation for *Lixing*.

The roots of a "fascist" parallel in China has to be found in the historical situation of China. The Chinese political scene was intensely ideological since the New Culture Movement. The competing claims of liberalism and socialism, muddied further by the eclectic concoction of Sun-wenism, neither delivered China from imperialist encroachment nor brought about a Marxian utopia. When emotions erupted in the May 30th movement, what was demanded was *action*. And it was Jiang and his cadets who provided the action, by launching the northern expedition, and reestablishing a credible central government.

When Jiang Jieshi gunned down the communists at Shanghai, the German Reichstag was not yet on fire. The party purge was *action*. And if that is the essence of fascism, then such actions could be called fascism, although there was no thought of using the term "fascist" until it was imported from Europe. At the same time the very importation of the term frightened those involved in the *action chinoise*, for they thought fascism was an ism comparable to socialism, which developed designs of taking over the Chinese revolution. Chinese "fascists" did not identify themselves as fascists.

Chinese fascism developed in the mid-1920s. Yet the very moment when Chinese fascism raised its head, it was threatened by the desertion of its duce, for Jiang deified Sun Yatsen to seek legitimacy in Sun Wenism. The emphasis on action had to be revived by the Lixingshe. If the leader refused to lead, he would have to be made to lead. The young officers were bent on capturing Jiang as their leader. Jiang was right when he perceived that both fascism and communism were out to get him.

The Dissolution of the Fuxingshe

In December 1936 Jiang was kidnapped by his own military allies at Xian and held captive for two weeks.[48] In March 1938 plans were drafted for the establishment of a GMD youth corps which took place in July.[49] In May 1938 Jiang ordered the dissolution of the Fuxingshe.[50] These were major events of the time. How did they relate to each other and how did they impact upon the Lixingshe?

The Xian incident expressed a serious disagreement between Jiang and his regional military allies concerning the relative importance of exterminating the communists and resisting the Japanese. The kidnappers tried to force Jiang to accept that resistance was the more urgent of the two. That military officers should attempt to put political pressure upon Jiang was not new, what was new was the open use of force in coercing him toward policy change.

The kidnap raised more policy issues than was intended. First it raised the issue of the location of policy-making power. Second it raised the question of succession should the worst happen to Jiang. How was the Lixingshe to respond to the dramatic turn of events?

Leaders of the Lixingshe felt partly responsible for the unexpected turn of events. The organization was not without influence in Xian prior to the kidnap, for Lixingshe agents were deployed at the headquarters of Zhang Xueliang and were in close contact with the Xiwei

Xuehui, a young officers pressure group under Zhang's command. The fact that Lixingshe leaders at Xian were either shot or put under military detention meant that the influence and authority of the Lixingshe itself were also challenged.[51] There was more than the life of Jiang at stake.

The Lixingshe was not established to take orders from the Nanjing government. It was an organization, a secret body, independent of the government and intent on performing actions which the Government could not do. In the case of the Xian incident the Lixingshe was able to take action faster than the Nanjing government, but not necessarily guided by the same political considerations. The secretary general of the Lixingshe at the time was Deng Wenyi. He responded to the challenge from Xian by deploying military units to surround Xian.[52] This action was no less damaging to the political authority of Nanjing than that of the kidnappers in Xian.

The action also resulted in a serious split within the Lixingshe. He Zhonghan was the most outspoken for a hard-line military response to Xian, treating the personal safety of Jiang as of secondary importance.[53] Indeed the hard-liners even thought of having He Yingqin nominated as their new leader should the worst happen to Jiang.[54] He Zhonghan is reputed to have leadership ambitions himself and the hard-line approach he advocated could turn the succession issue into a reality.[55] He did succeed in persuading the bulk of the Lixingshe core and over one hundred seventy young officers to make a joint public statement demanding a firm stand against Xian.[56] A sizeable number of Lixingshe members did not sign the declaration, including Teng Jie.[57]

In taking a hard-line military response to Xian with its own authority, the Lixingshe was putting the authority of the organization above the authority of Nanjing and treated the personal safety of Jiang Jieshi as of secondary importance. And in making this hard-line military response, the Lixingshe demonstrated to the Nanjing government that it was more than just a secret political pressure group, and it was capable of commanding the movement of government troops openly without the prior authorization of the government.

The Xian incident was resolved through negotiations conducted between the mutineers and Madame Jiang, first through her personal emissary William Henry Donald, then followed up by T.V. Soong, and finally by herself directly. And all the time she had to plead with the Lixingshe leaders not to aggravate the situation by military action.[58] Neither the Nanjing government nor the Jiang family was happy with the response of the Lixingshe.

Upon his safe return to Nanjing, Jiang was confronted with the need to reassert his authority over the Lixingshe. He Zhonghan was reprimanded and dispatched on an overseas assignment, while two other key Lixingshe office-bearers were put under detention.[59] The factionally divided Lixingshe accepted the censure of these members. Teng Jie was personally commended for abstaining from supporting the hard-liners,[60] which would have had the effect of reviving some of his lost influence within the Lixingshe. Liu Jianqun resigned from all positions associated with the Lixingshe.[61] Dai Li retained the confidence of Jiang by risking his own life in joining Jiang at Xian and helping with the negotiations.[62] Seeing that the leading figures of the Lixingshe did not resist punishment, Jiang weakened the organization further by dissolving the Fuxingshe in May 1937.[63]

The dissolution of the Fuxingshe went beyond the bounds of disciplinary action, it was an act of political sabotage against a key support base of the GMD. Did Jiang have an alternative arrangement in mind for harnessing the young officers of the Lixingshe? Addressing the extraordinary congress of the GMD on March 29, 1938, he said: "Our Party has already become virtually an empty shell, without any real substance; the form of the Party persists, but the spirit of the Party has almost completely died out."[64]

These words echoed those of Liu Jianqun in his article on the blue-shirt society, calling for GMD party reform as the means to strengthen China. What was different this time was that Jiang was not looking to the Lixingshe for action. Instead he was preparing the GMD for a subsequent appeal, an appeal for the abolition of all existing parties to bring about the formation of a new party of national unity. China must have "one faith, one party, and one will," Jiang declared.[65] Consultations with various political parties followed: "He even offered to change the organization and name of the KMT [GMD] if that would facilitate the creation of a single and unified political body. The Young China Party accepted Chiang's plan, and the Nationalist Socialist Party of Carsun Chang expressed itself ready to negotiate the question."[66] If the CCP did not object, Jiang had a good chance to succeed in organizing a new party of national unity. It was a bold stroke, which fell short of success.

What was salvaged out of the exercise was the establishment of the People's Political Consultative Conference which one author has seen fit to refer to as "China's wartime parliament."[67] But this was no substitute for support from the young officers and the troops which they commanded. The dissolution of the Fuxingshe reduced the effectiveness of the young officers' movement as a political pressure group. What Jiang could not change was his political dependence upon the continued support of these young officers. Damaging the Lixingshe could seriously endanger his own political future.

Did Jiang suffer any political losses in this grand exercise of political self-indulgence? The damage can be gauged from the reaction of his supporters in the young officers' movement. According to Deng Wenyi: "When the Lixingshe [and] Fuxingshe announced the cessation of their activities, many office holders met at Wuhan, and they wept for [the bleak] future of the revolution."[68] The young officers were bitterly disappointed with their leader.

Fortunate for Jiang, his grand gesture of dissolving the Fuxingshe was not that easy to accomplish. What was to be done with the existing membership of the Fuxingshe, for they could not be wished away with the stroke of a pen?

Prior to the dissolution of the Fuxingshe, Jiang instructed Kang Ze to draft a plan which would unite rival factions in the party and those in the Lixingshe.[69] Jiang did have plans for accommodating his supporters. They were to be regrouped into a united pro-Jiang body where a young officers' faction was to be balanced by a party faction represented by Chen Lifu and his Qingbaishe. In March 1938 these plans were submitted to the extraordinary congress of the GMD, and they were publicly approved and announced *before* the dissolution of the Fuxingshe.[70] Jiang appointed a committee of seven to oversee the establishment of the GMD youth corps, three representing the CC Clique, three representing the young officers, and one representing the GMD left faction.[71]

Confronted with a fait accompli, leaders of the Fuxingshe met at Wuhan in June to formalize dissolution.[72] In July the GMD youth corps was established. Former members of the Fuxingshe now became members of the GMD youth corps.[73] The veil of secrecy behind which the Fuxingshe thrived was thrown away. The despondency of the young officers contrasted strongly with the exuberant expectations of Jiang Jieshi: "The Youth are the revolutionary vanguard and the new life of the nation. There is no social progress or political reform that does not depend upon the stimulus of youth as its primary force. [They were] to serve as the vanguard in creating a new China, to establish in the very near future the cadre foundation of the nation's social reconstruction."[74]

As Lloyd Eastman puts it so well: "Jiang's purpose in forming the Youth Corps was to form a new revolutionary organization that, by eliminating the divisive quarrels of the past and by attracting the nation's youth, would take up the revolutionary tasks the Kuomintang [GMD] had forsaken."[75] This was the public image which Jiang promoted, while in practice he was preserving the existence of organized factions among his supporters and redeploying them. The GMD youth corps accommodated Kang Ze and Teng Jie from the young officers' movement and the Qingbaishe of the CC Clique. They were to balance each other inside the youth corps, while in public they cooperated to promote open mass support from the nation's youth. The young officers who were redeployed into the GMD youth corps were no longer part of an organization that could combine political work with access to effective military command as it was in the case with Lixingshe. Dai Li and his intelligence network was kept separate from the GMD youth corps, and with the dissolution of the Lixingshe structure in July 1938, the former intelligence arm of the Lixingshe now became indisputably the intelligence arm of Jiang. Other key Lixingshe members retained their various military commands, but they no longer had the benefit of the organization through which to exert their joint influence. Jiang was not really trying to get rid of factionalism in his camp, but only rearranging the factions to ensure his personal ascendancy.

The GMD youth corps, established in July 1938, was handicapped by historical antecedent. It was a shotgun marriage in which the young officers were clearly unhappy. They were the losers in this process of reorganization where the Fuxingshe was abolished and Zhu Jiahua was appointed to the position of acting secretary general of the youth corps.[76] Deng Wenyi commented that the youth corps lacked "revolutionary spirit and revolutionary action".[77] This is evidence to say that the former leaders of the Fuxingshe did not have their hearts in the "new" body. The loss of enthusiasm among the young officers was fatal for the GMD youth corps. Its membership was not new, as indicated by a constitutional provision where "youth" was defined as the age group 18–38.[78] The upper age limit comfortably fitted the young men and women of the mid-1920s into the scheme of things. Contrary to the rhetoric, the GMD youth corps did not begin with a fresh injection of new and young membership. It was, for all practical purposes, the Fuxingshe renamed and partially reorganized, but deprived of the sense of purpose and commitment that the Lixingshe had before its leaders were chastized and demoralized.

Retaining the bulk of the membership without retaining the enthusiasm and dedication of its leaders was a fatal formula. Chen Cheng explained the low percentage of young people in the corps in the following terms: "The Corps Leader [Jiang Jieshi] instructed us that who is youth in the Youth Corps is something not necessarily determined by age. In our view, anyone who has revolutionary enthusiasm and possesses a youthful and forward-looking spirit, even though he is over age, is still a revolutionary youth."[79]

What Jiang did in establishing the youth corps was to remove the enthusiasm of its leaders and to assume that his enthusiasm was shared. This is probably a case of a politician sold on his own rhetoric! The establishment of the youth corps effectively demoralized a network of political support cultivated by the Lixingshe. Instead Jiang inherited its shell in the form of a youth corp which attracted neither the young of the 1930s nor retained the enthusiasm of the youth of the 1920s. Jiang was in danger of alienating himself from the enthusiasm of the young of these two successive decades.

7 Xinan Lianhe Daxue: Associated University of the Southwest

In 1937 the decision to resist the Japanese invasion brought about a dramatic reconciliation between the GMD and campus communities in north China. Patriotic students again looked to the GMD for leadership. Even those students who had trekked to Yanan found the CCP asking for an anti-Japanese united front under GMD leadership. For students in north China all roads led to Nanjing.

For three weeks after the Marco Polo Bridge incident, it was unsure whether the Japanese would resort to war. But once their decision was made, it only took them two days to march into Beijing. The speed of the Japanese advance precluded any organized resistance by students in the city. Evacuation had hardly begun when Japanese troops entered Beijing and Tianjin. In the midst of disaster, the heroic stand of the Generalissimo became China's symbol of hope. In the words of Wen Yiduo: "At that time . . . faith and trust in Chairman Jiang was boundless."[1]

Since the twenty-one demands of 1915, Chinese students directed their ire mainly against Japan. The occupation forces were determined to teach the Chinese campus communities a lesson. On July 29 the Nankai campus at Tianjin was razed to the ground by artillery fire.[2] On September 12 the Qinghua campus at Beijing was turned into a military hospital.[3] With or without bidding from Nanjing, students and staff were looking to Jiang Jieshi for leadership and protection.

Government response was slow. The education department issued belated evacuation directives to Beijing University, Qinghua University, and Nankai University on September 10.[4] By then the cities of Beijing and Tianjin had fallen into Japanese hands for over a month. Still the evacuation directives gave those who fled or were planning to escape some hope for protection and employment in a projected temporary university at Changsha. Their initial expectations of Nanjing were met, but staff and students had to find their own way out of Japanese occupied zones. The favored escape route was by rail to the international concession at Tianjin, and then by sea and rail to Changsha.

Even though government action was slow, the directives from Nanjing represented a radical change of government attitude. Its acceptance of evacuation and resettlement responsibilities stood in stark contrast to earlier efforts in suppressing protest movements led by students. The invasion made reconciliation between students and the GMD not only possible but imperative. Government decision to establish a temporary university at Changsha was an open expression of GMD readiness for such a reconciliation.

What were the immediate response of staff and students at Nankai University, Qinghua University, and Beijing University? The majority of the Qinghua population was in or close to Beijing when the city fell into Japanese hands on July 29. It was summer vacation time. First-, Second-, and Third-year students were attending summer camp west of Beijing—participating in military drills. Over two hundred graduates were staying on campus looking for work or preparing for scholarship examinations. They were used to tense situations with the Japanese military and half-expected the Japanese to go no further than making threatening noises. When the Japanese military launched the invasion, only some engineering students, doing practical field work at Jinan, were beyond Japanese reach. They fled south with the equipments they were using in field work.[5]

Fear of harsh treatment at the hands of the Japanese military saw many members of these campus communities voting with their feet, and about half of their total number eventually made their way south. The determination of staff and students to flee south was a clear demonstration of support for resistance. Where the December 9th movement saw students distancing themselves from the GMD by trekking to Yanan, the Japanese invasion turned their march toward Nanjing once again.

How large was this academic refugee constituency in 1937? And what was the scale of assistance offered by the GMD government? The establishment of the temporary university at Changsha was guided by a small committee of five, representing the central government, the Hunan provincial government, and the three universities concerned.[6] The annual budget allocated was to be 35 percent of that of the previous year.[7] The size of the budget allocation reflected an official estimate that about a third of the staff and students were able to find their way south to Changsha. This estimate proved conservative, for when the first term started on November 1, 1937, the temporary university had a staff complement of 148 and a student enrollment of 1,452. Of these over eleven hundred students were from the three northern universities: 631 from Qinghua University, 342 from Beiing University, and 147 from Nankai University.[8] New arrivals were reported daily and refugee students from other institutions were also admitted. The size of campus population at Changsha was close to 50 percent of the preinvasion figures. Given the dangers of fleeing from the occupied areas, as well as the cost and scarcity of transport, the population size of the temporary university indicated renewed confidence in GMD leadership. Later the temporary university was relocated to Kunming, renamed the Associated University of the Southwest, and its total enrollment restored to the three thousand level.

Accompanying resettlement was a political debate on how these intellectual refugees could best serve the national cause. To most of the refugee students the course of action was self-evident. There was a war on and they wanted to be part of the war effort. To a government flushed with military support of all descriptions and somewhat overwhelmed with the number rather than quality of its fighting men, adding a mere thousand or two university students to a huge and cumbersome force had little military significance. Students and academics were politically articulate, but their immediate military value was negligible. Students, however, felt otherwise. They petitioned the education ministry to institute "wartime education,"[9] an emotional appeal which the government found difficult to accept or reject.

Without firm government direction, university administrators did what they could to carry on normal academic duties. When the new term started on November 1, 1937, it was generally assumed by the campus community that academic life would continue as before.[10] While students demanded intensified political involvement, university administrators were hoping to maintain as much of their normal educational roles as possible. Meanwhile the GMD government even contemplated contracting its financial support and diminishing the political role of students. It had more urgent military considerations to attend.

The course of the war allowed no delays in making firm decisions. Nanjing fell in November and the Nanjing massacre showed the horrific extent to which the Japanese military were prepared to go to terrorize a civilian populace. Anti-imperialist core groups, such as the refugee students, could not expect leniency from the advancing Japanese army. The GMD government, now relocated at Wuhan, could no longer assure the safety of Changsha. The merits or otherwise of restructuring university education to coordinate with the war effort, the question of another evacuation, and the morale of the local populace and the defending troops at Changsha all had to be taken into consideration. The local press aired objections to another evacuation, arguing that the educated elite should not evade their responsibility of contributing to the defense of Changsha. [11] Zhang Zhizhong, chairman of the Hunan provincial government, expressed his open support for students who wanted to take a more active part in the war.[12] These were local pressures to push martyrdom onto the campus community in order to maintain local morale, and they were in tune with the mood for self-sacrifice among students at the time.

It was General Chen Cheng, then coordinating defenses from Wuhan, who decided what the temporary university should do.[13] Chen was attracted to the proposition of a mass-based resistance effort and keenly aware of the power of propaganda. At Wuhan he recruited the services of prominent left-wing writers, headed by Guo Moruo, to organize propaganda, after having first approached Liu Jianqun of blue-shirt society fame.[14] Chen, however, retained strong suspicion for these former critics of the GMD government and had the activities of leftist allies closely monitored by secret agents. He Zhonghan, a Whampoa alumnus and a leading figure of the young officers movement, headed a political department within this propaganda unit.[15] What precautionary measures were General Chen Cheng to take with the larger body of students and academics from campuses which were at one time openly critical of the Nanjing regime?

Chen Cheng advocated evacuation and went personally to the temporary university to persuade staff and students that the best course of action was to move to the relative safety of Kunming in the distant southwest. He argued that university students were "China's last drop of blood" and stressed that their mission was to ensure the survival of Chinese culture.[16] It was a plea to the campus communities to return to the classroom rather than to go to the front. The argument combined prudence with valor, and Chen Cheng's personal involvement also relieved university leaders of the need to make a difficult decision themselves.

Even though the decision to evacuate the temporary university to Kunming was made, response to the decision in government, staff, and student circles was divided. Chen Cheng avoided arbitrary highhanded actions. Staff and students were given a free choice in opting for evacuation or for enlisting in the army. Chen was careful not to create unnecessary political distance between the GMD and the refugee students.

The choice of Kunming as the location for resettling the three prestigious universities, however, indicated that Chen Cheng perceived a political distance between the GMD and this campus community. Institutions with stronger GMD ties from central China were evacuated to the wartime capital Chongqing. This perceived political distance was reinforced by the geographic distance between Chongqing and Kunming. The political support rendered by these prestigious northern universities since the outbreak of war was rewarded with a considered coolness from the GMD government.

Political coolness was accompanied with caution, for, in spite of wartime shortages, the interests of those in the temporary university were well looked after. Some efforts were made to minimize the cost of relocation and able-bodied male students were encouraged to march to Kunming on foot. But the vast majority traveled to Kunming via a roundabout route in relative comfort: taking the Canton-Hankow railway to Canton, then to Hong Kong, then by sea to Haiphong, and then by land to Kunming.[17]

The overland party consisted of over two hundred volunteers. The journey was long and arduous, but, armed with government documentation, the party was well received by local authorities along the way. Usually billetted in local schools, the youngsters were treated quite generously by the local gentry. The trek to Kunming was more of an adventure, and the travelers could find spare moments to enjoy the beautiful scenery, visit historic sites, and observe the customs of the minority groups en route. This "long march" was no epic. Of the sixteen hundred miles traveled, one third was by boat. The experience, however, did instill a sense of common purpose, lifting the morale of the participants.[18]

The overland party started on February 19, 1938, and arrived at Kunming in late April. The main party was well settled by then and came out to greet the arrival of the overland party, whose arrival symbolized the completion of the relocation from Changsha to Kunming.[19] Most of the staff and two-thirds of the students of the temporary university at Changsha were evacuated to Kunming. Others enlisted in the army and various services closer to the front. A few senior academics, such as the presidents of Nankai University and Beijing University, found political office at the wartime capital Chongqing.[20] There were 350 faculty members and 992 students at the National Associated University of the Southwest when second term started on May 4, 1938.[21]

Relocating the three prestigious university of north China at Kunming indicated government intention to keep some political dis-

tance from these onetime critical campuses. The attitude was recipro-
cated when the Associated University chose May 4th, 1938, as its formal starting date. The choice was a symbolic reminder that the new
campus inherited the iconoclastic traditions of the new culture and
May 4th movement. While the Japanese invasion effected reconciliation between the GMD government and the critical voice of intellectuals from north China, a distance was deliberately maintained. Kunming provided the safety of geographical isolation, while study and
research provided an intellectual escape from the turmoils of war and
political intrigue. "Leave current affairs alone" (*mo tan quosi*) was a
popular catch phrase expressing this passing surrealism at Kunming,
but wartime privation faced the campus community from the start.

Conditions at Kunming

During the first year the Associated University used rented and bor-
rowed premises. By the second year new buildings were ready, but
these were makeshift structures of wood and bamboo. Roofs were
thatched and walls plastered with a mixture of mud and straw. Such
building materials were ill- suited to the heavy rains at Kunming, and
extensive repairs were needed every year after the rainy season. Student dormitories were overcrowded, badly lit, and in a constant state
of disrepair. Sleeping under umbrellas was a common sight.
Throughout the eight long years of its existence, the dormitories were
not equipped with basic amenities such as bathrooms. Students had
to bathe themselves next to a well or seek access to private facilities
off campus.[22] Some of the support staff lived and worked in conditions that were utterly unhygenic. The kitchen staff worked and slept
in the kitchen, and their bedding was covered with a blackish layer of
dust and grease.[23]

The living standards of staff and students were further ravaged
by wartime inflation. In spite of regular salary adjustments, income
could not keep pace with the escalating cost of living. By the beginning of 1945 the purchasing power of a full professor's salary was
equal to about a thirty-fifth of a prewar salary.[24] Many staff members
kept going by taking on part-time jobs. Needless to say, the students,
most of whom were dependent on government subsidies of one form
or another, fared much worse. The following recollection gives some
vivid details of their privation:

In the 27th year of the republic [1938] the monthly student loan could still [enable students] to eat eggs and weekly meal with chicken or pork. In the 30th year [1941] the loan was increased to two hundred yuan, in the 33rd year [1944] the loan was increased to a thousand yuan, and food consisted of Babao rice, discarded vegetables, pig skins, diluted rice gruel for breakfast, peanuts and some preserved vegetables, four basins of food and two buckets of soup for dinner, rice rationed by the government and mixed with sand[26]

In spite of primitive living conditions and extreme privation for staff and students, the academic community remained dedicated and high-spirited. The university attracted numbers in the first year by an "open door" policy, admitting anyone who cared to apply. Enrollment was boosted to just under two thousand.[27]

Such an "open door" practice was certainly an expediency and reflected the concern of the university about the viability of the institution in terms of student demand. From the following year onward, the viability of the university was assured by the Chongqing government, which instituted a centralized entrance examination and placement allocation systems for all tertiary institutions in areas under GMD control. Enrollment for the Associated University was set at around three thousand—that is, the equivalent of prewar enrollment levels at Beijing and Tianjin.[28] In this way access to non-local student intake was maintained and academic standards restored. Annual acceptances were maintained at around the three thousand mark throughout the war years, but of the twenty-one thousand admitted, only twenty-five hundred graduated. The vast majority of students were compelled by circumstances to suspend or terminate their studies.[29] An attrition rate of just under 90 percent meant that most of those who enrolled at the Associated University could neither dedicate themselves to academic pursuits nor be actively engaged in the resistance effort.

It should be noted in passing, however, that among the alumni were the Nobel Prize winners Li Zhengdao and Yang Zhenning.[30] For the relative few who did complete their tertiary education at Kunming, the basic training they received was of a high standard and the Associated University maintained the prestige of being a center of academic excellence.

There were five teaching faculties: liberal arts, science, education, engineering, and commerce and law.[31] The distribution of students in 1942 was about four hundred for liberal arts, three hundred for science, eight hundred for engineering, and nine hundred for commerce and law. There was an obvious student preference for vocational training as against liberal arts or theoretical science subjects. This was partly the consequence of government policy.[33]

Staffing did not follow the same pattern as student distribution. In 1942 liberal arts had 77 staff, and science 106, as against 73 for engineering and 42 for commerce and law.[34] The science faculty, enrolling the least students, had the largest number of staff. The relatively low student ratio for the faculties of liberal arts and science might in part explain the distinguished academic contributions of some of their faculty members.[35]

Within the Associated University there were four different hiring authorities: the Associated University, Qinghua University, Nankai University, and Beijing University. Most staff held two concurrent contracts, one with one of the three component institutions and the other with the Associated University. A contract with the Associated University indicated temporary appointment, lasting as long as that university would be in Kunming. The other contract represented tenure, for the three northern universities expected to resume their separate identity once the war was over.[36]

Of the three component institutions, Qinghua had a presiding influence. In material terms Qinghua succeeded in evacuating more books and equipment. Apart from government subsidies, Qinghua had a separate source of income from the Boxer indemnity remissions of the United States. Even the administration of the Associated University was dominated by Qinghua because the presidents of Nankai and Beijing universities opted to advance their fortunes by accepting political offices at Chongqing, and so Dr. Mei Yiji of Qinghua was left in charge.

Kunming was geographically isolated. Its attraction was the relative safety from the front. But Kunming was not immune from periodic Japanese air raids. Fei Xiaotong provides a vivid recollection of how the campus community responded to air raids:

> Responding to air-raid sirens was a daily routine. . . . The sirens were likely to sound around ten [o'clock] and taking shelter might last three to four hours, returning around one or two [o'clock] in the afternoon. . . .
>
> Our evacuation route was predetermined. . . . Most people we meet en route were friends from the Associated University. The exercise became a social occasion. . . . Air raids invariably occurred on fine days. . . .

Kunming developed its own popular air raid stories. The rumor was that Japanese pilots only flew return trips to Kunming as part of their graduation ceremony, a license test. . . .

On the 13th we had our social gathering on the hill slope as usual. . . . After one [o'clock], twenty-seven silvery planes appeared from the east. . . . I was driven by curiosity and raised my head... Fear hid itself and all I felt was excitement. . . . The bombs were released, under the sparkling silver wings were dropped a series of attractive little things. Then came the explosions, fairly loud and familiar.[37]

The regular air raids influenced the life pattern of staff and students. In one sense they made scholarly life more leisurely by disrupting work routines, but in another sense the raids imposed new physical demands. To minimize casualties, many staff and students moved their quarters to surrounding villages. This led to longer commuting time and more physical hardship. For one faculty member it was "tiring of course. Walking over a distance of six miles each day on gravel road was also disastrous for shoes and socks.[38]

GMD Influence

Lienta [Lianda] was unquestionably
China's most liberal wartime
university[39]

There was a mutually accepted distance between the Associated University and the GMD government. The university adopted the symbolism of May 4th to assert its autonomy and academic freedom. This was paralleled by a formal government direction that the wartime mission of the university was to preserve Chinese culture.[40] The consequence was a relatively liberal atmosphere at Kunming throughout the war. The university was particularly forceful in defending its academic autonomy against the efforts of the education ministry to increase central control over its curricula.[41] GMD acceptance of some measure of academic autonomy helped to maintain a rapport between the government and the campus community in spite of poor working conditions and a rapidly declining standard of living. Of the twenty-five hundred graduates, more than eight hundred were known to have enlisted in the armed services.[42] The degree of support for the government arguably increased toward the final years of the war, for Kunming became a principal receiving point for American support.[43] There was both an increase in opportunities for employment and for active service. The Associated University was the principal supplier of interpreters as Kunming shed its image of being political backwater.[44] Even after Chinese troops had suffered disastrous reverses at the hands of the Japanese during the Ichigo offensive, students were responding enthusiastically to the generalissimo's call for the youth of the nation to enlist,[45] for American entry into the war brought confidence of an eventual victory. Each time the GMD government gave the opportunity for the staff and students from the Associated University to serve, the response proved favorable. But such opportunities were rarely offered, suggesting continued GMD distrust for the prevailing liberalism at Kunming. Even though campus support for the government was consistent, the GMD did not leave the issue of faculty and student support to chance. Party presence on campus was expressed through a party branch, a GMD youth corps, and the directorate of moral guidance—the last being a term for the office of the dean of students. The party branch secretary sat, ex officio, in all major administrative bodies of the university.[46] The GMD was generally vigilant of the daily activities of the campus community.

Open and formal connections with the GMD government were sources of pride and honor for the campus community. The party branch focused its recruitment efforts on the faculty and a list of party branch membership read like an honor roll. When senior government functionaries visited Kunming, the university president, Dr. Mei Yiji, would hold formal dinner parties at his residence. Staff members invited to such functions were usually invited to join the GMD local branch.[47] It was a special honor to be invited, since the invitation was a formal gesture to show that one was a member of the in circle at the university. In this way practically all senior faculty members became GMD party members. There were those who resisted such direct party intrusion into the university as compromising academic freedom, but these were few and they became easily identifiable.

Further down the campus hierarchy, students who aspired to affiliate with the GMD could do so by joining the GMD youth corps. The youth corps conducted military drills and organized periodic meetings to arouse the nationalist feelings of fellow students. The youth corps was a fashionable front organization of the nationalist party. Connections with the party could bring tangible benefits, for such connections often formed part of the recommendations from the office of the dean of students when processing scholarships and other forms of financial assistance.[48]

Expressions of dissatisfaction with the government were rare, if not totally absent. The "anti-Kong" affair can be singled out as an example of how effective the authorities were in handling murmurs of discontent. Dr. H.H. Kong, finance minister of the GMD government and brother-in-law of the generalissimo, was rumored to have misused his personal influence when he flew his maid and pet dog from Hong Kong to Chongqing just before the fall of the British colony into Japanese hands. Two students, who were themselves GMD party members, created considerable stir on campus by openly criticizing H. H. Kong in big character posters. Three days later students paraded through the streets, carrying anti-Kong slogans written on white sheets. Jiang Monlin, president of Beijing University, personally intervened to admonish the students concerned. The local party branch summoned the two who started the affair and gave them stern warnings. The acting director of the GMD youth corps, Kang Ze, expressed openly that he would have made arrests if not for pleadings from university authorities.[49] The anti-Kong affair also reflected factional grouping within the GMD, with the two instigators acting under directions from the CC Clique, with Kang Ze taking the opportunity to reassert the influence of the Whampoa faction, and with both rival factions taking delight in embarassing H.H. Kong. The finance minister could be seen as a representative figure of the "family interests" of Jiang Jieshi. The affair was indicative of internal GMD factional tensions as well as of a growing disquiet on rampant official corruption.

Dissenting voices at the Associated University remained few. The Chinese communists, for example, found it impossible to operate in the open even though they did plant a few of their members on campus. These included the historian Hua Gang.[50] Those few academics who did dare to dissent in the open were often leading figures of minor political parties. During the resistance war they too generally avoided criticizing the government.[51]

Among the students there were no organized voice of dissent, although there were student organizations before the formation of the GMD youth corps on campus. Among these the two notable ones were the Cunshe and the Christian Fellowship. The Cunshe was established at Changsha. It organized public debates on current affairs and assisted in recruiting for the armed forces. The activities of the Cunshe were therefore supportive of the GMD-led war effort and the organization was no potential hotbed for dissidents. In its hey day the Cunshe claimed a membership of over two hundred—that is, less than 10 per cent of the student population. Between 1938 and 1941 the youth corps, the Christian Fellowship, and the Cunshe between them occupied most of the key positions in the student union. In 1941 the GMD tightened its control over the student union, and the youth corps gained ascendancy at the expense of the Cunshe and the Christian Fellowship.[52]

The primary concern of the GMD government was to ensure that campus dissent did not develop. To this end the government achieved almost complete success during the war. On the side of the teachers and students there was the annual ritual of May 4th memorial meetings, reminding themselves that student nationalism and intellectual iconoclasm did have a larger role to play. Ceremonial symbolism was no substitute for real critical expression. It only served to remind the government of the hostile attitude of students and teachers in the 1930s. While a rapport between the government and the campus was sustained throughout the war years, there was the absence of an active working partnership between the two. Mutual suspicion persisted. During the war the GMD muffled dissenting voice with comparative ease, but the calm setting at Kunming changed radically soon after the defeat of Japan.

8 Regimentation at Yanan

Under the leadership of Mao Zedong, the party Center and the core of the red army reached Yanan in October 1935. They escaped military encirclement and avoided political annihilation. However, Yanan was no promised land. There the Chinese communists retained control of only one and a half million people in a poverty-stricken area. They were pushed to a tight corner in the northwest and surrounded by hostile regional forces.

Political stability was essential if Jiang were to succeed in eliminating this last pocket of Chinese communist presence. However, politics in north China was volatile at the time. Japanese pressure was on the increase since the Manchurian incident of September 1931. Two high points in the 1930s should be noted—namely the December 9th movement and the Xian incident.

The December 9th movement of 1935[1] was a response to widespread rumors that Colonel Doihara Kenji was orchestrating the establishment of an autonomous state in north China.[2] Students in Beijing protested in the streets, demanding that Song Zheyuan, whose forces controlled Hebei and Charhar provinces, should deny any involvement with this autonomous movement. In December 1935 disenchantment with the militarist regime at Beijing and with the lack of GMD presence in north China saw many students joining the Chinese communists at Yanan. The December 9th movement enabled Yanan to bid for the support of patriotic students. How did Yanan cope when it was faced with an unexpected influx of students? Could the party live up to their patriotic expectations? Was the party to redirect its focus away from rural reforms and to concentrate on national defense? Was there the danger that nationalism could overtake socialism as the party adapted to the political wishes of its new supporters? Or would the patriotic young find their energies being rediverted by the party more toward issues of social reform?

Japanese pressure continued to destabilize north China after December 1935. In 1936 Jiang remained firm in his resolve to promote a final advance on Yanan. Possibly to allay the fears of major militarists such as Yan Xishan and Feng Yuxiang, nationalist units were not deployed in the northwest. Instead Manchurian units commanded by Zhang Xueliang were moved into Xian to act as the fulcrum of a new encirclement campaign. In this war by proxy, the allies of Jiang had a vested interest in keeping the Chinese communist threat alive. Without communist presence at Yanan, financial and material subsidies from Nanjing would cease. Dissatisfied with the performance of his allies, Jiang personally flew to Xian. There he was captured by Zhang Xueliang, and released only after Jiang had agreed to suspend the anticommunist campaign in favor of forming an anti-Japanese united front.[3]

The CCP Adapting to Student Nationalism

The December 9th movement of 1935 and the Xian incident of 1936 were unexpected opportunities for the CCP. Though communists had chanted "marching north to fight the Japanese" in their flight from central China, the Yanan base was in reality far from any sphere of Japanese influence. Slogans served to sustain morale, but the influx of young students who took the communist slogan in earnest was a political embarassment. The reduced capabilities of the CCP made it difficult for them to offer substantial resistance to Japan. Could Yanan survive such a predicament?

The institution that absorbed the shock of student influx was the red army school, hastily renamed the Anti-Japanese Resistance University.[4] Most of the new arrivals were enrolled in this "university," an institution with much pretension and little resource. Though a red army school existed in the Jiangxi Soviet, its entire institutional structure disintegrated when the Long March began. The red army school was reestablished in June 1936, with Lin Biao and Lo Ruiqing appointed as head and deputy.[5] Students were recruited from senior officers in the red army, including divisional commanders and political commissars.[6] The "university" was not originally designed to accommodate tertiary students.

In 1936 the red army school was a small establishment with meagre resources. According to Lin Biao and Lo Ruiqing, the initial enrollment in June 1936 was between two hundred forty and three hundred.[7] The entire teaching faculty consisted of three members, supported by a single secretarial aide. That is to say, apart from the head and deputy, there was only one other faculty member.[8] The campus was at first located at Wayaobao, a small village some six miles from Yanan. Accommodations there proved unsatisfactory and the school quickly moved to Baoan, another small village some three miles from Yanan. Campus buildings at Boaan consisted mainly of stables. Staff and students cleaned and converted these for use as living and studying quarters.[9]

The resources of the red army school were limited to the human endeavors of its members. Since those students of the first class were all senior cadres, what they valued most was a break of six months from active military service and time to think and talk with their fellow students. That the red army school had practically no staff complement was not a main concern in the short term. Both Lin Biao and Luo Ruiqing, the head and deputy of the school, regarded themselves as "students." The two hundred forty students of the first class were from the core leadership of the red army. It was a privilege for the inner group to study at the school.

Since the character of the red army school was defined by the type of students enrolled, its character was changed with the influx of students from Beijing and Tianjin. The second class started in late January or early February 1937, and the institution was renamed the Anti-Japanese Resistance University.[10] The change of name was to project an anti-Japanese image for the CCP. Intake was no longer restricted to senior cadres and student number was increased to twelve hundred.[11] The second class consisted of lower- and middle-ranking cadres. Enrolling them represented an effort to integrate the different regional units of the red army as they arrived at Yanan. This Resistance University, in spite of its new name, made only minor preparations to admit tertiary students from beyond red army circles. The Resistance University only set aside two hundred places to accommodate them.[12] The actual number of tertiary students enrolled in the second class was six hundred, three times what was expected.[13] How did the influx of students affect the Resistance University? The rapid expansion of student intake from two hundred forty to twelve hundred was a formidable task. When the intake was boosted by another six hundred, with little material or personnel backing, the morale and commitment of the campus community took a plunge. Luo Ruiqing explained the decline in morale in terms of strained relationships between regular army cadres and educated youths. Regular army cadres were shown up to be lacking in confidence and ability to compete in academic studies.[14] What the students and the army cadres did share was a sense of gloom caused by material shortages and inaction.[15] Material shortages caused hardship, but political inaction could cause more ephemeral emotional commitments to evaporate. The onus was on the Chinese communist leadership to demonstrate that it was committed to the anti-Japanese cause in both words and deeds, otherwise the political credibility of the CCP would suffer a fate similar to that of the GMD. This was a time when Yanan was effectively hemmed in by the GMD and its allies, and the opportunity for the CCP to live up to its anti-Japanese rhetoric was lacking.

This impossible situation changed with the outbreak of war in the summer of 1937. The GMD national government encouraged communist troops to assist in defense, temporarily suspending its siege of the Yanan area. The eighteen hundred students of the second class of the resistance university, made up of a mixed body of tertiary students and army cadres, were immediately assigned to military service. The credibility of the CCP soared among the educated. [16]

Japanese invasion also increased the rate of flow of students into Yanan. But the CCP remained ill-prepared to receive them. An estimated five thousand students poured into the isolated township of Yanan that summer, worsening the situation of a general shortage in food, clothing, and housing. By October it was evident that unless something was done to solve the housing problem, these newfound supporters would not be able to face the severities of the coming winter. It was in this atmosphere of urgency that the Resistance University decided on October 18, 1937, to organize self-help among the students. The predominant type of housing in the Yanan area was loess caves. In a flush of panic and exaggerated expectations, the Resistance University launched a cave-digging campaign. three thousand students were organized into teams of five, each given the target of completing one cave per fortnight.[17]

The inexperienced students, with the help of some "peasant engineers," were unused to hard labor. Progress was slow and made slower by the choice of many unsuitable sites. Some of the caves collapsed, and some were found to be too wet for use after completion. Of the projected six hundred caves, only 170 were completed—that is, a low completion rate of 28 percent. Declaring the campaign successful had more to do with propaganda than reality.[18]

In spite of the low completion rate, the campaign solved immediate housing problems. On November 15 Mao Zedong formally declared the caves open to mark the start of a new term.[19] This was the beginning for the third class, one made up entirely of incoming students. By November 1937 the resistance university was no longer a school for red army cadres. The former military institute was physically captured by middle-class students of doubtful ideological commitment to the communist cause.

The Resistance University was one of two institutions that catered for the incoming students. The second was the public school of northern Shaanxi province (hereafter referred to as the public school), established in July 1937 specifically for looking after students who trekked to Yanan.[20] Again preparations were grossly inadequate, reflecting critical material shortages at Yanan and CCP underestimation of the appeal of its patriotic rhetoric. Cheng Fangwu, a well-known literary figure, was assigned to the task of establishing the public school and given a meagre starting grant of eighteen hundred yuan. Cheng recruited what staff he could and arranged housing for about two hundred students initially.[21]

With no promise of further funding, Cheng planned a user-pay system, charging tuition fees and the full cost of room and board. Books and clothing were also to be the responsibility of the students themselves.[22] This user-pay system was simply impractical. For the students, who walked on foot to Yanan and owned only what they could carry with them, it was unrealistic to expect them to be financially self-supporting. Cheng reported the difficulties to Mao. The CCP had no option but to take up financial responsibilities for staff and students. The students were charged no fees, given room, board, and clothing, as well as a monthly allowance of one dollar. Staff members were given identical treatment.[23]

The case of the Resistance University and the public school showed how unprepared the CCP was for the influx of students. But the presence of these youngsters compelled the party to think of what to do with this newfound support, of how to turn an immediate liability into a new source of political strength.

Training and Organization

Cheng Fangwu, headmaster of the public school, observed bluntly that the party could not afford the luxury of providing education for students who were deprived of normal schooling by the war.[24] Neither the Resistance University nor the public school was established to provide normal schooling for all who walked to Yanan and professed political support for the CCP. The Resistance University was initially established to upgrade the quality of active cadres in the red army. This was changed by the outbreak of war as active cadres were recalled to the front and as the educated young from other parts of China poured into Yanan. The task of the Resistance University was to transform these new arrivals into loyal party cadres, new cadres to be used to expand the territorial and population base under communist control. Such an expansion was imperative if the Chinese communists were to become more effective in resisting the Japanese invasion.

The age of the students arriving at Yanan ranged from fourteen to twenty-eight.[25] It was a regionally representative group, with students from every province. There were some overseas Chinese as well.[26] Such a broad regional spread indicated first that students at Yanan were a representative national group, and second that CCP appeal to anti-Japanese emotions was being felt nationwide. This broadly based support contrasted strongly with the regional support that Mao brought from Hunan-Jiangxi or the local support which Liu Zhidan and Gao Gang established at Yanan. The young students who walked to Yanan were better suited to act as a national cadre force.

Yanan, however, was ill-prepared for giving these youngsters much formal training. In July 1937 the Resistance University and the public school were the only institutions available to enroll them. The Public School accepted younger students, those aged below eighteen. The Resistance University enrolled the older group, those between eighteen and twenty-eight.[27] By the beginning of 1938 the Lu Xun College of the Arts was established, providing an alternative for those who aimed for careers in journalism, graphic art, music, and the performing arts.[28] The educational background of the three thousand to five thousand students who walked to Yenan in 1937 spanned a wide spectrum, as did their age group.

These three institutions trained political cadres. In additional there were some modest technical training institutions. The Red Army Medical University trained only a handful of doctors in spite of the urgent need for medical services at the front. By 1942 this medical university produced between thirty to forty doctors a year. Its quality of training was severely hampered by chronic shortages of textbooks, medical supplies, and equipment. Much of what was used was makeshift and provisional.[29] A nursing school, named after Norman Bethune, was not established until early 1942 and it trained only thirty nurses in the first year of its operation.[30] With such limited facilities, Yanan could not meet the educational needs of the students even in the latter part of the resistance war. If the young students were after academic opportunities at Yanan, they would have been disappointed. In the summer of 1937 most of the students took what was the only option available: enroll in either the Resistance University or the public school. The chronic shortage of resources dictated that the CCP could only offer the bare minimum through the two institutions. When the Resistance University and the public school suggested a training period of six months, they were told by the party to offer a training period of two months only. The eventual compromise was three months.[31]

What did the two institutions offer to students in this short period? Were the organization of the school and the university substantially different? How were the students organized during training? And how were they employed after completing the short training course?

The Public School

The public school offered only one course of study: political training.[32] According to the assessment of Cheng Fangwu, the progress rate of his students was phenomenally high. His assessment was based on a comparison between a test that the students sat for at the beginning of the course and the results they attained at the end of three months. According to Cheng most of the students failed the politics section at the initial test, but the average grade attained at the final examination was above 90 percent.[33] This self-assessment could hardly be used to assert quality training. It was rather confirmation that after three months students were attuned to politics at Yanan and could answer political questions in ways expected of them.

The public school began with a staff complement of one—the headmaster Cheng Fangwu himself. How did he try to provide instructions for the few hundred students under his charge? What Cheng did was to co-opt voluntary service from party leaders in what were called "lectures by famous men." Mao Zedong, Zhu De, and Ai Siqi were called on to provide occasional lectures. Since the public school had no classrooms or lecture theaters, these talks were given in the open air. Up to five hundred students attended at a time —that is to say, the entire school would congregate to listen to these party leaders.[34] This practice was reminiscent of similar expediencies at Whampoa, where the party leaders, who were invited to speak, often did not turn up. Similarly at Yanan, scheduling lectures by party leaders was no guarantee that the speakers would turn up. A similar scheme adopted by the Resistance University did not work because party leaders often could not honor lecture commitments.[35] The Chinese communists at Yanan did not appear to be better organized than their GMD counterparts at a comparable stage of development. How could Cheng Fangwu succeed in instructing the students with next to no help? Judging from what Cheng claimed to be very high average grades in the final examination, he seemed to have achieved the apparently impossible. What were some of the improvisations that helped Cheng to instruct his students in the preferred political views of the CCP?

With no staffing resources to rely on, the only alternative left was one of self-help. Older or better educated students were often required to teach. Thus the way in which students were organized into groups became important. The student body was organized into a command structure and divided into units. The largest unit was the brigade (*dui*), numbering between one hundred twenty and one hundred sixty—that is, containing either three or four units of forty. Below the brigade was the branch brigade (*fendui*), each made up of forty members. And each branch brigade was further subdivided into platoons (*ban*), each consisted of ten members. Units at every level elected their own leaders and deputy leaders from its own ranks. These elected office-bearers were given the right to command, though they could be dismissed by a majority of those who voted.[36] The platoon was the effective cell. Its members lived in the same dormitory and acted as a small group. The headmaster Cheng Fangwu operated through the command structure and its elected officebearers. Such an approach was again reminiscent of GMD practices in militarizing campus communities.

Even though the public school was coeducational, in practice the sexes were segregated. The platoons were single sex units. There was also a tendancy to assign tasks on the basis of sex. Women, for example, were said to have more "natural" abilities in acting, singing, and dancing.[37] The public school certainly did not exhibit an enlightened social attitude. There were less opportunities for female students to play leadership roles. This command structure provided the organizational as well as social framework within which to promote and enforce individual conformity to the group. Divergent views within each group could be sharply pulled into line. Militarization, as evidenced in a command structure, was the order of the day.

Since the students were of diverse regional backgrounds and of varied educational levels, when left to instruct themselves, as the self-help principle suggested, group conformity to arty doctrines could be difficult to attain. The students had to be led to perform party-directed, but self-administered tasks, if party indoctrination was to succeed.

By making virtue out of necessity, students were required to "make their own books." This did not mean writing their own texts and sharing diverse opinions. "Making their own books" was a scissors-and-paste exercise, compiling study material from journals and newspapers then in circulation at Yanan. Since the media outlets at Yanan were directly controlled by the propaganda bureau, students were studying propaganda messages from the party. It is no wonder that at the end of three months of intensive self-administered "training," students could attain an average grade of over 90 percent in their final politics examination.

The way in which the public school was organized turned schooling into a process of high-pressured study of party propaganda. Why did the students agree to subject themselves to such a process? For students who fled as the Japanese advanced, there was a sense of urgency to participate in the resistance effort. Japanese air raids as far afield as distant Yanan helped to remind them of the danger the nation was facing. They volunteered to dig their own air raid shelters,[38] and they longed for the opportunity to be deployed to the front to participate actively in fighting the Japanese. The intensive study of CCP propaganda was legitimized as preparatory training for active involvement in the resistance effort. At the end of the three months, students were assigned cadre work at the front or in one of the border areas under communist control. There could not be any meaningful separation between the expansion of communist influence and the intensification of communist-led resistance. The two were inseparable and each legitimized the other. Besides, the ideal of the unity of thought was a long-standing Chinese scholastic tradition. Now this tradition was invoked in the name of patriotism, in the name of revolution, and the enthusiasm of the young carried them along in their effort to discipline themselves to the ideas of the party and to act as the party instructed. Chinese communist indoctrination and patriotism became acceptable as one and the same. Seen in this light, the efforts of the students to school themselves in the ideas of the CCP leadership were emotionally uplifting. In their small-group discussions, they prodded each other to learn what the party said and to conform to what the party demanded of them. They organized national salvation rooms where news items were edited, and posters designed.[39] Not only did they accept propaganda, they actively sought to be creative to improve the propaganda they were receiving. The public school provided them with what they perceived as the road to national salvation.

The public school graduated two hundred students in November 1937, four hundred in January 1938, and six hundred in March 1938. These were immediately assigned to the front and the various border areas.[40] The CCP was living up to the immediate expectations of the students. The question is whether the students could live up to the expectations of the CCP. Could the party retain loyalty from these hastily "trained" cadres once they were away from Yanan? This aspect will be treated in the following chapter.

The Resistance University

Students above the age of eighteen enrolled at the Resistance University. The size of its student population was ten times larger than that of the public school. While problems of organization and training facing the two institutions were similar, the magnitude of the tasks facing the Resistance University was greater. It also meant that it received more attention from the party. The performance of the Resistance University was a measure of whether the CCP succeeded in retaining and effectively using the services of the educated young. In evaluating the Resistance University attention will be focused on three related issues: funding, staffing, and the everyday life of the students.

When the CCP made Yanan the party's new headquarters, the township had a population of less than five thousand. Toward the end of the war a group of Chinese and foreign correspondents who visited Yanan estimated the population to be over forty thousand, and more than half were in government service.[41] In retrospect the resistance war turned Yanan into a boom town. Bearing in mind that in 1937 the entire population base under CCP control was a meagre million and a half,[41] the sudden doubling and tripling of the urban population at Yanan were potentially crippling blows to the CCP.

The war, however, also brought some relief and unexpected financial assistance. The military encirclement of Yanan was suspended, so the influx of the young educated was counterbalanced by the outflow of cadres and troops, as CCP influence expanded beyond the confines of the Yanan area. Graduates were mostly deployed outside the Yanan base area, so the period in which they needed to be supported within the confines of Yanan was between three to six months. The GMD government provided a monthly subsidy of 600,000 yuan as its contribution to assist the CCP to keep three divisions in the field to fight the Japanese. Only about 20 percent of this subsidy was used on the eighth route army,[42] and some of this subsidy was diverted to the Resistance University.[43] According to Lin Biao the estimated cost for maintaining a student was 8 yuan per month, including a monthly allowance of 2 yuan each.[44] The cost of maintaining five thousand students, therefore, came up to a grand total of 40,000 yuan, including teaching and various maintenance costs. A small portion of the GMD subsidy was sufficient to finance the entire operation of the Resistance University.

How did the Resistance University keep per capita costs so low? And did the low standard of living, which this implies, generate discontent and low morale?

What was considered an acceptable standard of living was based on comparative experiences that the students went through. Their journey to Yanan was both a financial and a physical drain, for though some form of transport could be hired up to Xian, the stretch between Xian and Yanan was covered on foot.[45] The only resources which the students had were what they could carry on their persons. When they finally reached Yanan, both their physical and financial resources were nearly exhausted; there was no turning back. The initial lack of preparedness to receive them did result in low morale. After arriving at Yanan in the early months of the war, they endured cold, hunger, and general privation. The favorite pasttime, according to one student, was searching for lice under the sun.

Privation and low morale marked a difficult start. From then on things improved. When the Resistance University organized students to dig caves in October and November 1937, the experience of finding something meaningful to do lifted morale. Keeping the students physically occupied became the standard formula for eliminating boredom, and for making the military and political training more effective. Spare moments were further used for subsidiary production to meet part of their daily food consumption. In short, the lack of resources resulted in additional pressures on students to study and to engage in production. There were hardly any spare moments left for the students to entertain thoughts critical of the Yanan regime.

Self-help became a guiding principle in keeping running costs down to a minimum. Five thousand pair of hands became a direct economic resource for the university. They dug caves to serve as dormitories and study rooms, reducing capital construction costs to zero. They attended lectures in the open air and dispensed with the need to pay for buildings. They cultivated their own vegetables, raised pigs, and even herded animals to supplement their meagre grain rations. [47] The daily cash payment to students for additional food was maintained at seven cents per head, while serving cadres at Yanan only had five cents per head to supplement what they could not produce themselves. Students were given a relatively easier time.[48] This quantifiable difference between them and those in active government service removed much grounds for complaint from students, though most of them were used to a higher standard of living. Hardship was seen to be equitably shared. A Spartan lifestyle and political militancy were well-suited to each other.

Minimizing wastage was another approach to keep running costs down. The student body was organized into a three-tiered structure similar to that at the public school: brigades (*dui*) consisting of 120-160 members, branch brigades (*fendui*) consisting of forty members each, and platoons (*ban*) of ten members each. Possibly because there were insufficient number of caves for use as dormitories, as many as fifteen to twenty platoon members shared the same dormitory. These were also known as small groups (*xiaozu*). At each level of student organization representatives were elected to promote thrift. This was in effect a kind of volunteer surveillance system. These representatives reported to their own small group on instances of wastage, thus invoking group social pressure against offenders. The CCP was using the principles of mutual surveillance employed by traditional Baojia police organizations. The university also organized competition between these small groups to see which would consume the least resources in the course of their daily work.[49] In this way small groups competed with small groups, and brigades against brigades—not unlike a scoring competition in sports performance between "houses" or "fraternities." Such organized social pressure could be unpleasant at times. Students did feel compelled to swallow every morsel irrespective of whether the food offered was palatable or not. Overall the low per capita running cost of the Resistance University does suggest that such tactics generally worked.

Of course not every expediency to keep costs down worked and there were some notable failures, for example, the organization of a campus cooperative and a fund-raising campaign. The campus cooperative was established as a self-help venture to reduce the cost of consumer items. Shares were set at half a Chinese dollar each.[50] Mainly because the student turnover rate was high and at frequent intervals, the cooperative found itself in a continual stop-and-start situation. To keep the cooperative going, the border government formally stepped in, providing operating capital, assigning permanent managers, and turning the cooperative into a government enterprise. There is no way of determining whether goods at the cooperative were offered at competitive market prices or not, so the original intention of having a consumer-run cooperative to supply consumer needs at minimal prices failed. There was also an element of compulsion in purchasing from the cooperative, for each time the Resistance University was short of cash, student allowances were issued in the form of cooperative coupons. These coupons could only be used to purchase goods at the cooperative.[51]

Another experience which the Resistance University did not wish to repeat was fund-raising. The target of the campaign was C$40,000 and the amount was to be raised from friends and relatives of the students. Letters were sent out soliciting funds. In the heat of the campaign, social pressures were exerted, resulting in cases where some students had to sell their own winter clothing to raise contributions. The fund-raising campaign was not repeated, even though the effort was ritualistically declared a success.[52]

The drive to economize promoted a lifestyle in which money was a rarity. Students received room and board, given uniforms to wear, encouraged to minimize consumption, and organized to produce. They often received cooperative coupons instead of cash as allowance. The government provided them with subsistence and they produced the "luxuries" of meat and vegetable. Material temptations were all but absent. Their lifestyle was puritanical and communal, almost monastic. Privacy was minimal and even married couples could only meet during weekends.[53] The following quote provides a vivid picture of the lifestyle of students at Yanan in those days:

> Our daily routine is as follows. Getting out of bed at half-past five, morning exercise, [group] singing, breakfast at seven, and self-study until lessons start at nine. Lessons finish at half-past twelve, lunch, and afternoon lessons run from one to four. [Then] one hour of self-study. Dinner at five, followed by extracurricular activities. Roll call at seven, shout slogans, and then begin small group study and discussion. Can't go to bed until ten. On every Saturday night there are entertainment programs (*wanhui*), popular and exciting gatherings.
>
> Courses we take include Political Economy, History of the Chinese Revolution, the China Problem, Issues on Japan, Wartime Political Work, Dialectics, Military Drills, Reconnaissance Drills, Guerrilla Tactics, Target Practice, and so on. It is busy-busy all day long. Life is tense and active.
>
> As a precaution against Japanese bombing raids, classes were halted for one week. We practiced air raid drills and built

air raid shelters. The men all participated [in building air raid shelters], and the people of Yanan were mobilized too. Female students had the choice of joining in or doing alternative propaganda work. With a body as healthy as mine, I joined in with the men in hauling dirt.

Those who came with me say I have grown thin. I am certainly thinner. The material aspect of life here is indeed harsh. Of the three meals a day it is usually dried millet or a thick soup, served with one pot of vegetable for every eight persons. We used to eat rice at times, but because of transportation difficulties, we have not had a rice meal for three to four weeks now. Our living quarters are also extremely crowded. Each person has a stool. It is used in lessons, at meals, during study time, for reading and writing—it follows you everywhere. Our work place is extremely crowded too: over one hundred persons cramped together, sitting on stools or on the floor. But everyone works well on the diaries and reads their books, certainly with no less interest than any well-equipped school. Though we suffer material shortages and I have indeed grown thinner, but I am in high spirits. Living in this city of freedom, in this new world, who would have any spiritual suffering?

You asked me what do I need? Thank you, sister. I don't need anything. Here everyone is poor. However, we don't need to buy anything. During my two months here I have not spent a cent. Here everyone, from soldier to officer, each should receive two dollars and fifty cents a month. But because of financial difficulties, we have not received any allowances for over two months. I don't need anything. I am not aware of material shortages: busily working all day. I just feel I have to try harder for the liberation of our Chinese people.[54]

This was a letter written by a female student, one of many who sought a future for China through Yanan. Her attitude and lifestyle were what the CCP tried to promote. Students responded to such expectations, not because they loved the CCP, but because they thought the Chinese communists could provide the direction and leadership for them to free China from Japanese domination. Their continued support depended not on bold words and promises, but performance. Could the CCP live up to such expectations? Were there no doubters among the students in Yanan?

Contrast the above letter with the following stage dialogue, a humorous but cynical piece performed by two comedians at Yanan:

Young Chen asked Mr. Wang about his impressions of life at the resistance university.

Mr.Wang: My first impression is plenty of singing. We sing on waking up. We sing before we go to bed. We sing at the playground. We sing even in the toilet. Constipation calls for more singing. Stomach upset would produce a chorus.

My second impression is plenty of meetings. There are sitdown meetings, discussion meetings, review meetings, evening meetings, morning meetings, this meeting, and that meeting. There may be as many as fifty-four meetings in one day!

My third impression is plenty of isms. The main one at the resistance university is called Marxism. Untidy clothing and casual manner is called free-ism (*ziyou zhuyi*). Spending the meagre monthly allowance on wine and cigarettes is called enjoyism. To relieve the boredom of studies by seeking the company of the opposite sex is called taking-advantage-ism. Sometimes when there is not enough food, one steals a couple of bowls of rice from the captain. [This] is called opportunism. [When] the eighth route army comes around to raise funds, concealing one's money is called closed-door-ism.[55]

But such comic relief was not appreciated by the authorities. The two performers were publicly cautioned on the spot. The laughter of the audience turned to embarassing silence.[56]

Comparing the harsh life and material shortages both at Yanan and Kunming, it is possible to say that those students who walked to Kunming were better provided for in the material sense than those who walked to Yanan. Yet those who walked south to express their political preference for the GMD were politically neglected on the whole. The neglect at Kunming is self- evident on comparing the annual enrollment figure of three thousand with a total graduate count of twenty-five hundred for the entire war period. At Yanan the CCP was capable of deploying more than three thousand graduates to the various base areas at quarterly intervals. It is only through such comparisons that one can appreciate the scale of lost opportunity for the GMD.

Now let us turn to the issue of staffing at the Resistance University. When the red army school was revived in June 1936, it had a staff complement of three for two hundred forty students. This staffing ratio, roughly at one to eighty, became the general yardstick for staffing in the early years. With the sudden expansion of the Resistance University after July 1937, how could staff be found at short notice to teach five thousand students?

The Resistance University began as part of the institutional framework of the red army. During the early period the staff and students were army cadres themselves. Could the red army provide the necessary increase in staffing when the sudden influx of students began? With the outbreak of war, active army cadres could no longer be spared and many active teachers had to be recalled to the front, thus worsening the staffing shortage. For example, the head of the resistance university, Lin Biao, was recalled, though he later returned to the resistance university to convalesce from injuries suffered at the front. His deputy, Luo Ruiqing, became the effective head of the Resistance University throughout the eight long years of the war.[57] So, at a critical time when additional staff was needed, the red army was not in a position to spare qualified and experienced personnel.

New teachers could only be found from among the new arrivals. Experienced teachers were few and most of them were not party members. Xu Maoyong, a teacher at the Resistance University, even claimed that Confucianism was honored at the Resistance University.[58] The mixed political backgrounds of newcomers did create difficulties for party indoctrination. To keep students in touch with the views of the CCP, party leaders provided some lectures themselves. They acted as part-time lecturers at the beginning. They were rewarded with a fee of two to three dollars, the right to a free meal at communal dining, and the privilege of using university bathing facilities.[59] The pressure of other duties often resulted in the cancelation of lectures at short notice,[60] and so the practice of part-time lecturing by members of the party leadership was stopped. Instead they were invited to provide an occasional public lecture, labeled as "talks by famous men," usually in the open air to an audience of six to seven hundred at a time.[61]

Another expediency was to assign teaching duties to administrative staff. During the fourth class—that is, from May to December 1938—the university had only forty faculty members. Basing on the staff-student ratio of one to eighty, there was a need for 64 faculty members to cater for five thousand students. At that time, however, the size of the support staff, numbering four hundred, was considerably larger than the teaching staff.[62] No explanation was offered for the size of the support staff. Besides, students too performed regular maintenance work. One suggestion was that many of the supporting staff were drill sergeants from the red army, because military drills were part of formal training.

New staff were mostly recruited from the graduates. Selected students were given a postgraduate preparation of six months before being assigned as apprentice teachers, taking relatively lighter duties and had their work supervised by an experienced staff.[63] By February 1939 a total staff complement of one thousand was reported, of these probably about one hundred were faculty members. At the time one-fifth of the staff complement were former cadres of the red army,[64] showing that as the war progressed, some army cadres while resting at Yanan took on some teaching, and thus allowed their experiences to be drawn on by the students.

Postgraduate training was not restricted to the training of new faculty members. By 1939 five different kinds of specialized professional training were provided for, namely:

(1) Military staff work
(2) Counter propaganda work
(3) Political work
(4) Labor organization
(5) The training of new faculty members.[65]

By the beginning of 1939 the Resistance University was firmly established and its graduates active in extending CCP influence throughout north China.

The founding of new guerrilla bases opened up opportunities and increased demands for the supply of cadres. For administrative purposes, the guerrilla base areas were divided into five zones: northwest Shaanxi, Shanxi-Charhar-Hebei, Shandong, Shanxi-Henan-Hebei, and central China.[66] In 1939 some staff resources were transferred from Yanan to these guerrilla zones, where they established branch campuses for the Resistance University. As these campuses were close to the front, their locations were kept secret. The fourth campus, for example, was in central China. Its location was unfortunately spotted by a GMD unit, and subsequently the entire campus population of about two hundred were either captured or killed.[67]

General Observations

How many cadres did the Resistance University and complementary institutions such as the public school and the Lu Xun College produce? The scale of the cadre training programs was related to the size of the population under Chinese communist control. In 1937, at the beginning of the Sino-Japanese war, this was under two million. The size of the red army then was somewhere between sixty thousand to eighty thousand. By the beginning of the Pacific war in December 1941, the corresponding figures—civilian and military—climbed to fifty million and half a million. By the end of the war the same figures climbed to one hundred million and one million. Without a steady supply of trained cadres, the political structure in command of one hundred million people and one million regular troops could not be maintained. Bearing in mind the speed and the scale of CCP expansion during the war years, the demand for new supplies of cadres could not be fully satisfied. In short the expanding CCP power structure could absorb as many cadres as the training institutions produced. Contrast this with a drastic reduction of territory under GMD control since the outbreak of war in 1937, together with the consequent loss of deployment opportunities in areas under GMD control. It was not until the outbreak of the Pacific War in 1941 that a policy of rapid expansion returned to the GMD camp. Political neglect of campuses at Kunming continued up to the final days of the war, while any murmur of discontent after the Japanese surrender would attract GMD suppression. Confrontation between students and the GMD in the postwar period will be treated in chapter 10.

How many cadres were produced at Yanan during the war years? During the first eighteen months the most productive institutions were the Resistance University and the public school, with the first reaching an enrollment level of five thousand and the latter a level of two thousand. Other institutions, principally the Lu Xun College of the Arts and the party school, were far more modest in scale; their contribution to the supply of cadres was negligible.

Between the Resistance University and the public school, the annual rate of graduating cadres could be up to eighteen thousand—with two thousand graduating at quarterly intervals from the public school and five thousand graduating at half-yearly intervals from the Resistance University. These were deployed to expand CCP influence further—that is, in building up the various guerrilla base areas in north and central China. The existence of these guerrilla base areas further stimulated demand for cadres, some of whom were trained locally in the branch campuses of the Resistance University.

By 1939 enrollment rate either stabilized or declined. The euphemism used was the "normalization" of the education system. The Resistance University, for example, began to offer postgraduate studies and other institutions tended to lengthen their period of training. This can be interpreted as reflecting a balance between supply and demand. CCP expansion could adequately deploy eighteen thousand to twenty thousand new cadres a year, and this scale was reached by 1939. During the seven years between 1939 and 1945, the size of the cadre force which had received some form of training at Yanan probably reached as many as one hundred forty thousand These were the crucial mid-level cadres whose dedication to the resistance effort enabled the CCP to reemerge as a viable contender for national power after the war. Seen in this light the December 9th movement which initiated the influx of students to Yanan was a crucial turning point in the political fortunes of the CCP.

Recruitment of students into the cadre structure during the civil war period is outside the scope of the present study. But there is every reason to expect that the scale of cadre training expanded with the rapid spread of communist power.

As the CCP expanded its power and control from north China to Manchuria, to central China, and eventually to south China, it was transformed from a party aspiring to power to a party in power. The established educational facilities, particularly those in major urban centers, became the responsibility of the new government. Instead of establishing new institutions for cadre training, the CCP had to coordinate the general program of educating intellectuals and cadres. With CCP control over all educational institutions, the nature of this process of reintegrating the elite entered into a different phase. The scope of the present study, as far as the harnessing of student nationalism by the CCP is concerned, is confined to the resistance period. The focus of this study is on the impact of student nationalism upon the GMD. The inclusion of a minor parallel study of the impact of student nationalism upon the CCP is to highlight what opportunities were lost by the GMD. The success of the CCP in building a viable alternative power structure during the resistance war reflected largely communist success in harnessing the forces of student nationalism. The next chapter will focus on how the CCP devised ways and means of controlling and harnessing the dynamic but volatile forces of student nationalism.

9 Regimentation through Rectification

In the 1920s and 1930s nationalism was the dominant force in Chinese politics. During the northern expedition Jiang Jieshi initiated a red purge. As communists were being hunted down in cities, they sought survival in rural areas and championed agrarian revolution. However, Jiang Jieshi was able to marshal sufficient military might to dislodge them from their rural bases in central China. When the Chinese communists started the Long March in October 1934, they were conceding defeat in central China. If the communist movement was to survive, the Chinese communists had to reestablish their credentials in the nationalist cause.

Anti-Japanese slogans were used by the Jiangxi Soviet, principally to embarass the GMD. But it was not until the protests of December 9, 1935, that students looked to the CCP for alternative leadership in the nationalist cause. From early 1936, the arrival of patriotic students at Yanan initiated a test of communist will power and ability to live up to its hard-line pledges against Japan. After arriving at Yanan, many students were disappointed to find the lack of physical means with which to counter Japanese incursions.

The outbreak of war in 1937 delivered the Chinese communists from a potential disaster. The urgency of the situation swept aside doubts about their capabilities. Students were ready to accept what modest contributions the CCP could give, for a stand against the Japanese invasion had to be made whatever the odds. Moreover, students who walked to Yanan were willing to assist in expanding communist influence and territorial control. The issue was no longer what the party could do for them, but what they could do for the party. Nationalist feelings propelled Chinese communist expansion after July 1937, for the strengthening of the CCP, became synonymous with strengthening the nation. Communist power could be a means to national salvation.

The point-and-line strategy of the invading forces, which chose to control communication lines and urban centers, determined that large tracts of territory remained outside Japanese control. The Japanese also regarded the Chinese communists as a minor threat, and they concentrated their forces on breaking GMD-led resistance. Japanese military strategy made communist expansion in north China comparatively easy. Thus, within the total resistance effort, the longer-term functional role of the CCP was enhanced by Japanese decisions.

Communist success in establishing guerrilla base areas restored the credibility of the CCP as an active champion of nationalism. The border governments in the guerrilla base areas were coalitions in which the CCP restricted its share of formal positions to no more than one-third. In the border governments, GMD and third-party partici-pations were openly seen. The CCP made the additional claim that they believed in a pluralistic political system and Mao explained this as new democracy.

The general populace of each guerrilla base area was given the vote to ensure popular perception that the people were active in their choice of local administrative and political leaders. But behind the outer wrappings of united front tactics and popular participation was tight party control over preselection. Candidates standing for election had to obtain prior approval from the CCP. GMD and third-party representations in the border governments were more apparent than real.

Contrary to early Japanese perceptions, Communist-led guerril-la resistance proved formidable. After the hundred regiments offen-sive of October 1940, the Japanese high command was awakened to the prowess of the CCP in north China. By flexing its muscles the CCP ended a phase of relative inattention from the invasion force and triggered off reprisal measures in the form of "security improvement" and "search and destroy" campaigns.[1]

To secure their hold over the countryside, the Japanese collected village communities into strategic hamlets. Villagers were organized to dig extensive trench works to inhibit the movement of men and resources between such defined points of Japanese power and areas where guerrilla activities thrived. This defensive strategy was paral-leled by offensive forays, military thrusts aimed directly at suspected centers of communist strength.[2] The year 1941 marked the beginnings of full-scale confrontation between communist-led resistance and Japanese forces in north China.

A hostile external environment made further CCP expansion difficult.[3] Indeed CCP-held territories contracted significantly. Early rapid expansion tactics were replaced by demands for improved internal cohesion, discipline, and command. The rectification movement[4] was part of this response, a reemphasis on the use of ideology for improving solidarity within the party. This should be contrasted with the check and balance approaches of Jiang Jieshi when he dissolved the Lixingshe, split the Whampoa faction, and deployed rival groupings to balance each other within the GMD, the GMD youth corps, and the military.

The CCP also responded to the loss of territory and population by economic measures. The popular slogan of "better troops and simpler administration"[5] was a call for cost cutting, including trimming the size of the army. Further economic measures announced at the end of a senior cadres conference in November 1941 indicated decisions to increase productivity.[6]

Launching the Rectification Campaign

The timing of the rectification campaign suggests that it was a direct response to Japanese pressure. The first two keynote speeches by Mao Zedong relating to the rectification campaign dated February 1 and February 8, 1942.[7] The public launching of the campaign was preceded by debates within the Party hierarchy, debates which led to the adoption of resolutions to "increase party solidarity."[8] Setting a goal for increasing party solidarity just as the Japanese were stepping up their military pressure could hardly be a coincidence.

Within the immediate context of the time, it is easier to appreciate that the rectification campaign was meant to be short and sharp, designed as an expediency to meet a current crisis. Following Mao's keynote speeches of early February, the propaganda department of the central committee issued a set of eighteen documents.[9] Collectively labeled as rectification literature,[10] these documents were prescribed reading for all cadres within a set study period of two to three months. At the end of the study period participants were to take a formal examination.[11] Instead of ending the campaign at the end of three months, the propaganda department issued an additional set of four documents and extended the study period to July.[12] But the rectification process, once initiated, was never brought to an end.

How was the rectification campaign to attain the goal of improved party solidarity? What were the tactics employed? What were the assumptions held? And what effects did the rectification instrument have on students and intellectuals who saw the Chinese communists as champions of nationalism?

The July resolutions to strengthen party solidarity reflected fears of the CCP that Japanese actions could weaken their control over the guerrilla base areas. The central committee expressed its apprehension in the following terms: "a broad agrarian environment, an environment characterized by long range, dispersed, independent, guerrilla warfare (may lead) certain Party members to develop individualism, heroism, anti-organizational attitudes . . . and other tendencies counter to the Party spirit."[13]

The perception that anti-Japanese feelings could become a centrifugal force led Mao to organize the rectification campaign to correct erroneous attitudes to study, to party work, and to the use of ideological language. A Marxian worldview and party discipline were regarded as more reliable than nationalist feelings. The rectification campaign was an organized process to stress that, within the CCP-led coalition of forces, nationalism was to be harnessed to serve the party and not vice versa. For Mao Zedong, Marxian rationalism should come before national feelings.

Nationalism could be subsumed within Marxian rationalism. The CCP put forth the argument that Chinese historical experience was of primary importance in understanding the Chinese revolution. Official release of the rectification literature in 1942 can be seen as the first move to establish an orthodox litany of Chinese communism.[14] Nationalism was to be redefined in Marxian terms. In the selection of documents Russian ideological influence was downgraded by separating specific Russian experience from general Marxian theory.[15] In compiling the rectification literature, Chinese national sensitivities were reflected by a focus on the Chinese revolution. Historical rationalism provided an intellectual bridge between Marxian rationalism and nationalism. National feelings were articulated in the form of an official litany of Chinese communism, but this nationalism was also to be harnessed to serve a Marxist party.

In a speech to students of the party school at Yanan on February 1942, Mao tried to legitimize the revolution in terms of the existence of national enemies: "Why must there be a revolutionary party? There must be a revolutionary party because our enemies still exist, and furthermore there must be not only an ordinary revolutionary party but a Communist revolutionary party."[16]

Later Mao stressed the point again in an address to delegates of the second border area consultative conference: "the only purpose for the Consultative Conference is for the defeat of Japanese Imperialism."[17]

The rectification campaign, though aimed at combatting the centrifugal tendencies of resistance groups, was publicly legitimized in terms of Chinese nationalism. The argument was that just being patriotic was not good enough, one should be a good communist patriot, otherwise patriotism might not have been effectively organized.

Legitimizing ideological control with nationalism also weakened Russian influence. The effort to create Sinicized Marxism and the release of rectification literature provided an ideological resource of indigenous origins. Mao's speech on foreign eight-legged essays[18] was a direct attack on Chinese cadres who dared to quote ideological authority from abroad. This downgrading of non-Chinese ideological authority hastened the decline in influence of the Russian-returned students within the CCP. Settling scores within the party leadership, however, did not develop into a principal goal of the rectification campaign.[19] It was sufficient for Mao to have the members of the central committee publicly accepting the primacy of Chinese experiences on ideological issues. As a principal contributor to the accumulating body of Sinicized ideological literature, Mao's personal authority was enhanced in the process.

The rectification campaign represented an effort to establish an indigenous ideological foundation for sustaining Communist power. National sensitivity expressed in the rectification literature was welcomed by those in the resistance. But the rectification campaign also brought with it the philosophical belief that human consciousness could be reshaped, reorganized, and regimented as the foundation for concerted national action. This made a coercive technique such as rectification outright dangerous to liberal intellectuals and a hindrance to future social reforms and technological modernization.

The technique and practice of imposing an official ideology upon those who aspired to bureaucratic office were well-developed in traditional China. The center piece of traditional practice was the civil service examination. Through the interplay of coercion and the lure of office—that is, the stick and the carrot—the spirit of ideological conformity permeated the entire education process. The civil service examination and official efforts to enforce ideological conformity were terminated one after the other because the Chinese came to believe, for a time, that such traditional forms of political organization were inadequate to enable China to withstand the might of foreign powers. The rectification campaign represented a change of mind, a renewed awareness that ideological conformity could be a source of organizational strength. For intellectuals who advocated a new culture to free the Chinese mind from ideological conformity, the rectification campaign was nothing less than a counterrevolution.

Implications for the Intelligentsia

What were the immediate implications of the reintroduction of ideological control for the intelligentsia? According to Mao, in a country such as China where the industrial proletariat was small and weak, the revolutionary task fell upon the shoulders of the intelligentsia. They were supposed to be the principal beneficiaries of the rectification campaign as Mao proclaimed to his cadres: "without a revolutionary intelligentsia, the revolution cannot succeed."[20]

What place did the intelligentsia hold within a Marxian perception of society and how could Mao assert that intellectuals were indispensable to the Chinese revolution?

The intelligentsia, in Marxian perception, is not a class. They form rather an element within a class. Nor is the intelligentsia considered an element exclusive to any one class. That is to say, all classes in society possess their own intelligentsia, and the class nature of the intelligentsia is decided by the interests they serve. This interpretation of the transferable service of the intelligentsia from one class to another became the theoretical basis upon which efforts to convert the class consciousness of the intelligentsia were based. The rectification campaign was one specific effort to convert the Chinese intelligentsia to the cause of the communist revolution.

How then were members of the intelligentsia to be converted to become revolutionaries? Most of the leaders who contributed to the building up of the Chinese communist movement were intellectuals—from professors Chen Duxiu and Li Dachao to library assisstant Mao Zedong. How did they become revolutionaries? To Mao such questions were at best rhetorical, for the only way to become a revolutionary was to engage in revolutionary work:

> How can half-intellectuals be transformed into intellectuals. . . ? There is only one way: to see that those with only book knowledge become practical workers engaged in practical tasks, and see that those doing the theoretical work turn to practical research. In this way we can reach our goal. . . . Thus Marx is to be regarded as a complete intellectual. The difference between

him and the half intellectual is that he participated in an actual revolutionary movement."[21]

Even as Mao continued to stress the central importance of action, he was installing the rectification process, which put the *words* of the party as the guiding force for future action. Mao Zedong, the activist of the 1920s, became the inspiration for an ideologically oriented generation of the 1940s.

In what ways did the rectification campaign relate to Mao's concept of practical revolutionary experience? The campaign was not directed against the intelligentsia as yet, but meant for party cadres who were formally engaged as professional revolutionaries. What the campaign tried to rectify were actions not guided by proper ideological principles—"proper" as defined by the central committee at the time. In Maoist terms the campaign was to ensure that theory and practice were brought together. In practical terms it was to ensure that party policy (theory) were implemented (practiced)—that is, the words of the central committee were to be translated into actual action by cadres at various levels. The hierarchical authority of the central committee was to be given added ideological teeth, for the party leadership also arrogated to itself the right, as wielders of the collective authority of the party, to monopolize ideological expressions. Where military command could fragment as the number of guerrilla bases multiplied, ideological command continued to sustain a unity of political will.

When so many students, teachers, artists, and men of letters joined the communists for patriotic reasons, the attempt of the party to impose ideological control was more than likely to meet with some resistance. Yanan was after all no heaven on earth, and the critical eyes of some sympathizers could lead them to express independent opinions. Independent opinion was one of the specified targets to be eliminated by the rectification campaign.

Writers who had made their reputation before going to Yanan were unlikely to subject themselves to intellectual regimentation without a murmur. Writers such as Ding Ling and Xiao Jun, prominent leaders of the League of Left-Wing Writers, were iconoclasts. It was this iconoclastic edge, exemplified by the writings of their hero Lu Xun, which the GMD government could not tolerate. And it was GMD intolerance which turned these writers to the CCP in their search for an alternative environment in which critical and iconoclastic spirits could be protected and nurtured. But exposé and criticism at Yanan could weaken party authority. Criticisms of the party by these independent spirits were regarded as resistance to party discipline.

Active efforts were directed at bringing such sympathetic cultural allies into line. On May 2, 1942, Mao delivered his famous speech at the Yanan forum, an "informal" talk addressed to cultural workers.[22] Here Mao laid down the general principles of intellectual regimentation and candidly referred to "the cultural army." Writers working in communist-controlled areas were treated as party cadres, they were part of the CCP's "cultural army," hence subject to command and discipline. Their work included exposing enemy weakness and glorifying party virtues. This was not merely administrative command, but also an imposition of ideological discipline to accept party authority to decide what was culturally acceptable. Criticisms against the CCP were considered to be counterrevolutionary acts, or at best signs of bourgeois individualism. Hence censorship was glorified in ideological terms and legitimized in the name of the revolution, whereas resistance against party authority was to be condemned. Culture was reduced to a mere political tool of the party and intellectuals were to submit themselves as soldiers in this "cultural army." Intellectuals and students who were capable of being forceful critics of a ruling government were denied the legitimacy of critical appraisals.

For writers who had been at the forefront of popularizing ideas of reform through their writings, there was an erroneous assumption that their personal perceptions of liberation and revolution were compatible, if not identical, with the perceptions of the party. On March 9, 1942, for example, Ding Ling continued her established role as a feminist reformer in writing an editorial for the *Liberation Daily* in which she criticized the ongoing sexism at Yanan. She complained that Yanan society looked down upon women either because they put their "personal" and "private" interests of love, marriage, and children before political activism, or because they were not feminine enough if they were to compete actively in the male preserve of politics.[23] Ding Ling and three other prominent writers were made examples of and put before what could only be described as a kangaroo court made up of party propaganda chiefs such as Chen Boda and Kang Sheng.[24] To indicate her acceptance of the new party discipline demanded of her, Ding Ling advised her readers that her article on women "represented only a personal point of view and neglected the standpoints of the party. Let me assure you repeatedly that it was a bad article. Please continue with your study of the [Party] documents."[25]

With the launching of the rectification campaign in 1942, intellectuals who opted for the CCP had to declare their renunciation of individualistic thoughts and to accept the party line. Ding Ling was one of the best-known victims of thought control in the 1940s. Worse still her pen was commandeered to praise the virtues of her detractors. In a work on thought reform edited by Ding Ling and published in 1949 she says:

> "Dare to fight and dare to denounce," this is what Mr. Lu Xun said [in directing his attack on] the northern warlords and their running dogs some twenty years ago. During the warlord period, encouraging the people to have the spirit to act was correct. But now the time has changed. The master of the house is now we the people, it is no longer right to repeat these words [of Lu Xun]. To be with the people is democracy. To act against the people, the people's government, and the war of the people's liberation would be antidemocratic."[26]

The point is reaffirmed by quoting the authority of Mao: "The people's nation protects the people. Only when there is a people's nation can the people, on an inclusive national scale, using Democratic methods, educate and reform themselves, so that they could be rid of all reactionary forces from in and out the nation."[27]

As if to make the irony as obvious as possible, the work included this broad explanation of what legitimacy stood for:

> What is legitimacy? In general the concept of legitimacy is popular acceptance of former rulers as "legitimate" [indicating] their willingness to serve as slaves, to be law-abiding persons, [and] to acknowledge the right of the ruler to oppress and exploit as being rational and legal. Such is the concept of "legitimacy.". . . The reactionary Jiang Jieshi clique also describes itself as the main stream of the Chinese people, as the [wielders] of national legitimacy. Whomever resisted them would be [charged] with "endangering the people" and "sabotaging the country," and be subjected to "antirebel" and "antibandit" campaigns."[28]

The rectification process went beyond labeling those who opposed or criticized the CCP as being illegitimate. The process tried to ensure that there was organized public rituals in which the educated were made to offer open adoration to the CCP. Those who resisted would be drowned in the vocal enthusiasm of the orchestrated social environment around them. Authority, ideological assertion, and the threat of social alienation were used concurrently to maximize pressure on members of the intelligentsia to ensure that those who were best equipped to think independently would not and could not do so. Accompanying negative pressures were the lure of office, social eminence, and continued opportunities to share in the exercise of power. These attractions made conformity gratifying and independence of spirit doubly unattractive.

At a time of national crisis, at a time when Japanese offensives threatened the survival of a communist-led resistance in north China, Mao devised the rectification process to maintain party authority over a number of territorially disconnected guerrilla bases. At a time of national crisis, this ideological weapon served its purpose of enforcing unity of will and in doing so became acceptable to the cadres, students, and prominent intellectuals at the time. But when the national crisis was over, the weapon of thought-control remained.

The presence of such an ideological system brought with it the danger that its manipulators could abuse the intent that brought it into being. The ideological system that imposed discipline upon CCP cadres since the 1940s brought chaos to China in the 1960s when its intent was abused. Jiang Jieshi said that political agents should not have any political views of their own so that they would not question orders from their leader.[29] Mao Zedong established the rectification process to ensure that cadres could have political views as long as they were those of the party.

Political coercion could help to instill political discipline. But in the context of longer-term socio-economic reforms and of technological modernization, coercion is no answer. Coercion has no real intellectual content and the "study,"which rectification processes demanded, was a collective effort to stop thinking so that the words of the party would not be contradicted. Coercive systems discipline social groups in the pursuit of prescribed tasks to enforce a unity of purpose. Coercion also eliminates alternative ideas even when the party is bankrupt of ideas. The spirit of the eight-legged essay permeated the "study" rituals of the rectification process.

During both the resistance war and the civil war, Mao found the rectification process effective in enforcing a unity of purpose among party cadres. Coercion removed critical view points from informed observers inside communist-controlled territories. During the civil war views critical of the CCP were rare. Campuses known for the independent views of their staff and students found themselves under the discipline of the rectification process. Intellectual vitality was sacrificed to strengthen the ideological authority of the party.

10 Confrontations with the Guomindang

Both the GMD and the CCP drew strength from student support. The Whampoa Military Academy captured student imagination with its "student army" and this symbolism breathed vitality into the party army. The CCP at Yanan captured the anti-Japanese mood of December 9th and was rewarded with a new injection of youthful followers. The GMD created an officers corps at Whampoa, while the CCP turned student supporters into an army of cadres. The common approach of both political parties was the regimentation of young student nationalists into an organized and disciplined force. To maintain this regimentation both parties developed control devices, exemplified by the underground network of the young officers movement and the Rectification process of indoctrination.

When the GMD was seen to falter under Japanese pressure in the early 1930s, the distance between the GMD and the students increased. This was reflected in the antigovernment protests on the one hand and police suppression on the other. The outbreak of the Sino-Japanese war, however, saw the GMD regaining support from campus communities. But the political distance of the 1930s persisted in the form of GMD political distrust of campus communities of northern Chinese origins. The activist Whampoa tradition of the 1920s was unable to rejuvenate itself in the 1930s.

During the resistance war the CCP regimented student support and deployed the hastily trained cadres to help expand communist power and influence. The CCP too suspected the longer-term political loyalty of these students who were of middle-class origins. This was dealt with by active indoctrination, in the form of rectification campaigns. Throughout the war years the GMD was hesitant in closing the distance between itself and the campus community at Kunming. In contrast, during the same period the CCP shortened that distance and channeled student support to serve its cause. The quality of the relationship between the educated elite and the two major parties was set during the resistance war, well before the resumption of civil conflicts after 1945.

In the postwar period the one single objective of the GMD was to reunify the country by force of arms. Yet this was one notable area in which the GMD failed to convince campus communities. In reading student publications of the time, articulations of critical comments against the GMD generally asserted propeace and anti-imperial intentions. There was a suggestion then that the GMD failed to gain student support because it was a war party and therefore out of tune with the mood of a war-wearied populace.

Yet the CCP was no less an advocate of war as the ultimate solution. Why then was the CCP free from antiwar and antihunger demonstrations by students in territories under its control? The educated in CCP-held areas were also militant, but their militancy was effectively channeled (principally through ideological control via the rectification processes) to provide active support for party policies in land reform and in a war of liberation. The contrast between a militant and critical student movement in GMD areas and a militant but subservient student populace in CCP areas was striking. Both parties were resorting to force and advocating a one-party state. Why was there a preference for one and not the other? Were students really against civil war and authoritarian government? Why then did the same critical student body become subservient once under CCP authority?

The response of the intellectual elite groups to the leadership of one party or another was a measure of the political performance of that party. This could not be left to chance and the two parties had to compete actively for support and be engaged actively in regimenting that support. Instead of student support, a confrontation between the GMD and the campus communities at Kunming and Beijing developed after the war. This was an indication of GMD policy failure as far as gaining student support was concerned. Why did the GMD fail to harness student support in the civil war period? The answer is obvious, for the GMD regarded student activism as hostile and did not hesitate to suppress it with force. In doing so the GMD assured itself of campus hostility.

Postwar Setting

During wartime the Chongqing government headed a nominally united coalition of forces. This fragile unity was a response to external threat. The strength of GMD authority over different parts of unoccupied China varied, and distrust between government and regional allies remained strong. It was this GMD distrust that determined government attitudes toward refugee students and academics from north China.

The war further weakened the GMD politically by uprooting it from its power base at the middle and lower reaches of the Yangtze River. The relocation of the seat of government to Chongqing made the GMD more dependent on regional support. And this regional support rested upon a delicate balance of three factors: the threat of enemy attack, the ability of the GMD to impose central control, and the willingness of local regimes to respect a central authority. What the central government and the local governments had in common was their enmity toward the invaders.

Within this coalition, the GMD perceived that the presence of weak provincial regimes would enhance central authority. This perception often led Chongqing to deny political and logistical support to its regional allies to fight the invading forces. As suggested by Lloyd Eastman, Jiang Jieshi was playing the politics of weakness[1]— to ensure that his rivals were weak, for "rivals" and "allies" were interchangeable terms. The CCP was to be isolated, the militarist allies were to be denied weapons, and suspect campus communities distanced. This politics of weakness also resulted in a weak GMD government.

The wartime coalition was not limited to groups with a definable territorial base. It also included diverse influential elements whose support was formalized through the Political Consultative Congress,[2] with the recruitment of prominent leftist writers such as Guo Moruo and Tian Han into the GMD propaganda machine,[3] and refugee students and faculties seeking GMD protection. While these former critics suspended their adverse comments in the face of a common national peril, they remained suspect in the eyes of the GMD. This suspicion led the GMD to practice the politics of weakness, to ensure its own ascendancy. The campuses at Kunming were treated as such a coalition partner. They were given enough sustenance to survive but not enough to nurture strength.

At the Associated University self sacrifice was accepted as the norm during the resistance war. Indeed the staff and students of the Associated University were more fortunate than most when they were left to sit out the eight long years of conflict in the comparatively secure remote southwest. But then no one was spared the effects of war however distant from the field of battle. At Kunming the damage can be seen from a continuous fall of living standards. According to one source, the income of the faculty fell by up to 96 percent between 1936 and 1945.[4] They were impoverished beyond expectation and they survived on government handouts and part-time employment.

The sacrifices they made during the war, however, did not earn them political trust from the wartime GMD government. Even though the defeat of Japan brought a sigh of relief, victory brought little prospects of improved relationships with the GMD government. Their fondest hope after the war was to be repatriated to North China and they became apathetic to the political fortunes of the GMD. The campus communities at Kunming were war-wearied.

The two major parties, however, were confronted with a renewed sense of urgency as the resistance war came to an end. The rationale for political rivals to accept GMD ascendancy was removed with the defeat of Japan. Each party had to reestablish its claim to national power and so a war-wearied people was dragged to the battlefield again by the GMD and the CCP. Confrontations at Kunming developed as direct consequences of GMD attempts to assert its authority

The GMD frantically dispatched troops all over the country to secure its claim as the legitimate government for all of China, a strategy based on an assumption of GMD military superiority. The CCP, on the other hand, marched its units into Japanese occupied north China and Manchuria to stake counterclaims. The two major parties were firmly committed to civil war.

Only the minor parties, who had neither territory nor troops, were in favor of the continuation of some form of coalition, so that civil war could be avoided and they might find the opportunity to develop as a third force by holding the balance of power. They were vocally against civil war and a one-party state for their own political survival. During the resistance war the minor parties formalized their third force existence within the Political Consultative Congress as the Democratic League. The antiwar stand of the league matched the war-wearied mood of the campus community at Kunming. It does not mean, however, that students and staff at the Associated University were ipso facto supporters of the Democratic League.

Developing Confrontation at Kunming

Yunnan Province was semiautonomous of GMD control between 1935 and 1945. Because of its remoteness, Yunnan stands at the periphery of national politics at the best of times. A measure of GMD influence was introduced into the province in 1935 as an incidental extension of central government authority when GMD troops pursued the communists fleeing from their Soviet bases.[5] The local militarist, Lung Yun, cooperated with the GMD and was allowed to retain much of his provincial autonomy. Lung Yun in general accepted GMD directions, but it was he and his army of about forty thousand who held de facto power in the province.[6] The Resistance War put the border province into the main stream of national politics. The arrival of refugee staff and students of the prestigious universities of north China turned the provincial capital into a cultural center. The loss of sea ports turned the inland provincial capital into a major entrepôt for the Chongqing government. GMD influence increased on all fronts with the establishment of party branches, the intrusion of secret service organizations, the building up of central government military presence, and the injection of paper money issued by the central government to pay its troops.[7] Local autonomy was on the decline. The Chongqing government, however, tolerated provincial autonomy at Yunnan to allay fears among other regional military coalition partners.

This semiautonomous setting provided opportunities for minor political parties to operate. The Democratic League found the acquiescent but politically frustrated campus community at Kunming a receptive audience. Its advocacy of liberal democracy gained further strength as Kunming became a major receiving point for American assistance in December 1941. The mild tone of political pluralism at Kunming was an irritating thorn for the GMD government during the resistance war.

After the war the GMD was ready and able to remove what it considered an unacceptable combination of regional autonomy and political dissidence at Kunming. In April 1945 Jiang summoned the commander of GMD forces at Kunming to brief them of his intention to have the regional militarist, Lung Yun, physically removed from his territorial base.[8] On October 2 the actual orders to transfer Lung Yun were issued[9] They were to be hand delivered to Lung Yun by General Du Yuming. Instead, Du moved his units to disarm the personal guards of Lung and precipitated an armed clash. Lung in fact ordered his men to lay down their arms and complied with central government orders.[10] The episode, however, did show that Jiang's generals at Kunming lacked political skills and were inclined to resort to force unnecessarily.

With the semiautonomy of Yunnan ending in October 1945, the GMD military at Kunming was soon to confirm its political ineptitude. One week prior to November 25 the new GMD leadership at Kunming learned that the student alliance was planning a public forum on current affairs and that some of the leading speakers were prominent members of the Democratic League.[11] There was the possibility, not a certainty, that opinions critical of the government might be expressed. How were the GMD military authorities going to handle potential critics at Kunming?

The leading GMD figures at Kunming at the time were Li Zonghuang, deputy chairman of the provincial government, Guan Linzheng, commander of GMD forces at Yunnan province, and Qiu Qingzhuan, the Kunming garrison commander.[12] In an emergency meeting of the three, Li Zonghuang argued that the public forum announced by the student alliance represented an opportunity for the government to assert its authority.[13] Li was proposing confrontation to silence dissent, because of his preconceived notion that the campus community was hostile to the GMD.

On the fateful day, local morning papers published emergency regulations prohibiting public gatherings, debates, and demonstrations.[14] Given less than twenty-four hours notice, it was practically impossible for the organizers to cancel the public forum. Government instructions were also dispatched to school and college administrations, urging them to warn students against taking part in the forum organized by the student alliance that evening. Li Zonghuang further contacted the presidents of Yunnan and Associated Universities requesting their cooperation. In the afternoon the garrison commander called on the president of Yunnan University in person to reiterate the request. At Yunnan University the campus security guards were called out, the main gates locked, and everyone leaving or entering campus screened.[15] The GMD authorities succeeded in manufacturing an emergency.

The notice given to all concerned was extremely short. Not only were the student alliance and the Democratic League surprised, but GMD elements among both the faculty and the students were also caught unprepared. Noting that GMD influence among staff and students was considerable, the sudden move by the local GMD authorities was hasty and ill-considered. They were making a major political move without first mobilizing GMD support on campus, thus making government supporters appear foolish and disorganized.

The student alliance and the Democratic League were also confused because of the speed and vehemence of GMD reaction toward the public forum. After a hasty consultation the organizers decided to conduct the forum regardless.[16] With government actions helping to publicize the occasion, the general public sensed the excitement of a potential confrontation. In the evening, crowds gathered at the front gate of Yunnan University, for the announced venue was the assembly hall on that campus. There a notice was posted to announce the new venue to be the front lawn of the main library at the Associated University.[17]

The GMD did not expect to have their authority flouted, nor did the forum organizers expect a sizeable attendance. The tense situation excited the populace of what was a humdrum township. Crowds first gathered at the main gate of Yunnan University and then strolled toward the Associated University, and curious passersby were collected along the way. Many probably did not even know the public forum was proscribed. The gathered crowd swelled to about ten thousand—a mixed group representative of the Kunming populace. [18]

Police and military units were hurriedly called out with no well thought-out plans to deal with an unexpected gathering of this size. The university campus was surrounded and electricity supply for the forum's public address system cut off. When speakers addressed the gathering regardless, agents were sent in to disrupt the proceedings. In the distance troops fired volleys into the air, adding confusion to a tense situation.[19] These moves were for dispersing the gathering and to cow the speakers, yet, when the gathering did disperse, troops surrounding the campus hesitated to allow anyone to leave for fear of possible street demonstrations.[20] In short the authorities were quick to flaunt their armed strength, but rather unsure of their own immediate objectives.

The consequence of the events of November 25 was an open confrontation between students and the government, with the Democratic League taking the political stance of supporting the voice of student protest. Considering how the campuses at Kunming remained supportive of the GMD government throughout the resistance war, the emergence of student protest in November 1945 was dramatic. The political frictions at Kunming was a direct consequence of GMD attempts to assert central control, but the confrontations of November 1945 were largely precipitated by the ineptitude of GMD military leaders on the spot.

The local blunders were further magnified when the Central News Agency reported the events in a news release the following day as a "local skirmish between bandit elements and the law".[21] Again the students were being labeled enemies of the government. Leaders of the student alliance met on November 26 and decided on a three-day strike to back up three demands which the alliance presented to the government. These were:

(1) revoke the emergency laws of November 25
(2) public apologies to those who attended the forum
(3) guarantee that similar incidents would not recur.[22]

University administrators were alarmed by this hardening confrontation between students and the GMD government. Strong pressure was exerted on students to stay on campus and to resume classes as soon as the publicly announced three-day strike was over. There was some hope that by reaffirming academic discipline and by keeping the students off the streets, further incidents could be avoided.

Kunming witnessed instead an unwarranted use of force. On December 1, 1945, armed personnel in civilian clothes raided various campuses to beat up students and staff at random. Starting from around 10 in the morning, groups of armed men varying from forty to two hundred raided the Yunnan University, the Associated University, a teachers college, a technical college, and one secondary school. Apart from numerous injuries, three students and one teacher were killed.[23]

Popular emotions ran high. The four victims became instant symbols of martyrdom. Their corpses lay in state at the main library of the Associated University, serving as a focal point for public expression of grief and anger at the high-handedness of the ruling government.[24] The murmur, which the GMD authorities tried to muffle on November 25, turned into a roar of indignation by December 1. Protests came from both inside and outside GMD circles. The professorial board at the Associated University openly supported the students and the students declared an indefinite strike.[25] In their anxiety to assert GMD authority, Generals Li, Guan, and Qiu generated popular ill-will for the GMD government.

The political ineptitude of Li, Guan, and Qiu demanded action from higher authorities in the central government. Two prominent academics with strong ties at the Associated University were sent by Jiang Jieshi to try to calm down the situation. Wu Yaoxun, a former dean of science, returned to Kunming to soften the mood among his former colleagues. He tried to discredit student activists by suggesting that they harbored ulterior political motives.[26] Fu Sinian, a serving trustee of the board of governors of the Associated University, and a close political adviser to Jiang, was sent to Kunming as a personal emissary of the generalissimo.[27] Fu was a student activist in the 1910s and could therefore command respect as a student leader and as a senior academic in his own right.

At Kunming, Fu admonished colleagues and students alike for taking political stands against the ruling government as improper and demanded that they put an end to the campus strike. At the same time he raised the hope that he was in a position to advise Jiang to cashier the offending GMD generals at Kunming.[28] Fu won the support of the professorial board of the Associated University, whose members consisted of all faculty members of associate professor status and above, by appealing to the students to end their protest strike.[29]

Some students heeded the appeal and returned to classes. Office-bearers of the student union, seeing that the strike action was ended without instructions from the student alliance, had the names of those who returned to classes struck off the membership list of the student union of the Associated University.[30] This started a confrontation between the student union and the professorial board, which argued that the union had no right to expel any of its members and that Union membership was a right for all students.[31] The Union immediately held a referendum and had its stand vindicated by the membership. But the union also compromised in a face-saving formula and agreed to end the student strike on receiving a pledge from the professorial board to take action against those responsible for the excesses of December 1.[32] Thus did the campus community come to seek a quid pro quo from the GMD government: an end to student strike actions in return for the cashiering of Li Zonghuang, Guan Linzheng, and Qiu Qingzhuan from their official positions.

With anti-GMD feelings redirected specifically at the three military figures, pro-GMD elements on the faculty tried to rally progovernment feelings. On February 24, 1946, 110 faculty members from the Associated University signed a joint declaration demanding the withdrawal of Russian troops from Manchuria.[33] The political wound could not be healed instantly and it was not until March 17, 1946, that the four victims of December 1 were given a formal funeral by the students, signaling an end to this particular round of confrontations with the GMD government.

The Assasinations of Li Gongpu and Wen Yiduo

In the first three months of GMD military control at Kunming, the ineptitude of its leaders generated an atmosphere of resentment against an authoritarian government. This atmosphere provided the minor parties with opportunities to adopt a relatively high profile in order to attract new support. In contrast to the committed stand of the GMD and the CCP for a one-party state, the minor parties championed the cause of political pluralism. Some leaders of the Democratic League saw the militancy of students over the December 1 incident as a potent weapon to oppose the civil war and to support a coalition government. This intention of Democratic League leaders, such as Li Gongpu, Wen Yiduo, and Fei Xiaotong, ran counter to GMD postwar determination to assert the authority of the central government.

Li Gongpu was the most active leader of the Democratic League at Kunming. Li was at one time a GMD member, but he became disillusioned with the GMD and the CCP, as the two parties waged civil war against each other in the late 1920s. He left for the United States to study, supporting himself with part-time employment. He returned to China soon after the outbreak of war with Japan and became active in youth work, at one time serving Yan Xishan at Shanxi province. He remained distant from the two major parties. His overseas experience also convinced him of the merits of a pluralistic political system. At the end of the war Li went to Chongqing where he openly advocated a coalition government and voiced his objections to the resumption of civil war. At Chongqing, Li was beaten up by GMD agents. He was not intimidated and continued his advocacy on his return to Kunming. His assassination on July 10, 1946, as he and his wife were walking home after an evening at the local cinema, was a blatant act of political terrorism.[34] This was barely four months after settling the student unrests. The GMD was too prone to using brute force to silence dissent at Kunming.

In face of overwhelming force, most members of the Democratic League and their sympathizers endured the murder of Li Gongpu in silence. Wen Yiduo was the notable exception. Wen was a famous scholar and a popular teacher. At Li's funeral service Wen openly accused the GMD of complicity in the political murder and challenged its secret service to have him killed as well.[35] The challenge was promptly taken up and Wen was gunned down on his way home straight after the funeral service.[36] Other prominent leaders of the Democratic League at Kunming ran for their lives, seeking sanctuary at the American consulate.[37] The assasinations of Li Gongpu and Wen Yiduo caused much hostility from overseas. At Kunming, however, the campus communities were cowed into guarded silence. When Liang Shuming and Zhou Xinmin were dispatched by the Democratic League to inquire into the deaths of Li and Wen in August 1946, they found the academic community generally reluctant to speak.[38] The fear of reprisal and the hope for government assistance to an early repatriation to north China both worked in favor of abstention from any actions or comments which could be construed as hostile to the GMD. The absence of open comment, however, did not indicate active political support. In suppressing political comments from academics critical of the GMD, the government further alienated itself from the campus community at Kunming. Meanwhile the tempo of repatriation quickened between May and October 1946,[39] and Kunming returned to its backwater existence. But the political mood of the staff and students was set even before their repatriation to their home campuses in north China.

After the defeat of Japan, GMD efforts to suppress student activism contrasted strongly with the rising expectations of the educated. They were not prepared to be bystanders. GMD failure to tap their energies created a pool of frustration. In 1946 there were 984 newspapers and periodicals registered with the GMD government, but the actual total was estimated at 1,832, with a combined circulation of two million.[40] The educated were ready to flaunt the power of their pens. One of the most influential publications was the *Guancha Zhoukan* [Weekly Observer], which started in Shanghai in September 1946. Its circulation rose from four hundred to a hundred thousand within a year.[41] The GMD lost the media battle from the start and this failure was related to GMD distrust of intellectuals and students in the postwar setting. Their desire to participate in politics was frustrated by the GMD and this led it to support the Democratic League or to criticize the GMD. But we must bear in mind that remonstrance, as distinct from political opposition, is a well-established tradition in Chinese politics.

Developing Anti-GMD Student Militancy at Beijing

Having had a taste of student hostility at Kunming, the GMD was relatively more willing to maintain campus tranquility in postwar Beijing. The governing party's attitude was one of caution, dominated by a negative concern that organized student movements should not emerge. Mutual suspicion between the government and the campus communities stayed just under the surface. The government maintained a calculated distance from the students and generally lacked any political will to turn an organized student movement into an active support base for the party.

Student antagonism threatened to surface with minor frictions. When the government announced a two-tiered scholarship system, giving a more generous grant to those repatriated from the south than those who studied in Japanese occupied territories, the students suspected this to be a politically motivated tactic of divide and rule.[42] This forced the GMD authorities to replace the two-tiered system with a uniform scholarship scheme. But those students who studied under the Japanese were required to enroll in a halfway house, a "temporary university," where they were individually screened before being readmitted to the repatriated institutions.[43] Given the fact that in north China the CCP had considerable political appeal throughout the war years, some GMD precautions against communist infiltration were to be expected.

In the general political turmoil of the postwar period, the negative approach of trying to prevent teachers and students from engaging in political debate could not be maintained for long. On Christmas eve of 1946, a female student from Beijing University, Shen Chong, was raped by two American soldiers. Her screams led passersby to alert the local police, and one of the offenders was apprehended on the spot.[44] This created a delicate political incident for the martial law authorities to handle, for they needed to avoid potential friction with both the educated elite and the government's indispensable ally, the United States. Here the GMD authorities tried to hush up the incident, and attempts were made to dissuade the daily papers from publishing the rape story. Such a move created the public impression that the martial law authorities hesitated to enforce the rigors of the law when the offenders were American nationals.[45] Failing to hush up the incident, the authorities tried to discredit the personal character of the victim with a news release from the Central News Agency.[46] This tactic stirred the campus communities to action.

Before the Christmas eve rape case of 1946 there was generally an absence of student activist organizations in Beijing. Initial attempts to provide a collective response on the rape issue were spontaneous. Fellow students from the dormitory of the victim called a meeting after dinner on December 27 and drafted a formal protest. [47] Earlier in the same afternoon the history society of Beijing University convened a meeting of class representatives and student clubs. Debates continued until eleven o'clock at night and three resolutions were adopted. These were:

(1) Severely punish the culprit and his commanding officer through a public trial under a joint Sino-American court in Beijing;

(2) Demand a public apology from the highest authorities of the American military in China, accompanied with a guarantee that

similar incidents will not occur prior to the repatriation of American troops;

(3) The immediate withdrawal of American troops from China.[48]

The rape case was being blown out of proportion and the issue magnified into the highly emotional plane of national dignity. To support their demands, the meeting also agreed to stage a one-day strike. [48] A latent anti-GMD mood now threatened to emerge as a new wave of student nationalism directed against its foreign ally, the United States.

Although this new wave of student political activism began at Beijing University, because the victim happened to be a Beijing University student, the suburban campuses of Qinghua and Yanjing were also affected. At Qinghua a popular sociology lecture was turned into a public forum on December 27 as news of the rape case came through. Qinghua students convened a mass meeting the following day and adopted the resolutions passed by Beijing University students the day before.[50]

The resurgence of student activism was interpreted by the authorities as basically antigovernment. Unable to prevent students from organizing for political action, the authorities tried to "counter organization with organization"—that is, agents provocateurs were mobilized to stage counteraction. On the evening of December 29 a student meeting at Beijing University called to discuss protest tactics had to be canceled because of interference by secret agents and right-wing students from off campus. The following day the intruders returned to tear down antigovernment posters and replaced them with posters of their own.[51] Physical confrontation followed as Beijing University students and progovernment elements faced each other in the playing field.[52] When news of off-campus elements physically intruding into Beijing University reached the Qinghua campus, students there decided to march into the city to give support to the students of Beijing University. At the same time Qinghua students strongly lobbied the students at Yanjing on New Year's Day, and Yanjing students too decided to join in the march to the city.[53] The actions of the agents provocateurs proved to be counterproductive.

With mass student demonstrations scheduled for January 1, 1947, university administrators from Qinghua and Yanjing appealed to the martial law authorities for restraint to minimize the political damage.[54] The government heeded this voice of caution and the students were allowed to march from one campus to the next without interference from the police and the military. The students took a circuitous route, passing by the campuses of Furen University, the teachers college, the technical college, and the law institute. The ranks of the demonstrators swelled to about five thousand.[55] Strict precautions were taken by the GMD military to prevent the students from any violence, and the demonstrators could do little more than chant slogans.

Responses from campuses at Tianjin, Shanghai, and Nanjing between January 1 and January 3 indicated widespread anti-American feelings among student groups in major urban centers. The GMD authorities imposed self-restraint, kept force on the alert,[56] and generally managed to confine student demonstrations to day-long affairs of slogan shouting. The government was set to weather the political storm and left the outcome of the rape case in the hands of the American military and its legal processes. The suspect concerned was tried by court martial; he was convicted, then sent home to the United States. There an appeal was lodged and he won the appeal on the ground that the court martial at Beijing was subjected to political pressure.[57] This legal outcome was a severe political embarassment to the GMD government.

The Christmas rape case redirected the arrow of student nationalism at the United States and the GMD government, with Beijing University again emerging as a nerve center of student activism. The approach of discouraging students to organize for political action failed. In the eyes of the students, the GMD failed to defend the interests of Chinese citizens on Chinese soil. Allowing the American military to conduct its own court martial was, in the eyes of the Chinese public, tantamount to the de facto exercise of extraterritorial rights, rights that the United States and the Western powers had already renounced. The educated elite could no longer be restrained from expressing open disenchantment with the GMD government.

Government resistance to student demands, albeit through the more tactful approach of procrastination, evasion, and nonaction, prodded the reappearance of an organized student voice. This voice was also increasingly hostile to the ruling government, thus inducing an increase in police surveillance and selective arrests. The GMD was pressured into adopting repressive measures by the sheer force of events. In a "household reregistration campaign" on February 17, 1948, over two thousand people were arrested and detained for interrogation.[58] Such repressive measures helped to defuse the anti-American mood and moved the focus to the issue of civil rights instead. The GMD was unable to avoid confrontation with the student movement. Thirteen professors from Beijing University made a public declaration asserting the civil rights and personal liberties of the citizenry.[59] And as the educated community became increasingly hostile, the GMD government also became increasingly high-handed. Arrests and detentions continued. Representations from the Beijing University administration and threats to boycott examinations made by Qinghua students failed to impress the authorities. The release of suspects became the exception rather than the rule.[60]

The mass arrests of February deeply affected the campus communities. Confronted with a renewed GMD readiness to use force, the educated elite was visibly cowed: strong words of protest were no longer followed by street demonstrations. A threatened strike by Qinghua students never did materialize, while the release of one single prominent student leader was taken as an excuse for student leaders to tone down protests.[61]

Voices critical of the government could be silenced as long as the GMD had the physical means to do so. But by 1948 the GMD was fast losing that physical attribute. Military defeats in Manchuria removed its claim of military invincibility in civil conflicts. The civil war was also ravaging the economy, causing hyper inflation. Teachers, students, civil servants, and others in government pay joined hands with merchants, wage earners, and laborers in demanding their right to live. With leadership provided by a hostile educated elite, the new wave of antihunger campaigns was turned into a new round of confrontation with the ruling government. The city of Beijing was ready to receive alternative masters before the GMD defenses collapsed. The GMD government, which swept to power in 1928 by harnessing the force of student nationalism, became an object of attack of that selfsame source of political energy in 1949.

11 Conclusion and Epilogue

In the 1910s the New Culture and May 4th movements articulated two tactical concerns in China—namely, cultural and political action. Leaders of the New Culture Movement stressed the unity of culture and society, articulating the view that Cultural renaissance was the a priori to political rebirth. Their students, activists of the May 4th Movement, did not reject the importance of culture, but changed their emphasis from cultural renaissance to political action.

Sun Yatsen responded to this call for action. He popularized the motto "knowledge is difficult, but action is easy." The slogan became a mantra for the faithful, and repeatedly invoked by Jiang Jieshi, the commandant at Whampoa. The military academy thrived in action. Organization and discipline captured the mood of the cadets and their dedication turned into a font of political energy for the GMD.

The readiness for action was pervasive in the 1920s. Mao Zedong articulated the point in grand poetic diction when he reported on the peasant movement in Hunan: "In a very short time . . . several hundred million peasants will rise . . . like a hurricane. . . . Every revolutionary . . . will be put to the test . . . Every Chinese is free to choose, but events will force you to make the choice quickly."[1]

The pressure of events was upon all sections of community; rural unrest and urban nationalism were bursting for action. In this sense the political fortunes of both Jiang Jieshi and Mao Zedong were made by the impatience of an age.

Nationalism propelled the GMD to power in 1928 and the CCP onto a similar path since the outbreak of war with Japan in July 1937. Chinese national identity was embedded in culture and national consciousness strongest among the educated. The two parties provided organization and leadership to turn national feelings into a powerful social and political weapon. The fortunes of the two parties were decided by their ability to defend Chinese national interests.

Initially neither party was well suited to lead the nationalist cause. The GMD was awakened to the potency of student nationalism after the May 4th protests of 1919. This prompted the GMD to reorganize. It was barely able to offer leadership and organization when national feelings erupted in the May 30th movement of 1925. It was the newly established Whampoa Military Academy that provided the means with which the fury of student nationalism was organized for action. Students enlisted, obtained basic training, and gained access to power by helping the GMD to build a party army. Whampoa cadets marched in the battlefield, acted as marshalls in street demonstrations in Canton, and extended the authority of the GMD into units of the regional military. The Whampoa Military Academy militarized student nationalism, giving its cadets the opportunity to lead the northern expedition and to witness the establishment of a new national government in Nanjing.

As a political partner of the GMD, the CCP shared in the excitement of achieving national reunification. But political plotting and subversion by the CCP led to a breakdown in the first united front, beginning with a bloodbath for the CCP at the hands of the GMD party army. While the CCP survived by championing rural revolution, it could not match the military might of the GMD.

The prospects of a reunified China alarmed Japan. Determined Japanese incursions were met with a policy of appeasement from Nanjing, for the GMD government decided it was not yet able to match the might of Japan. Appeasement put the political credibility of the Nanjing government in doubt at a time when patriotic students were impatient for action.

The CCP repeatedly tried to project the image that it could protect nationalist interests better. At first its anti-Japanese propaganda was unconvincing. But when the Japanese military occupied Manchuria and pressed into north China without any effective check from Nanjing, student support turned toward the Chinese communists at Yanan. Nonetheless students who walked to Yanan were not joining the communist cause; they were seeking alternative leadership for the nationalist cause. The story of the Resistance University showed how the CCP gained credibility and consolidated support from patriotic students. Further, the rectification process was developed to subject students and intellectuals to party discipline.

Both Whampoa and the Resistance University offered very little professional military training. But the students who enrolled were prepared to offer supreme sacrifice in defense of the nation. The hardships demanded of them were accepted as necessary preparation for service. In this sense the Whampoa spirit and the Yanan way were different labels for Chinese nationalism and student work.

Outbursts of national feeling were periodic, largely responses to immediate crises. The GMD and the CCP provided student nationalism with an institutional base to get organized for action. Whampoa initiated militarization, promoted a military lifestyle for its cadets, offered the same formula to tertiary institutions such as Qinghua, and later tried to broaden the military lifestyle throughout the nation by launching the New Life Movement. The Resistance University took an almost identical path, but Mao introduced the rectification process to reinforce party authority.

It was Japanese challenge from the early 1930s that undermined the credibility of the GMD as an effective defender of Chinese national interests. The young officers' movement developed from among Whampoa graduates to stiffen Chinese resistance. They established the Lixingshe, which coordinated an underground network to promote patriotic feelings and to deal with enemies of the state. The Lixingshe turned former Whampoa alumni into an organized political movement, co-opting Jiang as their leader along the way. They were to unify the military, bypass the faction-ridden party structure of the GMD, deal with communist subversion, and act against the Japanese where the hands of the Nanjing government were tied by diplomatic and other considerations. It was largely the work of this young officers' movement that maintained the credibility of the Nanjing government in the difficult years between the Japanese occupation of Manchuria and the outbreak of the Sino-Japanese war—that is, between 1931 and 1937.

Japanese challenge in the 1930s gave rise to the activist tradition of the December 9th generation in north China. Initially they looked to the CCP for leadership, but many returned to support the GMD as the Sino-Japanese war unfolded. Those who walked to Yanan found their commitment to action fulfilled, and the CCP was able to maintain authority over them, particularly after the introduction of the rectification process in 1942. Those who walked south to join the GMD were evacuated to Kunming, outside the mainstream of wartime politics at Chongqing. The GMD did not actively enlist students at Kunming to rejuvenate the party. This was partly because the northern campuses had been critical of the GMD in the early 1930s

The effectiveness of the young officers' movement was predicated upon the existence of a tightly knit inner leadership core. Even though its front organizations drew membership from all sections of the community, its inner core was exclusive to Whampoa alumni.

Exceptions were rare. This exclusiveness enhanced organizational cohesion, but it also meant that other students were denied access. The young officers' movement was in danger of becoming little more than an organized faction.

The assertiveness of the young officers' movement also made its leader, Jiang Jieshi, feel uneasy. To ensure that his former students would not dictate, Jiang encouraged factionalism in the young officers' movement. Three factional divisions were identifiable from the inception of the Lixingshe. Prior to the Xian incident of 1936, the factional divisions within the young officers' movement did not obscure their common purpose. During the Xian incident, the Lixingshe showed that it could marshal troops without reference to the Nanjing government. After his release from Xian, Jiang took action to guard against future insubordination by members of the young officers' movement. He reorganized the young officers' movement and ordered the dissolution of the Fuxingshe, the political wing of the Lixingshe. The intelligence wing of the Lixingshe under Dai Li was taken over from the movement altogether. The central body, the Lixingshe, was also dissolved to ensure that what once constituted the combined military, intelligence, and political wings of the young officers' movement could no longer be coordinated by one unified command. The power of the young officers' movement frightened Jiang, and he actively weakened that movement by encouraging factions to develop and to balance them against each other. The activist tendencies of the young officers' movement languished into inaction as a result of factional infighting.[2]

In contrast the rectification process enabled the CCP to centralize authority with ideological coercion. Critical opinions were silenced by elaborate political rituals. Self-criticisms and group discussions were manipulated to ensure unquestioned acceptance of party decisions. Those critical of the CCP had to recant, admit their "mistakes," and join in open praise of party decisions.

The faction-ridden camp created by Jiang was also intolerant of critical dissent. The intelligence arm of the young officers' movement practiced political assasination and found the method both effective and popular when it was directed against pro-Japanese figures in the 1930s. In the postwar period the GMD military leaders at Kunming employed the same method to silence dissent. Their political ineptitude confirmed campus disillusionment with the GMD. Rapport between the Associated University campus community and the GMD was never fully restored, not even after repatriation to their home campuses in Beijing. The GMD had lost the support of the educated in north China before it lost the civil war. Indeed the Christmas rape case at Beijing reactivated student protest movements and opened up what Mao described as a second front in the civil conflict.[3]

The GMD came to power by championing nationalism, and the young officers' movement sustained that commitment through the 1930s. But the seeds of factionalism sowed by Jiang ennervated that movement, while the high-handed tactics of the GMD military at Kunming antagonized the educated. In the civil war, student protest movements were directed against the GMD, largely the result of accumulated tactical errors made by Jiang and his officers from Whampoa.

The Whampoa spirit and the Yanan way articulated two legends. In reality neither the military academy nor the resistance university could offer much professional training. They offered a place for patriotic students to converge and to get organized. The student work of the military academy and the resistance university turned patriotic students into an organized force. The young men and women who gave their support to the GMD or the CCP were motivated by their own intense patriotic feelings for the plight of China: the prospect of China's political dismemberment by foreign interests and the distinct possibility of subjugation by Japan. High points of their support for one party or another were related to the facts of vehement humiliation at the hands of foreign powers—the May 30th movement in 1925 and the December 9th movement of 1935, for example.

The Whampoa spirit and Yanan way were expressive of the intense nationalist feelings of the 1920s and 1930s. Student nationalists did what they could to strengthen the GMD and the CCP as a means to strengthen China. The extreme demands made on the young at Whampoa and Yanan were accepted with a readiness for self-sacrifice. Young students were prepared to die for China before Jiang demanded readiness for sacrifice in battle, and before Mao demanded unquestioned ideological discipline. Young students were ready to sacrifice so that the GMD or the CCP might save China.

Student nationalism was based on emotions, hence volatile. The readiness to sacrifice all was a momentary response. How could this volatile element be stabilized? Introducing students to a militarized lifestyle was a common approach adopted by the GMD and the CCP. For the young officers, the Lixingshe was a secret command core to extend military coordination. Similarly the CCP developed a rectification process to coerce ideological conformity.

Epilogue

The establishment of the people's republic in 1949 ushered in a period of ideological control. The control system was manned by an army of cadres. The nurturing of cadres and ideological indoctrination became vital functions of formal education. Students were both objects of political manipulation and potential future manipulators.

Until late 1986, student demonstrations were orchestrated by the CCP. But the party leadership developed serious disagreements over policy matters since the late 1950s. The great leap forward in particular created visible distances between Mao Zedong and his senior colleagues. The cultural revolution witnessed the translation of party-room disputes to the open political stage. Students, organized as red guards, became a powerful weapon used by Mao Zedong to topple his powerful detractors. However, the red guards were also objects of control in the eyes of Mao and the gang of four. Once their political ascendancy was assured, the red guards were dispersed by a nation-wide campaign of *Xiafang*, of forcing educated young men and women to acquire labor experience in the villages. The relocation of a generation of students from city to village created serious disillusionment among young party faithfuls and many defied party orders to return to live in the cities as illegal urban dwellers. This resistance transformed regimentation into repression, and former red guards became political fugitives. They formed a pool of socio-political malcontents from among the educated elite and a potent source of political opposition.

Since 1978 more liberal policies were introduced to practice damage control. Many victims of the cultural revolution and the Xiafang campaign were rehabilitated. Many members of the new party leadership had suffered at the hands of the reds guards, and student movements were political instruments that they were reluctant to orchestrate. A student populace with a tradition of political involvement was left with no legitimate roles in the political process. Party and students were distanced one from the other.

Campus dissent in the 1980s was partly a reaction against the efforts to depoliticize students, but students too were apprehensive of the excesses of the cultural revolution. Periodic attempts to write big-character posters, to make anonymous public accusations, had minimal impact. But students did make open complaints against living and working conditions on campus. Elements common to this restlessness were a protestation of their love of country and of demands to protect the right to stage further protests. Such restlessness indicated there was considerable untapped political energy on campus.

The response of the post-Mao leadership was mixed. The choice was between positive channeling and suppression. On the one hand the police were beefed up as a paramilitary force, and on the other hand signals for a more open environment were made. Filmmakers and novelists spoke of a new realism and of discarding false propaganda. Fang Lizhi, an astrophycist and president of the University of Science and Technology at Hefei, Anhui Province, encouraged student participation in decision-making on campus.[4] In November 1986 the *People's Daily* praised the innovations of Fang Lizhi.[5] The authoritarian leadership was inviting some degree of liberal expression by artists and students.

In December 1986 a series of student demonstrations took place in Shanghai. These were "the first series of student demonstrations in the People's Republic not directly sponsored or explicitly encouraged by top party officials."[6] There was no single cause for the re-emergence of student dissent in the streets of Shanghai. Rather the demonstrations represented a mixed chorus of diverse dissatisfactions with the ruling regime, protesting against authoritarianism on campus, against poor and deteriorating living conditions, against the inflationary efforts of recent economic reforms, against too much government intervention in this and too little government intervention in that. Above all, the students were demonstrating for the right to dissent— that is, claiming moral responsibility and authority to comment on current affairs.

Government response to the events of late 1986 and early 1987 was predictable. The police were called out to suppress the demonstrations, and the more liberal voices within the party were silenced. Fang Lizhi was dismissed from his administrative duties and expelled from the Communist Party. Hu Yaobang was later relieved of his position as general secretary of the CCP. Such actions made political martyrs of Hu Yaobang and Fang Lizhi, but each attained distinctly different symbolic importance.

Hu Yaobang spoke of "socialist democracy." This was a formula for loyal positive comment, extending no further than remonstrance by loyal party members. He suffered his disgrace in silence, but we are yet uncertain of what specific political groundworks he tried to lay in response to his disgrace and possible future comeback. He died suddenly of a heart attack in April 1989 and his death precipitated the tragedy of June 4.

Fang Lizhi spoke of "true democracy" after his disgrace. Fang was arguing for the importance of intellectual freedom in modernizing China.[7] He put loyalty to the nation as being higher than loyalty to the party. That Fang was tolerated to speak up to the eve of June 4 indicated considerable support from the technocracy and its pivotal importance in the current technological modernization process.

The June 4 democracy movement was precipitated by the death of Hu Yaobang, not by the outspoken views of Fang Lizhi. Hu died of a heart attack on April 15, 1989. On April 16 a few hundred students gathered at Tiananmen Square to mourn his death. On April 18, more than six thousands students gathered at Beijing University and then marched to Tiananmen Square. An organized group of student activists took possession of the symbolic center of China and mounted a direct confrontation with the Communist Party leadership by staging a sit-in in front of Zhongnanhai, where the top leadership lived and worked.[8]

From present indications I would suggest that the June 4 democracy movement began within the framework of Hu Yaobang's call for "socialist democracy"—that it, was integral to the factional power struggles within the top leadership of the CCP. The occupation of Tiananmen Square, the symbolic center of the Chinese world, was political drama. One observer commented: "during some early demonstrations educated youths even roped their brigades off from the general populace to prevent members of the population at large from joining their marches."[9] The demonstrators, however, appealed directly to members of other establishment groups such as teachers, journalists, policemen, and soldiers.

We are still uncertain of the details of party factional struggles during May and June of 1989. We do know that Zhao Ziyang lost out. The decisive defeat of one faction in the party rooms could have been critical in making the crucial decisions to use force against the students at Tiananmen Square. What we saw, however, were the high dramas presented by the international media and the bloody massacre executed by the Chinese military. And in between we are puzzled by the undefined use of democracy and the appearance of the statue of the goddess of liberty. The student demonstrators were playing to the world press. Such tactics could prove counterproductive and misleading within the context of an ongoing factional power struggle. But elements of spontaneity and symptoms of a deep-seated longing for Western democracy cannot be ruled out.

The massacre on June 4 reflected government fears in panic proportions, but such ferocious acts were restricted to the cities of Beijing and Chengdu. At the same time, government response in Shanghai was visibly restrained. Were such differences in tactics made by decision-makers on the spot or were they measured responses from the central leadership? These are questions that cannot be answered without further information.

Enlightenment and Discipline

Finally let us attend to the symbolism of Fang Lizhi. His call for intellectual freedom was a direct challenge to use a state ideology to deliver a strong state structure. This practice is a traditional practice. Although the revitalization of this tradition by the CCP did deliver a strong unified state, nonetheless the practice was a hindrance to technological modernization. In European historical experience, continuous progress toward modernity was brought about by an ever-widening mental horizon; Modernity began with the Enlightenment. In Western historiography, Enlightenment refers to the age of reason in 18th-century Europe, an age which questioned traditional beliefs, and attacked the values of church and state.

As Europe overwhelmed the rest of the world in the eighteenth and nineteenth centuries, there developed a self-perception that modernity was cast in a European mold. This culture-based perception leads us to ask whether the Enlightenment would ever reach China. When would the minor pattern of Chinese historical development merge into the larger European or global pattern?

Are we facing the events of June 4 with similar preconceptions? We need to be aware of our inbred assumptions in commenting on how China *should be* even if we may not be able to transcend our own cultural experience in practice.

Are Enlightenment and ideological discipline incompatible? This question is being readdressed by Fang Lizhi. Is commitment to socialist principles incompatible with intellectual enlightenment? Is the persecution and eventual exile of Fang Lizhi confirmation of their incompatibility?

The collapse of the ancien régime in China, signaled by the 1911 revolution and the demise of the dynastic order, was not brought about by the age of reason. It was brought about by the age of imperialism. This is a focal difference in historical experience between Europe and China. The forces that breached the Confucian state were not internal reasoning but external force. The most pressing issue, though by no means the only issue, is that of containing external force whether that be British, French, Japanese, German, American, or Russian. The primary concern is not social or intellectual liberation, but the defense of the state. Nationalism, not democracy, remained the motivating force behind intellectual debates, student movements, and political reforms. This common purpose means that reconciliation among competing groups is feasible and that the debate about the best means to serve the nation will continue.

Whether the Enlightenment and ideological discipline are compatible has been a live debate since the opium war. The June 4 democracy movement tried to establish a symbolic connection with this debate on May 4 with a memorial service. Events of June 4, 1989, illustrated once again the highly-charged emotions of that debate in contemporary China. But there were no real winners on June 4. State authority has been seriously compromised and repression will weaken that authority further. The task for Fang Lizhi and his supporters is to argue convincingly that intellectual freedom is the route to national strength.

Notes

Chapter 1

1. L. A. Schneider, "National Essence and the New Intelligentsia," in Charlotte Furth, ed., *The Limits of Change* (Cambridge, Mass., 1976, 57.

2. Benedict Anderson, *Imagined Communities* (London: Verso, 1964).

3. See Lin Yusheng, *The Crisis of Chinese Consciousness, Radical Antitraditionalism in the May Fourth Era* (Madison, 1979). In his opening chapter, Lin Yusheng introduces the idea that the May 4th intellectuals sought a total rejection of the past. But they also argued that total rejection was only the a priori, not the substitute, for cultural rebirth. They continued with efforts toward finding an alternative, toward proposing a total substitution, toward re-creating a cultural-political order in which the intellectual elite remained central.

4. Diane Lary, *Region and Nation* (Cambridge, 1974).

5. Ralph Thaxton, *China Turned Rightside Up* (New Haven, 1983).

6. Schneider, "National Essence."

7. Chow Tse-tsung, *The May Fourth Movement* (Stanford 1967). 58–61.

8. The equivalent Pinyin translation is Huangpu. Whampoa is a more familiar Cantonese rendering.

9. Whampoa is the popular name for the Central Military Academy, headed by Jiang Jieshi. Kangda is the abbreviated form for the Anti-Japanese Resistance University established by the CCP at Yanan. Lianda is the abbreviation for the Associated University at Kunming, formed jointly by Beida, Qinhua, and Nankai during the resistance war.

10. Schneider, "National Essence."

11. Compare Ambrose King, *The Modernisation of Intellectuals* (Hong Kong, 1971), 71–72.

12. The Self-Strengtheners used the Ti Yong formulation, the 1898 reformers modified it to the Ti Qi formulation, the nationalists stressed Sun's three principles of the people, and the Chinese communists emphasized the Chinese historical experience as specific. Their parallel efforts to state the central importance of a Chinese element turned the universal pretensions of Chinese culture upon its head, and signaled the transformation of traditionalism into nationalism.

13. John Israel, *Student Nationalism in China, 1927–1937* (Stanford, 1966), 5.

14. The phrase has been used as title of the collection of essays edited by Charlotte Furth, *The Limits of Change* (see n. 1, above).

15. See Schneider, "National Essence."

16. Donald A. Jordan, *The Northern Expedition: China's Revolution of 1926–1928* (Honolulu, 1976); C. Martin Wilbur, *The Nationalist Revolution in China, 1923–1928* (Cambridge, 1983).

Chapter 2

1. The inaugural speech of Sun Yatsen at the Whampoa Military Academy. Author's translation. The full text can be found in Dang Dexin and Huang Kailing, eds., *Diyici Guogong Hezou Shiqide Huangpu Junxiao* (Beijing: Wenshi Ziliao Chubanshe, 1984). The extract is from pp. 2–3. A slightly different translation of this extract is provided by F. F. Liu in *A Military History of Modern China: 1924–1949* (Princeton, 1956), 8.

2. A good introduction to the connection between educational reform and political power is *The Dewey Experiment in China: Educational Reform and Political Power in the Early Republic* (Cambridge, Mass., 1977).

3. For Sun Yatsen's connection with the Japanese, see Marius B. Jansen, *The Japanese and Sun Yatsen* (Cambridge, Mass., 1954).

4. Norman D. Palmer, *Sun Yat-sen and Communism* (New York, 1960), 48; C. Martin Wilbur, *Sun Yat-sen: Frustrated Patriot* (New York, 1976), 113–14.

5. For a translated text of the Karakhan manifesto, see Allen S. Whiting, *Soviet Policies in China 1917–1924* (Stanford, 1968), 269–71.

6. Dov Bing, "Sneevliet and the Early Years of the CCP," *China Quarterly*, no. 48, October/December 1971, 677–97.

7. Guangdong Geming Lishi Bowuguan, ed., *Huangpu Junxiao Shiliao* (Canton, 1982), 11.

8. Richard B. Landis, "Training and Indoctrination at the Whampoa Military Academy," in F. Gilbert Chan and Thomas H. Etzold, eds., *China in the 1920s: Nationalism and Revolution* (New York, 1976), 74.

9. Bowuguan, *Huangpu*, 13—an extract from Mao Sicheng, *Minguo Shiwunianqian zhi Jiang Jishi Xianshen* (n.p., 1937).

10. Liu, *History*, 5.

11. Bowuguan, *Huangpu*, 12–13, based on Mao, *Minguo*.

12. T. McNelly, ed., *Sources in Modern East Asian History and Politics* (New York, 1967), 99–100. Sun was against the divisive connotations of the theory of class struggle, but he was a strong advocate of socio-economic reforms.

13. Bowuguon, *Huangpu*, 21—an excerpt from the *Shanghai Minguo Ribao*, March 16, 1924. Author's translation. Similar sentiments were expressed when Sun addressed the gathering at the opening ceremony of the Whampoa Military Academy on June 16, 1924. See Dang and Huang, *Diyici*, 1–12.

14. Dang and Huang, *Diyici*, 24–25—an extract from *Liao Zhongkai Ji*, edited by Zhongguo Kexueyuan Guangzhou Zhexue Shehui Kexue Yanjiusuo (Canton, 1963)

15. Zhongyang Lujun Junguan Xuexiao, *Zhongyang Lujun Jungguan Xuexiao Shigao* (Nanjing, 1936), vol. 1, chap. 2, section 2: Bowuguan, *Huangpu*, 26.

16. Junguan Xuexiao, *Shigao*, vol. 1, chap. 2, section 2.

17. Liu, *History*, 9.

18. Mao, *Minguo*, vol. 6, pp. 6–7: Jiang tendered his resignation on February 21, 1924. only eleven days after the first meeting of the preparatory committee. On February 27 he left for Shanghai. Vol. 6, 47: Jiang returned to Canton on April 26, 1924.

19. Wang Jianwu, Zhu Jiming, Yang Zhanrong, *Huangpu Junxiao Shihua* (Henan Renmin Chubanshe, 1982), 11.

20. Bowuguan, *Huangpu*, 30–31.

21. Mao, *Minguo*, vol. 6, 3; Bowuguan, *Huangpu*, 28; see also 29–31 for correspondence between Liao Zhongkai and Jiang Jieshi. Luo Jialun, *Geming Wenxian* (December 1955), vol. 10.

22. Mao, *Minguo*, vol. 6, 47.

23. Junguan Xuexiao, *Shigao*, vol. 1, chap. 2, section 2. Lujun Junguan Xuexiao, *Lujun Junguan Xuexiaoshi Chugao* (Taipei, 1964), vol. 1, p. 2144. Bowuguan, *Huangpu*, 3.

24. Lujun Junguan Xuexiao, *Chugao*, vol. 1, 2102. Junguan Xuexiao, *Shigao*, vol. 1, chap. 2, section 4.

25. Junguan Xuexiao, *Chugao*, vol. 1, 2102. Junguan Xuexiao, *Shigao*, vol. 1, chap. 2, section 4. Zhongyany Dangshi Shiliao Bianzuan Weiyuanhui, *Huangpu Jianjun Sanshinian Gaishu* (Taipei, 1954), 5.

26. Junguan Xuexiao, *Shigao*, vol. 2, chap. 3, section 2, narrates instances of obstruction by various militarists.

27. For example, both Li Dachao and Mao Zedong were delegates of the first national congress of the GMD.

28. Junguan Xuexiao, *Chugao*, vol. 2, 3107–8, gives rounded figures on enrollment for the first class.

29. Bowuguan, *Huangpu*, 33.

30. Ibid., 34.

31. Ibid., 37–39. Communist influence was not entirely excluded at the screening test, for this source reports that Mao Zedong was one of the examiners administering the tests at Shanghai. According to Chen Guofu, Jiang did not gain full control over admission procedures until recruitment for the fourth class began—that is, toward the end of 1924. See Wu Xiangxiang, *Chen Guofu de Yisheng* (Taipei, 1971), 93–94.

32. Landis, "Training" (n. 8, above), 74–75.

33. Liu, *History* (n. 1, above), 6.

34. Ibid., 13–14. Shikan Gakkoo graduates included Jiang Jishi, He Yingqin, and Wang Boling, Baoding graduates included Zhang Zhizhong and Chen Cheng. Yunnan Military Academy graduates included Zu De.

35. Landis, "Training," 78–79.

36. Bowuguan, *Huangpu*, 180–81.

37. Ibid., 27–28.

38. Ibid., quoting from "Gongqingtuan Guangzhou Diwei Baogao, no. 7."

39. Ibid., 37–39, Guo Yiyu, "Guanyu Huangpu Junxiao de Pianduan Huiyi."

40. Ibid.

41. Ibid., 39.

42. Renmin Chubanshe, *Dangshi Yanjiu* (Bejing, 1980). Bowuguan, *Huangpu*, 61.

43. See D. W. Klein and A. B. Clark, *Biographical Dictionary of Chinese Communism* (Cambridge, Mass., 1971).

44. Bowuguan, *Huangpu*, 4. The secret branch of the CCP at Whampoa was under the control of the Guangdong province party leadership.

45. Fei Yunwen, *Dai Li de Yisheng* (Taipei, 1980), 5–12.

46. Bowuguan, *Huangpu*, 59–63.

47. Ibid.

48. Ibid., 346–47. Order issued by Jiang on April 7, 1926.

Chapter 3

1. Guangdong Geming Lishi Bowuguan, *Huangpu Junxiao Shiliao* (Guangzhou, 1982), 66–69. Author's translation of an address, "Huangpu Jingshen yu Guomin Gemingh," given by Zhang Zhizhong to the cadets at the Changsha branch campus. The plight of Liao Zhongkai is reaffirmed by Madame Liao in Lujon Junguan Xuexiao, *Lujun Junguan Xuexiao Chugao* (Taipei, 1964), vol. 1, 2110. See also Gong Lequn, *Huangu Jianshi* (Tappei, 1976), 18.

2. Wang Boling, "Huangpu Chuangshi zhi Huiyi," in *Huangpu Jikan*, vol. 1, no. 3, 1939.

3. Lydia Holubnychy, *Michael Borodin and the Chinese Revolution 1923–1925* (New York, 1979). Chap. 3 gives a detailed scrutiny of Borodin's arrival. Holubnychy establishes October 6, 1924, as the date of Borodin's arrival in Canton. See esp. 259.

4. Louis Fischer, *The Soviets in World Affairs* (New York 1930) vol. 2, p. 640. Holubnychy, *Borodin*, 412–41, suggests that Whampoa was receiving Canton $100,000 per month in subsidies from the Soviets. See also Wang Tianwu, *Huangpu Junxiao Shihua*, Henanrenmin Chubanshe, 18–19.

5. Boling, "Huangpu."

6. Lujun Junguan Xuexiao, *Lujun Junguan Xuexiaoshi Chugao* (Taipei, 1964), vol. 2, 3111.

7. Ibid., vol. 2, 3127. Junguan Xuexiao, *Shigao*, vol. 2, chap. 4, section 1.4.

8. Bowuguan, *Huangpu*, 66–69.

9. Xianggang Huazi Ribao, *Guangdon Kouxie Chao* (Hong Kong, 1924), 1. Xu Gaolin, "1924 nian Sun Zhongshan de Beifa yu Guangzhou Shangtuan Shibian," in *Lishi Yanjiu*, March 1956. The author estimates that only four thousand members of the merchants' militia were armed. Cuncui Xueshe, ed., *1924 nian Guangzhou Shangtuan Shibian* (Guangzhou, 1924), 1–2, indicates that Sun himself thought the hard core of the merchants' militia numbered only between thirty and forty.

10. Ribao, *Guangdon*, 2. The congress met on May 27, 1924, and was attended by over three hundred delegates.

11. Sun Yatsen, letter to Jiang Jieshi dated August 9, 1924. The text can be found in Cuncuishe, *1924 nian Guangzhon Shanghuan Shikian* (Guangzhou 1924), 1–2.

12. Ribao, *Guangdong*, 3–4.

13. Ibid., 6–7.

14. Ibid., 7–9.

15. Sun Yatsen, letter to Jiang Jieshi dated August 9, 1924. Text found in Cuncui Xueshe, *1924*, 1–3. See also Jiang Jieshi, "Pingding Shangtuan Jungguo," in Bowuguan, *Huangpu*, 241.

16. Du Congrong, *Huangpu Junxiao zhi Chuangjian Dong ji Dongzheng Beifa zhi Huiyi* (Taipei, 1975), 24–27.

17. Ribao, *Guangdong*, 11–46.

18. Sun Yatsen, correspondence dated August 20, 1924, in Cuncuishe, *1924 nian*, 7.

19. Jiang Jieshi, "Pingding Shangtuan Jingguo," in Bowuguan, *Huangpu*, 241. For diplomatic exchanges between Sun and the British, see Xuexiao, *Chugao*, vol. 1, chap. 2, section 2.1.

20. Sun Yatsen, letter to Jiang Jieshi dated October 11, 1924, found in Bowuguan, *Huangpu*, 55–57, and in Xuexiao, *Chugao*, vol. 1, following the table of contents.

21. *Wu Tiecheng Huiyilu*, in Cuncuishe, *1924 nian*, 136. Refer also to 75–86 for a report favorable to the merchants' militia.

22. Xuexiao, Chugao, vol. 2, 3129.

23. See *Wu Tiecheng Huiyilu*, in Cuncuishe, *1924 nian*.

24. Jiang Jieshi, "Pingding," in Bopwuguan, *Huangpu*, 241.

25. Sun Yatsen, letter to Jiang Jieshe, dated October 11, 1924. Text found in Bowuguan, *Huangpu*, 55–57, and in Xuexiao, *Chugao*, vol. 1, following the table of contents.

26. Wu Xiangxiang, *Chen Guofu de Yisheng* (Taipei, 1971), 87–89.

27. Ibid.

28. Ibid., 88.

29. Ibid.

30. Ibid., 90.

31. Du Congrong, *Huangpu*, 35–40. Bowuguan, *Huangpu*, 252.

32. Xuexiao, *Chugao*, vol. 1, chap. 2, section 3.2.

33. Guofangbu Shizhengju, *Beifa Jianshi* (Taipei, 1961),28–29. See Bowuguan, *Huangpu*, 263–66, for battle plans, and pp. 266–68 on public condemnation of Yang and Liu issued jointly by Liao Zhongkai and Jiang Jieshi, and pp. 268–72 for a description of the "recapture of Canton."

34. Bowuguan, *Hangpu*, 272-73. Hong Jianxiong, *Guangzhiou Shaji Tushazhong Dangli Junxiao Sinanzhe* (Canton, July 1925).

35. Ibid., 23–26.

36. Ibid., 23. This same work provides biographical sketches of Whampoa cadets killed by the British during the demonstrations. Bowuguan, *Hangpu*, 276–80, reports on a memorial service for the 13 cadets who died during the Shaji incident.

37. Guangdong Zhexue Shehui Kexue Yanjinsuo Lishi Yanjiushi, *Shanggang Dabagong Ziliao* (Canton, 1980), 165–75. The strike call was issued on June 19, 1925. Armed pickets numbered over 2,000 and directly controlled territory adjacent to Hong Kong. At the time, the armed pickets were as strong a force as the Whampoa cadet units. See also Jean Chesneaux, *The Chinese Labor Movement, 1919–1927* (Stanford, 1968), 290–318.

38. Xuexiao, *Chugao*, 6016.

39. Ibid., 2026–27.

40. Ibid.

41. Bowuguan, *Huangpu*, 74–78.

42. Ibid.

43. Junguan Xuexiao, *Chugao*, vol. 7, p. 11,003. Wu Xiangxiang, *Chen Guofu de Yisheng*, 93–94.

44. Xuexiao, *Chugao*, vol. 2, 31,111.

45. Ibid., vol. 2, 31,115–17 and 31,125–27, where detailed figures on regional origins are provided.

46. Jane Price, *Cadres, Commanders, and Commissars* (New York, 1976), 56. Price is quoting from *The Whampoa Military School, A Report Compiled from Soviet Documents*, file 2657-I-281/120, Modern Military Records Division, U.S. National Archives, 12–16. Wang Boling, "Huangpu" (n. 2, above), vol. 1, January 1939, 11–12. Here Wang explains that Dai Jitao was a principal examiner and placed much emphasis on the candidates' command of classical Chinese. Wang himself was much more lenient. He admitted Hu Zongnan even though he failed both the written and physical tests. Hu later rose to be one of Jiang's most trusted generals.

47. For selections of speeches to Whampoa cadets by Jiang Jieshi He and Yingqin, see Jiang Zhongzheng, ed., *Huangpu Xunlianji*, and He Yingqin, *He Yingqin Zhongzhanganlunji*. There are frequent references to the absence of invited lecturers as the reason for either Jiang or He to be giving an address. Guojun Zhenggongshi Bianzuan Weiyuanhui, *Guojun Zhenggong Shigao* (Taipei, 1960), vol. 1, 89, explains how Zhou Enlai became the effective head of the political department by default.

48. Bowuguan, *Huangpu*, 178–79—an extract from *Huangpu Chao*, 1925. Author's translation. See also Wang Tianwu, *Huangpu Junxiao Shihua*, Henan Renmin Chubanche, 1982, 22–23, where it is reported that Zhou Enlai succeeded in enrolling 99 cadets of communist affiliation into the fourth political studies class.

49. There was so much time for infantry drill that the cadets were drilled individually first before marching in formation. Xuexiao, *Chugao*, chap. 4. Bowuguan, *Huangpu*, 143–44.

50. Bowuguan, *Huangpu*, 154–55.

51. Ibid., 144–45.

52. Xuexiao, *Chugao*, chap. 4. Bowuguan, *Hangpu*, 155.

53. For the full text in Chinese, see appendix 2 in Guofangbu Shizhengju, *Beifa Jianshi* (Taipei, 1961). See also Bowuguan, *Huangpu*, 170–71.

54. Bowuguan, *Hangpu*, 278. The text of a memorial speech for those who died during the Shaji incident indicates that only 16 cadets died during the first eastern expedition.

55. Ibid., indicates that 27 cadets were killed during the Shaji incident of June 23, 1925.

56. Xuexiao, *Chugao*, chap. 1, section 1.2. Xuexiao, *Zhongyang* (see chap. 2, n. 15), vol. 1, p. 2153.

57. Bowuguan, *Huangpu*, 398–99. Xuexiao, Chugao, vol. 1, chap. 3, section 3.1.

58. Bowuguan, *Huangpu*, 399. Xuexiao, Chugao, vol. 1, chap. 3, section 3.1. Xuexiao, *Zhongyang*, vol. 1, p. 2501.

59. Bowuguan, *Huangpu*, 399.

60. Ibid., 398–429.

61. Xuexiao, *Zhongyang*, vol. 4, chap. 4, section 5.2. Xuexiao, *Chugao*, vol. 1, p. 2501.

62. Xuexiao, *Zhongyang*, vol. 4, chap. 5. Xuexiao, *Chugao*, vol. 1, 2501–2.

63. Xuexiao, *Zhongyang*, vol. 4, chap. 4, section 5.2 Xuexiao, *Chugao*, vol. 1, 2502.

64. Xuexiao, *Chugao*, vol. 1, 2502.

Chapter 4

1. John Israel, *Student Nationalism in China, 1927–1937* (Stanford, 1966), 1.

2. Ibid., 3–4.

3. Qinghua Daxue Xiaoshi Bianiezu, *Qinghua Daxue Xiaoshi Shigao* (Beijing, 1981), 94.

4. Ibid., 94–95. *Guoli Qinghua Daxue Xiaokan*, no. 10, November 19, 1928.

5. Bianxiezu, *Quinhua*, 94–95.

6. Wang Niankun, *Xuesheng Yundongshi Jianghua* (Shanghai, 1951), 26.

7. Bianxiezu, *Qinghua*, 93.

8. Ibid., 93. Qinghua, *Xiao Xia Zhoukan*, no. 3, July 23, 1928, 9.

9. Ibid., no. 1, July 1928, p. 11. Bianxiezu, *Quinhua*, 94.

10. Li Jingqing, "Qinghua Xuechao Qianhou," in *Xiao Xia Zhoukan*, no. 6, January 9, 1930, 22. Bianxiezu, *Qinghua*, 95.

11. Ye Gongchao, "Yi Mei Xiaozhang," in Qinghua Xiaoyou Tongxin-she, ed., *Mei Xiaozhang Yuehan Xiansheng Shishi Sanzhounian Jiniankan* (Taipei, 1965), 1–3.

12. *Zhongyang Ribao*, March 20, 1931. Bianxiezu, *Qinghua*, 95.

13. Bianxiezu, *Qinghua*, 96–97.

14. for more in-depth discussions of the Manchurian incident, see S. N. Ogata, *Defiance in Manchuria* (Berkeley, 1964); L. Li, *Japan over Manchuria, 1931–1936* (Hong Kong 1992).

15. Donald Jordan, "Chinese Students in the Anti-Japanese Movement after the Manchurian Incident of 1931." Paper delivered at the international conference on the September 18 incident, Shenyang, 1991, 5.

16. League of Nations, *Report of the Commission of Enquiry of the League of Nations Signed at Peiping, 4th September 1932* (Shanghai, 1932), 81. Wang Niankun, *Xuesheng* (n. 6, above), 34–38. E Ji, *Zhongguo Xiandai Xuesheng Yundong Jianshi* (Hong Kong, n.d.), 50.

17. Wang Niankun, *Xuesheng*, 34–38. E Ji, *Zhongguo*, 49–53.

18. Wang Niankun, *Xuesheng*, 36.

19. M. B. Jansen, *Japan and China* (Chicago, 1975), 386.

20. Jerome Grieder, *Intellectuals and the State* (New York, 1981), 337.

21. L. Li, *The Japanese Army in North China* (Tokyo, 1975), 28.

22. Wang Niankun, *Xuesheng*, 44. Author's translation.

Chapter 5

1. Within the Fuxing Yungdong, the most senior in rank was Major General Liu Jianqun. He was a secretarial aide to General He Yingqin—really a civilian in military uniform. He Yingqin was also on the faculty at Whampoa, never a cadet. Whampoa cadets were accorded the rank of captain upon graduation.

2. Deng Yuanzhong, "Sanmin Zhuyi Lixingshe Shi Chugao" (3), in *Zhuanji Wenxue*, vol. 40, no. 1, 86. The thirty were selected from the first 6 classes—five from each.

3. Some older cadets were also close to Jiang, but they were not selected for further studies. Dai Li, Hu Zongnan, and He Zhonghan, for

example, were relatively older, all close to Jiang, and none of them were sent overseas for further training.

4. Gan Guoxun, "Minzu Fuxing Yundong Ji—Lixingshe Fuxingshe Shihua," in *Zhongwai Zazhi*, vol. 16, no. 1, July 1974, p. 40. Idem, ed., *Lanyishe, Fuxingshe, Lixingshe* (Taipei, 1984), 170.

5. Gan Guoxun, *Lanyishe*, 170. Deng Yuanzhong, "Sanmin" (4), in *Zhuanji Wenxue*, vol. 40, no. 6, 105.

6. Deng Yuanzhong, "Sanmin" (4), pp. 105–6, based on an interview with Deng Yuanzhong and Teng Jie on April 26, 1972.

7. Ibid., based on the same interview.

8. Deng Yuanzhong, "Sanmin" (3), 82, based on an interview with Deng Yuanzhong and Teng Jie on July 4, 1972.

9. Ibid.

10. Deng Yuanzhong, *Sanmin Zhuyi Lixingshe Shi* (Taipei, 1984), 63–66.

11. Paul G. Pickowicz, *Marxist Literary Thought in China: The Influence of Ch'u Ch'iu-pai* (Berkeley, 1981).

12. Huang Meizhen, Shi Yuanhua, Zhang Yun, eds., *Shanghai Daxue Shiliao* (Shanghai, 1984).

13. Deng Yuanzhong, "Sanmin" (3), 82.

14. Qiao Jiacai, *Hao Yen Ji* (Taipei, 1981), vol. 4, 484.

15. Ibid.

16. Ibid.

17. Chen Dunzheng, "Fuxing She, Qingbai She, Lanyi She—yige 'Fuxing She' canjiazhe de xushu yu guancha," in Gan Guoxun, ed., *Lanyishe*, 49.

18. Deng Yuanzhong, "Sanmin" (1), in *Zhuanji Wenxue*, vol. 39, no. 4, October 1981, 67.

19. Ibid., (4), pp. 107–8. Qiao Jaicai, *Hai Yen Ji*, vol. 4, 490.

20. Gan Guoxun, "Sanmin," in Gan Guoxun, ed., *Lanyishe*, 170–72. Deng Yuanzhong, "Sanmin," (4), 106.

21. Liang Xiong, *Dai Li Zhuan* (Taipei, 1982), vol. 1, 48.

22. Xuan Jiexi, "Lanyishe zhi Lailong Qumo," in Gan Guoxun, ed., *Lanyishe*, 15.

23. Ibid., 14–24.

24. Ou Weiwen, "Lanyishe yu Zhongguo Guomindang," in *Nanfang Zazhi*, no. 6, September 1933. The journal was published by the Guangxi branch of the central executive committee of the GMD (see p. 13). Deng Yuanzhong, *Sanmin*, 16. Liu Jianqun, *Fuxing Zhongguo zhi lu* (Nanjing, 1933), 107–9. Author's translation.

25. Ou Weiwen, "Lanyishe," 30. Author's translation.

26. Xuan Jiexi, "Lanyishe," 30. The handful of supporters were Xie Boyuan, principal secretary to He Yingqin, Zhu Jingjun, party representative of the 39th army corps, Huang Xianjin, a student of politics at the central university (Zhengdai), and Xuan Jiexi, a fellow political adviser to He Yinqqin.

27. Ibid.

28. Ibid.

29. Ibid., 30–31.

30. Ibid., 31.

31. Ibid., 32.

32. Ibid.

33. Ibid. Deng Yuanzhong, "*Sanmin*, 65.

34. Xuan Jiexi, "Lanyishe," 31. We are informed that the twelve were recruited by Xuan Jiexi at Nanzhang and by Huang Xianjin at Zhengdai, so this twelve consisted of students from Zhengdai and political advisers of He Yingqin at Nanzhang.

35. Ibid., 32. Deng Yuanzhong, *Sanmin*, 108.

36. Liang Xiong, *Dai Li Zhuan*, 29–31.

37. Ibid., 32.

38. Ibid., 33.

39. Ibid., 37.

40. Ibid., 38.

41. Ibid., 39.

42. Ibid., 38–39. Qiao Jiacai, *Hao Yen Ji*, vol. 4, p. 33.

43. Liang Xiong, *Dai Li Zhuan*, 333. Dai Li, "Geming Gongzuo yu Geming Xingdong," in Zhang Sayuan, *Dai Xiansheng Yixun* (1948, restricted to internal circulation), vol. 1, 9.

44. Qiao Jiacai, *Hao Yen Ji*, 489.

45. Ibid.

46. The movement is identified as the Minzu Fuxing Yundong, which can be translated as the national revival movement. The term "minzu" has racial overtones, here referring to the Hanzu or the Han ethnic majority. But this reference to race relates to indigenous people, not to the racist ideas of the German Nazis.

47. Qiao Jaicai, *Hao Yen Ji*, vol. 4, 486. Deng Yuanzhong, *Sanmin*, 106.

48. Gan Guoxun, "Sanmin," 171. Deng Yuanzhong, "Sanmin" (4), 106. Qiao Jiacai, *Hao Yen Ji*, vol. 4, 486.

49. Qiao Jiacai, *Hao Yen Ji*, vol. 4, 486.

50. Gan Guoxun, "Sanmin," 171. Deng Yuanzhong, "Sanmin" (4), 106. Qiao Jiacai, *Hao Yen Ji*, vol. 4, 487.

51. Ibid.

52. Gan Guoxun, ed., *Lanyishe*, 171. Gan specifically states that the guest list included three names suggested by Zang, so that the other seven must have been nominated by Yeng.

53. Deng Wenyi was requested by Teng Jie to report to Jiang about the secret group, when an alumnus threatened to expose his secret activities to Jiang. This is an indication that Deng Wenyi was a trusted member of the Teng Jie faction, and that Deng could be relied on to put his loyalty to the faction above that to Jiang.

54. Gan Guoxun, "Minzu" (n. 4, above), 40. Deng Yuanzhong, "Sanmin" (4), 106. Qiao Jiacai, *Hao Yen Ji*, vol. 4, 487.

55. Qiao Jiacai, *Hao Yen Ji*, vol. 4, 487. Deng Yuanzhong, "Sanmin" (4), 106.

56. See chap. 2, n. 30 above.

57. Qiao Jiacai, *Hao Yen Ji*, vol. 4, 489.

58. Ibid.

59. Ibid.

60. Ibid., 487. Note that a dinner for twelve of the first meeting cost $5, so $300 at that time could pay for 60 dinners for 12, or a feast for 720 persons. It was a considerable sum.

61. Ibid., 488.

62. Gan Guoxun, ed., *Lanyishe*, 172. Note that only the Teng Jie faction was exclusive to Whampoa alumni. As the revival movement expanded, other elements were represented.

63. Qiao Jiacai, *Hao Yen Ji*, vol. 4, 489.

64. Ibid.

65. Ibid.

66. Ibid. Deng Yuanzhong, *Sanmin*, 107, suggests that Jiang was considering the Ten Jie organization as early as January 1932.

67. Deng Yuanzhong, "Sanmin" (4), 108.

68. Qiao Jaicai, *Hao Yen Ji*, vol. 4, 490. Gan Guoxun, ed., *Lanyishe*, 173–74.

69. Qiao Jiacai, *Hao Yen Ji*, vol. 4, 490.

70. Ibid.

71. Gan Guoxun, "Sanmin Zhuyi Lixingshe," in Gan Guoxun, *Lanyishe*, 178.

72. Ibid.

73. Ibid., 178–79.

74. Ibid., 179.

75. Ibid.

76. Ibid., 180.

77. Ibid., 181.

78. Gan Guoxun, "Dai Li, Teng Jie, Liu Jianqun," in *Zhongwai Zazhi*, vol. 16, no. 3, September 1974, 36. Author's translation.

79. Ibid., 37. Author's translation.

80. Gan Guoxun, "Sanmin Zhuyi Lixingshe," in Gan Guoxun, ed., *Lanyishe*, 184.

81. Ibid., 185.

82. Ibid. The quote is: "Zhi Nan Xing Yi Zhi Zhi Li Xing." The name Lixingshe is derived from the two last words in this quote, Li Xing.

83. Ibid., 186.

84. Ibid.

85. Ibid.

86. Ibid.

87. Ibid., 186–87.

88. Xuan Jiexi, "Lanyishe" (n. 22, above), 32.

89. Gan Guoxun, "Sanmin" (n. 48, above), 178.

90. Ibid., 180.

91. Ibid., 6 and 176. Deng Yuanzhong, "Sanmin" (1), 66.

92. Gan Guoxun, "Lanyishe," 36.

93. Ibid., 10–11 and 36–37.

94. Chen Xiaoxiao, *Hei Wang Lu* (Hong Kong, 1966), 14.

95. Gan Guoxun, ed., *Lanyishe*, 187.

96. Qiao Jiacai, *Hao Yen Ji*, 489.

97. Gan Guoxun, ed., *Lanyishe*, 187.

98. Gan Guoxun, "Lixingshe yu Zhuntongju," in *Zhongwai Zazhi*, no. 179, January 1982, pp. 69–70.

99. Ibid., 69.

100. Ibid., 70.

101. Ibid.

102. Lloyd Eastman, *Seeds of Destruction* (Stanford, 1984), 131.

103. Qioao Jiacai, *Hoa Yen Ji*, vol. 4, 492. Gan Guoxun, "Lixingshe," 70.

104. Qiao Jiacai, *Hoa Yen Ji*, vol. 4, 494.

105. Liang Xiong, *Dai Li Zhuan*, 50.

106. Ibid., 51.

107. Qiao Jaicai, *Hoa Yen Ju*, vol. 4, 41–42.

108. Liang Xiong, *Dai Li Zhuan*, 50.

Chapter 6

1. Deng Yuanzhong, "Sanmin yi Lixingshe Shi Chugao" (4), in *Zhuanji Wenxue*, vol. 40, no. 6, 107.

2. Ibid.

3. Ibid. Liu Zhenghong, "Kang Ze ban Zhongguo Ribao," in *Yiwen Zhi*, July 1973, no. 94, 27–28.

4. Deng Yuanzhong, "Sanmin," 107.

5. Ibid.

6. Ibid.

7. Deng Yuanzhong, "Sanmin Zhuyi Lixingshe Shi Chugao" (1), in *Zhuanji Wenxue*, vol. 39, no. 4, October 1981, p. 68. Based on an interview with Lim Beixin, deputy secretary of the Lixingshe since 1933. Interview dated April 19, 1972.

8. See chapter 5, above.

9. Deng Yuanzhong, "Sanmin Zhuyi Lixingshe Shi Chugao" (3), *Zhuanji Wenxue*, vol. 40, no. 1, January 1982, 81.

10. Gan Guoxun, ed., *Lanyishe, Fuxingshe, Lingishe* (Taipei, 1984), 45–79 and 80–104.

11. Ibid., 58–59.

12. Ibid., 45–47.

13. Ibid., 26. The evidence quoted refers the proposed blue-shirt organization, and is therefore an indirect indication of arrangements within the Lixingshe.

14. Qiao Jiacai, *Hao Yen Ji* (Taipei, 1981), vol. 4, 44–46 and 492.

15. Deng Yuanzhong, "Sanmin" (3), 81. Gan Guoxun, ed., *Lanyishe*, 58. This is a conservative estimate. Another estimate can be arrived at by adding the separate categories together, giving an approximate figure of 130,000 members. See also Deng Yuanzhong, *Sanmin Zhuyi Lixingshe Shi* (Taipei, 1984), 13, where he gives an upward review of his figure to half a million.

16. Deng Yuanzhone, "Sanmin" (1), 66.

17. Ibid.

18. Liu Jianqun, *Yinhe Yiwang* (Taipei, 1966), 1–2.

19. Gan Guoxun, ed., *Lanyishe*, 14–44.

20. Xuan Jiexi, "Riben Xianbing Beiping 'bu' wo 'ji'," in *Zhuanji Wenxue*, vol. 38, no. 5, 55–60.

21. Refer to chap. 5 and Deng Yuanzhong, *Sanmin*, chap. 4.

22. Gan Guoxun, ed., *Lanyishe*, 110.

23. Ou Weiwen, "Lanyishe yu Zhongguo guomindang," in *Nanfang Zazhi*, no. 6, September 1933, 13–14.

24. Gan Guoxun, ed., *Lanyishe*, 10. also Gan Guoxun, "Kangzhan Qianqi de Tongyi Yundong (shang)," in *Zhongwai Zazhi*, vol. 16, no. 5, November 1974, 43.

25. Gan Guoxun, ed., *Lanyishe*, 10 and 36.

26. Ibid., 10.

27. Ibid., 10–11.

28. Liu Jianqun, *Yinhe*, 1.

29. Gan Guoxun, "Kangzhan," 44.

30. Ibid.

31. Liu Jianqun, *Yinhe Yiwang*, 96. Misuzu Shobo, *Nitchu Senso*, vol. 1, 60–72.

32. Liu Jianqun, *Yinhe Yiwang*, 1–2 and 97.

33. Consult Misuzu Shobo, *Chunitchi*, vol. 1, 128–36, being a Japanese report on the autonomous movement in north China.

34. Liu Jianqun, *Yinhe Yiwang*, 76–77.

35. Ibid., 78–79.

36. Ibid., 80–81.

37. Ibid.

38. F. F. Liu, *A Military History of Modern China, 1924–1949* (Princeton, 1956), chap. 7, 60–70; A. N. Young, *China's Nation Building Effort* (Stanford, 1971), 350–51.

39. Gan Guoxun, "Lingshe yu Zhuntongju," in *Zhongwai Zazhi*, no. 179, January 1982, 70.

40. Young, *China*, 353–54.

41. Dengo Yuanzhong, "Sanmin" (1), 67.

42. Gan Guoxun, ed., *Lanyishe*, 49.

43. Deng Yuanzhong, "Sanmin" (1), 66.

44. Lloyd E. Eastman, *The Abortive Revolution* (Cambridge, Mass., 1974), chap. 2.

45. Maria Hsia Chang, " 'Fascism' and Modern China," *China Quarterly*, September 1979, 304.

46. M. R. Godley, "Lessons from an Italian Connection," in David Pong and Edmund Fung, eds., *Ideal and Reality* (Lanham, 1985), 93–123.

47. N. Greene, *Fascism, An Anthology* (New York, 1968), 40.

48. Gongzheng Chubanshe, *Xian Shibian Huiyilu* (Hong Kong, n.d., reprint), contains recollections of the generalissimo and his wife.

49. Deng Yuanzhong, *Sanmin*, 663.

50. Gan Guoxun, ed., *Lanyishe*, 76–79.

51. Deng Yuanzhong, *Sanmin*, 570–71.

52. Ibid., 572–73.

53. Ibid., 583.

54. Ibid., 577–78. *Nelson T. Johnson Papers*, memorandum of conversation with G. W. Shepard, Nanjing, May 17, 1937. Shepard was a confidant of Madame Jiang.

55. Deng Yuanzhong, *Sanmin*, 477–79.

56. Ibid., 579–82.

57. Ibid., 623–24.

58. Ibid., 599–600.

59. Ibid., 629.

60. Ibid.

61. Ibid., 628. Gan Guoxun, ed., *Lanyishe*, 4 and 99.

62. Liang Xiong, *Dai Li Zhuan*, vol. 1, 88–92.

63. Gan Guoxun, ed., *Lanyishe*, 76–79.

64. Eastman, *Seeds*, 89.

65. Gan Guoxun, ed., *Lanyishe*, 77.

66. Eastman, *Seeds*, 89.

67. Lawrence N. Shyu, "China's 'Wartime Parliament': The People's Political Council, 1938–1945," in Paul T. K. Sih, *Nationalist China during the Sino Japanese War, 1937–1945* (Hicksville, NY, 1977), 273–313.

68. Deng Wenyi, *Maoxian Fannanji* (Taipei, 1973), vol. 2, 110.

69. Gan Guoxun, ed., *Lanyishe*, 78.

70. Ibid.

71. Ibid.

72. Ibid.

73. Ibid.

74. Eastman, *Seeds*, 92.

75. Ibid.

76. Gan Guoxun, ed., *Lanyishe*, 78. Deng Yuanzhong, *Sanmin*, 688, where Zhu Jiahua is cited as a known critic of the Lixingshe.

77. Deng Wenyi, *Maoxian*, 110.

78. Huang Jianli, "The Guomindang Youth Corps: Policy on the Recruitment of Students, 1938–1940," unpublished conference paper, 5th national conference, Asian Studies Association of Australia, Adelaide, May 1984, p. 1.

79. Eastman, *Seeds*, 93.

Chapter 7

1. Xinan Lianda Chuxi Fukan, ed., *Liana Banian* (Kunming, 1946), 4. After the war, Wen emerged as a vocal critic of the repressive tactics of the GMD, and he was assassinated by GMD agents at Kunmiog. See also Hu Lin, *Yieryi de Huiyi* (Hong Kong, 1949), 3.

2. Cha Liangzheng, "Kangzhan Yilaide Xinan Lianda," in *Jiaoyu Zazhi*, vol. 31, no. 1, January 1941. See also Israel Epstein, *The People's War* (London, 1939), 50–51.

3. Ibid.

4. Li Zhongxiang, "Guoli Xinan Lianhe Daxue Shimo ji (shang)," in *Zhuanji Wenxue*, vol. 39, no. 2, August 1981, 72.

5. Qinghua Daxue Xiaoshi Bianxiezu, *Qinghua Daxue Xiaoshigao* (Beijing, 1981), 289.

6. Ibid., 290.

7. Ibid., 291. Figures based on reports of the establishment committee of the temporary university of Changsha.

8. Li Zhongxiang, "Guoli," 73.

9. Cha Liangzheng, "Kangzhan," 1.

10. Wen Yiduo, "Banianlaide Huiyi yu Ganxiang," in Lianda Chuxi Fukan, *Lianda*, 3–7.

11. Cha Liangzheng, "Kangzhan," 349.

12. Ibid.

13. Guo Moruo, *Moruo Zizhuan* (Hong Kong, 1978), vol. 4, chap. 1.

14. Ibid. Within this propaganda unit was a political department headed by He Zhonghan. He was a Whampoa alumnus and a leading figure in the Lixingshe. See p. 177 of Guo's autobiography for his report on how members of this political department tried to have themselves evacuated from Wuhan as the city was about to fall. Guo's account is colored, but it does confirm that left-wing writers working for the GMD were watched closely by Whampoa elements known for their hostility to the CCP.

15. Bianxiezu, *Qinghua*, 390.

16. Ibid., 290.

17. Ibid., 291. Liangzheng, "Kangzhan," 1. Xinan Lianda Chuxi Fukan, *Lianda*, 5–6 and 8–17. Zhongxiang, "Guoli," 73.

18. "Zhangzheng Riji—you Changsha dao Kunming," in Fukan, ed., *Lianda*, 8–17.

19. Ibid.

20. Zhongxiang, "Guoli," 74.

21. Ibid., 292 and 312.

22. Zou Xintian, "Wo Zuzai Xinxiaoshe," in Fukan, ed., *Lianda*, 73–77.

23. Ibid., 70–71.

24. Yang Ximeng, "Jiunianlai Kunming Daxue Jiaoshou de Xinjin ji Xinjin Shizhi," in *Guancha*, vol. 1, no. 3, p. 7. The author was professor of economics at Beida. For a biographical sketch of Yang, see Fukan, *Lianda*, 186.

25. Fukan, ed., *Lianda*, 96–102; Shi Jing, *Wen Yiduo de Gusi* (Hong Kong, 1978), 78–79; Bianxiezu, *Qinghua*, 318–19 and 400. Babao rice or eight-treasure rice was a term coined for rice mixed with sand or other impurities.

26. Zhongxiang, "Guoli," 86. Author's translation.

27. Bianxiezu, *Qinghua*, 316.

28. Ibid.

29. Feng Youlan, "Guoli Xinan Daxue Jianshi," in Fukan, *Lianda*, 1–2.

30. Zhongxiang, "Guoli," 63–65.

31. Cha Liangzhao, "Kunming Huban—Shisannianqian de Yiduan Huiyi," in *Zhuanji Wenxue*, vol. 1, no. 2, 29–30. Bianxiezu, *Qinghua*, chap. 4.

32. Bianxiezu, *Qinghua*, 316.

33. The minister for education, Chen Lifu, actively advocated vocational and technical training. See John Israel, "Hsinan Lienta's (Xinan Lianda) Response to Government Educational Policy and Party Control," in Zhongyang Yanjiusuo Jindaishi Yanjiusuo, *Kangzhan Jianguoshi Yantaohui Lunwenji* (Taipei, 1985).

34. Bianxiezu, *Qinghua*, 312.

35. Well-known faculty members included the social historian Ho Ping-ti and the sociologist Fei Xiaotong. John Israel, "Chunking and Kunming: Hsinan Lienta's Response to Government Educational Policy and Party Control," 371–72. Fukan, ed., *Lianda*, 55–60.

36. Bianxiezu, *Qinghua*, 312.

37. Fukan, ed., *Lianda*, 55–60. Author's translation.

38. Li Zhongxiang, "Guoli Xinan Lianhe Daxue Shimo (xia)," in *Zhuanji Wemxue*, vol. 39, no. 4, 82–88.

39. Israel, "Chungking and Kunming," 346.

40. Bianxiezu, *Qinghua*, 390. Israel, "Chungking and Kunming," 344.

41. Israel, "Chungking and Kunming," 349–56.

42. Feng Youlan, "Guoli," 1–2. Bianxiexu, *Qinghua*, 319.

43. Note that the alliance with the United States also entailed considerable political costs for the GMD. Building airfields for B29 heavy bombers taxed manpower resources heavily, and for the local populace it was forced labor. But American involvement improved material standards in general and created employment opportunities for the educated.

44. Zhang Zu, "Fanyiguan," in Fukan, ed., *Lianda*, 125–29. The associated university supplied over 500 interpreters.

45. Zhongxiang, "Guoli," 87. In 1944, 291 out of 386 graduates enlisted in the armed services. Every time the GMD called for help from the students at Kunming, the response was enthusiastic. Campus discontent developed

mainly because of GMD neglect of this valuable support more than the lack of latent support for the GMD throughout the resistance was period.

46. Bianxiezu, *Qinghua*, 296, citing the education ministry directive under file number Gaozi 09717.

47. Ibid., 296–97.

48. See Israel, "Chunking and Kunming," 363–66, the section on the dean of students, Cha Liangchao (Cha Liangzhao).

49. Fukan, ed., *Lianda*, 18–19.

50. Zhu Wenzhang, "Wen yiduo shi Ruhe Chengwei 'Minzhu Doushi' de?," in *Zhuanji Wenxue*, vol. 39, no. 5, May 1981, 20–22.

51. Bianxiezu, *Qunghua*, 298–99.

52. Zhong Dao, "Xuesheng Zizhihui Yange," in Fukan, ed., *Lianda*, 136–39.

Chapter 8

1. John Israel, "The December 9th Movement: A Case Study in Chinese Communist Historiography," in Albert Feuerwerker, ed., *History in Communist China* (Cambridge, Mass., 1968), 247–76.

2. Misuzu Shobo, *Nitchu Senso*, vol. 1, 125–50.

3. James Bertram, *First Act in China: The Story of the Sian Mutiny* (New York, 1938).

4. Luo Ruiqing, "Kangda de Guochu yu Xiancai," in *Jiefang*, no. 48, August 1938, p. 17. The full name is Kangri Junzheng Daxue.

5. Luo Ruiqing and Cheng Fangwe, *Shaanbei de Quingnian Shenghuo* (Shanghai, 1939), 40–41. Tian Jiagu, *Kangzhan Jiaoyu zai Shaanbei* (Jankow, 1938), 18–19.

6. Dongyuanshe, *Kangda Dongtai* (Wuhan, 1939), 39.

7. Ibid., 18 and 37. Luo Ruiqing and Cheng Fangwu, *Shaanbei*, 41.

8. Dongyuanshe, *Kangda*, 42. Luo Ruiqing and Cheng Fangwu, *Shaanbei*, 16–20.

9. Dongyuanshe, *Kangda*, 28 and 37.

10. Ibid., 20, citing December 9, 1936, as the date when the new name was adopted. December 9, 1936, was the first anniversary of the December

9th movement. Tian Jiagu, *Kangzhan*, claims that August 1936 is the correct dating. Luo Ruiqing and Cheng Fangwu, *Shaanbei*, put the date at December 9, 1936.

11. Dongyuanshe, *Kangda*, 20. Luo Ruiqing and Cheng Fangwu, *Shaanbei*, 43–44.

12. Dongyuanshe, Kangda, 21, Cheng Fangwu, "Bannianlai de Shaanbei Gongxue," in *Jiefang*, no. 38, May 1938, 23–24.

13. Cheng Fangwu, "Bannianlai," 23–24. Luo Ruiqing and Cheng Fangwu, *Shaanbei*, 21.

14. Luo Ruiqing and Cheng Fangwu, *Shaanbei*, 44–45.

15. Dongyuanshe, *Kangda*, 21. Xu Shuhuai, *Kangda Duilai* (n.p., 1938), 18–23.

16. Dongyuanshe, *Kangda*, 21. The same practice continued with the third class. Sending trainees away from Yanan, often before training was complete, became an expediency in lessening pressure on the resistance university.

17. Ibid., 39–42.

18. Ibid., 38–42.

19. Ibid., 42.

20. Cheng Fangwu, "Bannianlai," 23–24. See Ren Tianma, *Huoyue de Fushi* (Shanghai, 1938), 100, where Tian cites November 1, 1937, as the starting date for the Shaanbei Gongxue.

21. Cheng Fangwu, "Bannianlai," 23–24. See Ren Tianma, *Huoyue*, 103, where enrollment for the Shaanbei Gongxue is cited as 2,000.

22. Luo Ruiqing, and Cheng Fangwu, *Shaanbei*, 22.

23. Ibid., 22. Cheng Fangwu, "Bannianlai," 23–24.

24. Cheng Fangwu, "Bannianlai," 23–24.

25. Ren Tiama, *Huoyue*, 41. Tian Jiagu, *Kangzhan*, 19.

26. Lu Ping, *Shenghuo zai Yanan* (Xian, 1938), 117. Dongyuanshe, *Kangda*, 28.

27. Yuan Jingxin, *Shaanbei Jianying* (Wuhan, 1938), 21.

28. Jiefang, no. 47, August 1938, pp. 4–5. Jiefang Ribao, June 10, 1941, 2. Zhao Chaogou, *Yanan Yiyue* (Chongqing, October 1944), 21.

29. *Jiefang Ribao*, February 11, 1942, 1.

30. Ibid., February 16, 1942, 4.

31. *Jiefang*, no. 37, May 6, 1938, 12. Luo Ruiqing and Cheng Fangwu, *Shaanbei*, 22.

32. Luo Ruiqing and Cheng Fangwu, *Shaanbei*, 5.

33. Ibid., 26. Cheng Fangwu, "Biannianlai," 23–24.

34. *Jiefang*, nos. 63/64, 31–32. Dongyuanshe, *Kangda*, 52–53.

35. Dongyuanshe, *Kangda*, 52. The admission that party leaders could not honor their lecture commitments was made by Lin Biao, head of the resistance university.

36. Cheng Fangwu, "Bannianlai," 23–24. Shao Shiping, "Shanbei Gongxue Shishi Guofang Jiaoyu de Jingyan yu Jiaoxun," in *Jiefang*, no. 37, May 1938, 13.

37. Dongyuanshe, *Kangda*, 176–83. Luo Ruiqing and Cheng Fangwu, *Shaanbei*, 7. In this source it is clearly stated that male students were sent to the front, while female students were sent to the rear, areas where less risk was involved. See also Tian Jiagu, *Kangzhan*, 18 and 65, where female students were praised for their contributions to laundry and needle work.

38. *Jiefang*, no. 58, December 1938, p. 3, and nos. 63/64, p. 32. The Japanese bombed Yanan on November 20 and 21, November 1938, causing extensive damage to some buildings. Most students of the public school were accommodated in houses, while the majority of the Yanan populace lived in loess caves.

39. Cheng Fangwu, "Bannianlai," 23–24. Dongyuanshe, *Kangda*, 118–22.

40. Cheng Fangwu, "Bannianlai," 23–24.

41. Qi Wen, ed., *Waiguo jizhe yanzhong de Yanan ji jiefanggu* (Chongqing, 1946), 11.

42. *Balujun Jungheng Zazhi*, vol. 1, no. 1, January 1939, 3. Dongyuanshe, *Kangda*, 46.

43. Dongyuanshe, *Kangda*, 45. The admission that GMD funds were diverted to the resistance university was made by Lin Biao. The actual amount of funds diverted was not revealed.

44. Ibid., 47.

45. Xu Shuhuai, *Kangda*, 6–12.

46. Ibid., 18–19.

47. Dongyuanshe, *Kangda*, 48–49.

48. Ren Tianma, *Huoyue*, 41.

49. Dongyuanshe, *Kangda*, 208–9.

50. Ibid., 49.

51. Ibid.

52. Ibid., 50–51 and 216–21.

53. Ibid., 177.

54. Lu Ping, *Shenghuo*, 119–21. Author's translation.

55. Yuan Jingxin, *Shaanbei*, 39–41. Author's translation.

56. Ibid., 41.

57. Dongyuanshe, *Kangda*, 16.

58. Ibid., 13–14. In these two pages, one of the teaching staff explained how the resistance university was an institution that practiced Confucian teaching.

59. Ibid., 52.

60. Ibid.

61. Ibid., 53.

62. Ibid.

63. Ibid., 54–55.

64. Xu Guangda, "Kangda Zuijin de Dongtai," in *Balujun Jungzheng Zazhi*, no. 2, February 1939, pp. 26–31.

65. Ibid.

66. *Jiefang Ribao*, July 7, 1942, 4.

67. *Jiefang Ribao*, May 24, 1941, 1.

Chapter 9

1. Boeicho Boeikyujo Senshishitsu, *Hokushi no Chiansen*, (Tokyo 1968–71), Vol 1, chapter 4.

2. *Ibid*, 539–552.

3. Renmin Chubanshe, *Kangri Zhanzheng Shiqi Jiefangqu Gaikuang*, (Beijing 1954), 2–3.

4. Zhengfeng Yundong.

5. Jingbing jianzheng.

6. Xinhua Chubanshe, *Jingji wenti yu caizheng wenti*, (Hong Kong 1949, 3rd edition).

7. Boyd Compton, *Mao's China: Party Reform Documents, 1942–1944*, (Seattle 1952), 9–54 contains translations of the two speeches. For Chinese texts see Xinhua Shudian, *Zhengfeng Wenxian*, (Canton 1950, revised edition).

8. Xinhua Chubanshe, *Op Cit*, 1–5.

9. *Ibid*, 5.

10. Zhengfeng Wenxian.

11. *Ibid*, 4. Wu Anjia, *Zhonggong Yanan Shiqi Zhengfeng Yundong zhi Yanjiu* (unpublished thesis, National Zhengzhi University, Taipei 1973), 70.

12. *Ibid*, 70–73.

13. Boyd Compton, *Op Cit*, 157.

14. Xinhua Shudian, *Zhengfeng Wenxian*, (Canton 1950, revised edition). Many of the documents were of collective authorship. The names of Mao Zedong, Liu Shaochi, and Kang Sheng were the few individual writers identified.

15. Xinhua Shudian, *Op Cit*, the few documents relating to Russia were concerned with the Russian historical experience.

16. Boyd Compton, *Op Cit*, 9. Xinhua Shudian, *Op Cit*, 250.

17. Boyd Compton, *Op Cit*, 246. Xinhua Shudian, *Op Cit*, 250.

18. Yang ba gu.

19. Jiang Xiaochu, *Yanan zhengfeng huiyilu*, (Harbin 1958).

20. Boyd Compton, *Op Cit*, 14. Xinhua Shudian, *Op Cit*, 10–11.

21. Boyd Compton, *Op Cit*, 17. Xinhua Shudian, *Op Cit*, 12–13.

22. *Ibid*, 287–292.

23. Jiefang Ribao, March 9, 1942.

24. Wu Anjia, *Op Cit*, 104–107.

25. *Ibid*, 108. Author's translation.

26. Ding Ling (ed.), *Lun Sixiang Gaizo*, (Tianjin 1949), 4. See also Wu Lan, *Ziwo piping shili*, (Hong Kong 1950). Author's translation.

27. Ding Ling, *Op Cit*, preface. Author's translation.

28. *Ibid*, 7–8. Author's translation.

29. Zhang Sayuan, *Dai xiansheng yixun*, (N.P. 1948), Vol 1, 7–17.

Chapter 10

1. Lloyd E. Eastman, "Regional Politics and the Central Government: Yunnan and Chungking," in Paul K. T. Sih, ed., *Nationalist China during the Sino-Japanese War, 1937–45* (New York, 1977), 329–62.

2. Lawrence N. Shyu, "China's 'Wartime Parliament': The Council, 1938–1945," in Sih, ed., *Nationalist China*, 273–313.

3. Guo Muro, *Murou Zizhuan* (Hong Kong, 1978), vol. 4, 489.

4. Yang Ximeng, "Jiunianlai Kunming daxue jiaoshou de xinjin shizhi," in *Guancha*, vol. 1, no. 3, p. 7. for a biographical sketch of the author of this article, see Xinan Lianda Chuxi Fukan, *Lianda Banian* (Kunming, 1946), 186.

5. This refers to the long march of October 1934 to October 1935. See Otto Braun, *A Cominterm Agent in China, 1932–1939* (St. Lucia, 1982), translated by J. Moore.

6. Eastman, "Regional Politics," 332.

7. Ibid., 335. Based on state department file 893.00 PR Yunnan/11, political report for December 1937, 6.

8. Ibid., 348.

9. Ibid., 349–50.

10. Ibid., 350–51.

11. Hu Lin, *Yieryi de Huiyi* (Hong Kong. 1949), 1–2. Yu Zai Xiansheng Jinian Weiyuanhui, *Yieryi Minzhu Yudong Jinianji* (Shanghai, 1946), 10.

12. Ibid., 2.

13. Ibid.

14. Wang Niankun, *Xuesheng Yudong Shiyao Jianghua* (Shanghai, 1951), 58. Hu Lin, *Yieryi*, 2–3.

15. Hu Lin, *Yieryi*, 2–3.

16. Ibid., 3.

17. Ibid.

18. Ibid., 4. Xinan Fukan, *Liana Banian*, 89. Wang Niankun, *Xuesheng*, 59. Shi Jing, *Wen Yiduo de Gushi* (Hong Kong, 1978), 89.

19. Hu Lin, *Yieryi*, 4–8. Shi Jing, *Wen Yiduo*, 89. Wang Niankun, *Xuesheng*, 58–59.

20. Hu Lin, *Yieryi*, 59. Xinan Fukan, *Lianda Banian*, 34. Wang Niankun, *Xuesheng*, 59. Yu Zai, *Yieryi*, 11.

21. Yu Zai, *Yieryi*, 11. Hu Lin, *Yieryi*, 7. Wang Niankun, *Xuesheng*, 59.

22. Wang Niankun, *Xuesheng*, 59–60. Xian Fukan, *Liana Banian*, 35. Hu Lin, *Yieryi*, 8. Yu Zai, *Yieryi*, 11.

23. Yu Zai, *Yieryi*, 1014. Xinan Fukan, *Lianda Banian*, 34–35. Qinghua Daxue Xiaoshi Bianxiezu, *Qinghua Daxue Xiaoshigai* (Beijing, 1981), 415–16.

24. Yu Zai, *Yieryi*, 1–9, provides biographical sketches for each of the victims. Xinan Fukan, *Lianda Banian*, 36. Hu Lin, 27–28. The public funeral was held in March 1936.

25. Quighua Bianxiezu, *Qinghua*, 419.

26. Xinan Lianhe Daxue Xuesheng Chubanshe, *Wu ai Wu shi Wu You ai Zhenli* (Kunming, 1946), contains press clippings and student articles, pp. 1–3.

27. Hu Lin, *Yieryi*, 34–35. Qinghua Bianxiezu, *Quighua*, 423.

28. Fu Sinian, public statement quoted in *Wu ai Wu shi Wu You ai Zhenli*, 51–52.

29. Qinghua Bianxiezu, *Quighua*, 423.

30. *Wu ai Wu shi Wu You ai Zhenli*, foreword, p. 3.

31. Ibid., 8.

32. Ibid., 37–38 and 49–50.

33. Ibid., 9.

34. Li Wen er Lieshi Weiyuanhui, *Renmin Yinglie* (Kunming, 1946), 3–9.

35. Qinghua Zhoukanshe, *Wen Yiduo Xiansheng Zhouwai Jinian Tekan* (Beijing, 1947), 48–49.

36. Ibid. 10–12 contain an eyewitness account of the murder.

37. Ibid., 14. A total of eleven prominent academics sought protection at the American consulate in Kunming.

38. Liang Shuming and Zhou Xinmin, *Li Wen an tiaocha baogaoshu* (Nanjing [?], 1946), 2–3.

39. Huabei Xuesheng Yundong Xiaoshi Bianji Weiyuanhui, Huabei Xuesheng Yundong Xiaoshi (Beijing, 1948), 1.

40. Xu Jiling, "Zhongguo Ziyouzhuyi Zhishifenzi de Canzheng, 1945–1949," in *Ershiyi Shiji* [Twenty-first century] Hong Kong 1991b, 40.

41. Ibid.

42. Beijing Daxue Xuesheng Zizhihui Beida Banyuekanshe, *Beida 1946–1948* (Beijing, 1949), 4.

43. Huabei Weiyuanhui, *Huabei*, 4.

44. Ibid., 12. Beijing Banyuekanshe, *Beida*, 4.

45. Huabei Weiyuanhui, *Huabei*, 12.

46. Ibid., 13.

47. Ibid., 15.

48. Ibid.

49. Ibid.

50. Qinghua Bianxiezu, *Quinghua*, 464.

51. Ibid., 465.

52. Huabei Weiyuanhui, *Huabei*, 15–20.

53. Qinghua Bianxiezu. *Quinghua*, 465.

54. Huabei Weiyuanhui, *Huabei*, 20–21.

55. Ibid., 21.

56. Ibid., 25–26.

57. Suzanne Pepper, *Civil War in China* (Berkeley, 1978), 57.

58. Qinghua Bianxiezu, *Quinghua*, 467.

59. Ibid.

60. Huabei Weiyuanhui, *Huabei*, 55.

61. Ibid., 55.

Chapter 11

1. Foreign Languages Press, *Selected Works of Mao Zedong* (Beijing, 1975), vol. 1, 23–24.

2. The phenomenon of a faction-ridden nationalist government was reported by American war correspondents. See Theodore White and Annalee Jacoby, *Thunder out of China* (New York, 1946), and Graham Peck, *Two Kinds of Time* (Boston, 1967; 2nd, revised edition).

3. Suzanne Pepper, *Civil War in China* Berkeley, 1978), 54–58.

4. Cheng Chu-yuan, *Behind the Tiananmen Massacre: Social, Political, and Economic Ferment in China* (Westview, Colo., 88). Fang argues that China must recognize its intellectuals as a leading force in promoting social programs.

5. J. N. Wasserstrom, *Student Protests in Twentieth-century China* (Stanford, 1991), 302.

6. Ibid., 304.

7. Cheng Chu-yuan, *Tiananmen Massacre*, 88.

8. Yi Mu and Mark V. Thompson, *Crisis at Tiananmen, Reform and Reality in Modern China* (San Francisco, 1990), 16.

9. Wasserstrom, *Student Protests*, 309.

Bibliography

Newspapers and Periodicals Quoted

Balujun Junzheng Zazhi　八路軍軍政雜志	Yanan 延安
Beida Qinghua Lianhebao 北大清華聯合報	Beijing 北京
Bianqu Jiaoyu Tongxun　邊區教育通訊	Yanan　延安
Daxue 大學	Beijing 北京
Guancha 觀察	Shanghai 上海
Guomin Gemingjun 國民革命軍	Nanjing 南京
Guomin Zhengfu Gongbao 國民政府公報	Nanjing/Chongqing 南京/重慶
Guoji Qinghua Daxue Xiaokan 國立清華大學校刊	Beijing 北京
Huangpu Jikan 黃埔季刊	Nanjing 南京
Hunan Wenshi Ziliao Xuanji 湖南文史資料選集	Changsha 長沙
Jiaoyu Zazhi 教育雜志	Chongqing 重慶
Jiefang Ribao 解放日報	Yanan　延安
Jiefang Zhoukan　解放周刊	Yanan　延安
Jindai Lishi Yanjiu　近代歷史研究	Beijing 北京
Kangri Zhanxian 抗日戰綫	Yanan　延安
Kangzhan Daxue　抗戰大學	Yanan　延安
Kangzhan Xiangdao 抗戰向導	Hankou 漢口
Nanfang Zazhi 南方雜志	Guilin　桂林
Qinghua Zhoukan 清華周刊	Beijing/kunming 北京/昆明
Qingnian 青年	Chongqing 重慶

Yunwen Zhi 藝文志   Taibei 台北

Xianggang Huazi Ribao 香港華字日報   Xianggang 香港

Zhongguo Qingnian 中國青年   Yanan 延安

Zhongwai Zazhi 中外雜志   Taibei 台北

Zhongyang Ribao 中央日報   Chongqing/Taibei 重慶/台北

Zhuanji Wenxue 傳記文學   Taibei 台北

Books in Chinese/Japanese

A Ji 阿話 *Zhongguo xiandai xuesheng jianshi* 中國現代學生簡史 (Hong Kong, no date).

Bai Dongsheng 白動生 *Zhanshi shehui fuwu zhidao* 戰時社會服務指導 (Changsha 1941).

Bao Zunpeng 包遵彭 *Zhongguo qingnian yundong shi* 中國青年運動史 (Taipei 1954).

Bei Ye 貝葉 *Kangzhan yu qingnian* 抗戰與青年 (Hankou, no date).

Beida Siyuan Zizhihui 北大四院自治會 *Fengbao siyue* 風暴四月 (Beijing 1948).

Beijing Daxue Xuesheng Zizhihui Banyuekan She 北京大學學生自治會半月刊社 *Beida 1946–1948* 北大 1946–1948 (Beijing 1948).

Beijing Daxue Yuanxi Lianhehui 北京大學院系聯合會 *Beida Yinian* 北大一年 (Beijing 1947).

Beiping Tushuguan Guoli Xinan Lianhe Daxue Hezu Zhongri Zhanshi Shiliao Zhengjihui 北平圖書館國立西南聯合大學合組中日戰事史料徵輯會 *Gongzuo Baogao* 工作報告 (Kunming 1939).

Beiyang Daxue — Tianjin Daxue Xiaoshi Bianxiezu 北洋大學-天津大學校史編寫組 *Beiyang Daxue-Tianjin Daxue Xiaoshi*, 北洋大學-天津大學校史 vol. 1, October 1895 to January 1949, (Tianjin 1990).

Beijingshi Danganguan 北京市檔案館 *Jiefang zhanzheng shiqi Beiping xuesheng yundong*, 解放戰爭時期北平學生運動(Beijing 1991).

Boeicho Boeikyushujo Senshishitsu 保衛廳保衛究修所戰史室 *Hokushi no Chiansen* 北支之治安戰 (Tokyo 1968).

Chao Ren 超人 *Zhanshi qingnian zuzhi he xunlian* 戰時青年組織和訓練 (Hankou 1938).

Chen Binyin 陳彬囷 *Ding Ling zhuan: minzu nuzhanshi* 丁玲傳: 民主女戰士 (Hankou 1938).

Chen Boda 陳伯達 *Renxing, dangxing, gexing*人性、黨性、個性(Hong Kong 1947).

Chen Bulei 陳布雷 *Guomin gemingjun zhanshi chugao* 國民革命軍戰史初稿 (Nanjing 1936).

Chen Cheng 陳誠 *Qingnian jieyue xianjin yundong* 青年節約獻金運動 (Chongqing 1939).

———. *Kangzhan jianguo yu qingnian zeren* 抗戰建國與青年責任 (Chongqing).

Chen Gaoyong 陳高傭 *Zhanshi wenhua yundong* 戰時文化運動 (Chongqing 1938).

Chen Gongshu 陳恭澍 *Lanyishe neimu* 藍衣社內幕(Shanghai 1942).

Chen Jianhua 陳建華 *Kangda yu qingnian* 抗大與青年 (Chongqing 1940).

Chen Lei 陳雷 *Xiang paokou yao fan chi* 向炮口要飯吃 (Shanghai 1947).

Chen Lifu 陳立夫 *Zhanshi jiaoyu fangzhen* 戰時教育方針 (Chongqing 1939).

Chen Mingzhang 陳明章 *Guoli Nankai Daxue* 國立南開大學 (Taipei 1981).

Chen Mingzhang 陳明章 *Guoli Xinan Lianhe Daxue* 國立西南聯合大學 (Taipei 1981).

Chen Ning 陳寧 *Wen Yiduo zhuan* 聞一多傳 (Beijing 1947).

Chen Wengan 陳文干 *Kangzhan junshi yu xinwen dongyuan* 抗戰軍事與新聞動員 (Chongqing 1938).

Chen Shaoxiao 陳少校 *Heiwang lu* 黑黃錄 (Hong Kong 1966).

Chen Xuezhao 陳學昭 *Manzou jiefangqu* 漫走解放區 (Shanghai 1949).

Cheng Fangwu 成仿吾 *Changzheng huiyi lu* 長征回憶錄 (Beijing 1977).

Cheng Jinwu 程今吾 *Yanan yi xuexiao* 延安一學校 (Shanghai 1949).

Cuncui Xueshe 存萃學社 *1924 nian Guangzhou shangtuan shijian* 1924 年廣州商團事件 (Hong Kong 1974).

Daxue Yuekanshe 大學月刊社 *Wen Yiduo jiaoshou xunguo zhounian teji* 聞一多教授殉國周年 特輯(Beijing 1947).

Dai Li 戴笠 *Zhengzhi zhentan* 政治偵探 (Nanjing, 1938, restricted).

Dang Dexin and Huang Kailing 黨德信、黃靄玲 *Diyici Guogong hezuo shiqi de Huangpu Junxiao* 第一次國共合作時期的黃埔軍校 (Wenshi Ziliao Chubanshe, Beijing 1984).

Dazhong Ribaoshe 大衆日報社 *Shanganning Bianqu jianzheng shishi gangyao* 陝甘寧邊區簡政實施綱要(Yanan 1943)

Deng Tuo 鄧拓 *Zhengfeng yundong zai guojia jianshe zhongde zhongyaoxing* 整風運動在國家建設中的重要性 (Beijing 1950).

Deng Wenyi 鄧文儀 *Congjun baoguo ji* 從軍報國記 (Taipei 1979).

————. *Huangpu jingshen* 黃埔精神 (Taipei 1976).

————. Huangpu qingnian 黃埔青年 (Taipei 1976).

————. *Huangpu junxiao zhijianshe* 黃埔軍校之建設 (Chongqing 1943).

————. Jiang Zhuxi 蔣主席 (Nanjing 1945).

————. *Maoxian fannanji* 冒險犯難記 (Taipei 1973).

Deng Yuanzhong 鄧元忠 *Sanmin Zhuyi Lixingshe shi* 三民主義力行社史 (Taipei 1984).

Ding Ling 丁玲 *Sixiang gaizao lun* 思想改造論 (Tianjin 1949).

Du Congrong 杜從戎 *Huangpu Junxiao zhi chuangjian ji dongzheng beifa zhi huiyi* 黃埔軍校之創建暨東征北伐之回憶 (Taipei 1975).

Duli Chubanshe 獨立出版社 *Kangzhanzhong qingnian zenyang zixiu* 抗戰中青年怎樣自修 (Chongqing 1938).

————. *Kangzhan yu yishu* 抗戰與藝術 (Chongqing, no date)

————. *Zhanshi jiaoyu lun* 戰時教育論 (Chongqing 1938).

Fang Dingying 方鼎英 *Fang jiaoyuzhang yanlunji* 方教育長言論集 (Guangzhou 1927).

Fang Jing 方敬 *Jiyi yu wangque* 記憶與忘卻 (Shanghai 1949).

Fei Yunwen 費雲文 *Dai Li de yisheng* 戴笠的一生 (Taipei 1970).

————. *Dai Yunong xiansheng nianpu* 戴雨農先生年譜 (Taipei 1966).

Gan Guoxun (ed) 干國勛 *Lanyishe, Fuxingshe, Lixingshe* 藍衣社復興社、力行社 (Taipei 1984).

————. *Sunwen Zhuyi yu Zhongguo zhengtong sixiang* 孫文主義與中國正統思想 (Taipei 1979).

Gan Naiguang 甘乃光 *Xiaozu de yunyong* 小組的運用 (Guangzhou 1921).

Gao Gang 高崗 *Yijiusiwunian bianqu de zhuyao renwu he zuofeng wenti* 1945年邊區的主要任務和作風問題 (Yanan 1945).

Gao Gang 高崗 *Bianqu dang de lishi wenti jiantao* 邊區黨的歷史問題檢討 (CCP Northwest Bureau 1943).

Geming Shijian Yanjiuyuan 革命實踐研究院 *Zhonggong de zhengfeng yundong* 中共的整風運動 (Taipei 1951).

Gong Lequn 龔樂群 *Huangpu jianshi* 黃埔簡史 (Taipei 1971).

Gongzheng Chubanshe 公正出版社 *Xi'an shibian huiyilu* 西安事變回憶錄 (Hong Kong reprint, no date, contains reminiscences of Jiang Jieshi and Madame Jiang).

Gu Sheng 古僧 *Dai Li jiangjun yu kangri zhanzheng* 戴笠將軍與抗日戰爭 (Taipei 1975).

Guangdong Geming Lishi Bowuguan 廣東革命歷史博物館 *Huangpu Junxiao shiliao*黃埔軍校史料 (Guangzhou 1982).

Guangdong Zhexue Shehui Kexue Yanjiusuo Lishi Yanjiushi 廣東哲學社會科學研究所歷史研究室 *Shenggang tabagong ziliao*省港大罷工資料 (Canton 1980).

Guangzhou Xinhua shudian Zhengfeng wenxian整風文獻 廣州新華書店 *Zhengfeng wenxian* 整風文獻 *(revised edition, Canton 1950).*

Guo Moruo郭沫若 *Lishi renwu*歷史任務 (Shanghai 1950).

———. Guo Moruo zizhuan 郭沫若自傳 (Hong Kong 1977).

Guo Tong 郭桐 *Guogong fengyun mingren lu* 國共風雲名人録 (Hong Kong 1977).

Guofangbu Qingbaoju 國防部情報局 *Zhongmei Hezuosuo shi* 中美合作所史 (Taipei 1961).

———. *Dai Yunong xiansheng zhuanji* 戴雨農先生傳記 (Taipei 1979).

Guofangbu Shizhengju 國防部史政局 *Dai Li lieshi zhuan* 戴笠烈士傳 (Taipei 1962).

———. *Beifa jianshi* 北伐簡史 (Taipei 1961).

———. *Mao Renfeng zhuan*毛人鳳傳 (Taipei 1962).

Guojun Zhenggongshi Bianzuan Weiyuanhui 國軍政工史編纂委員會 *Guojun zhenggong shigao* 國軍政工史稿 (Taipei 1960, 3 vols.).

Guoli Xinan Daxue Jingjixi 國立西南大學經濟系 *Guoli Xinan Daxue Jingjixi yijiusiwunian biye jiniance* 國立西南大學經濟系 1945 年畢業紀念册 (Kunming 1946).

Guomin Gemingjun 國民革命軍 *Jundui neiwu gangyao* 軍隊內務綱要 (Nanjing 1931).

Guomin Gemingjun Zongsilingbu zhengzhibu 國民革命軍總司令部政治部 *Guomin Gemingjun Zhengzhibu zuzhi caoan* 國民革命軍政治部組織草案 (Canton 1925).

Guomin Gemingjun Zhengzhi Xunlianbu國民革命軍政治訓練部 *Chi huo lu* 赤禍録 (n. p., 1927).

Guomin Zhengfu jiaoyubu 國民政府教育部 *Jiaoyubu zhanqu zhongxiaoxue jiaoshi fuwutuan gongzuo gaikuang* 教育部戰區中小學教師服務團工作概況 (Chongqing 1941).

Guomin Zhengfu Jiaoyubu Shehui Jiaoyushi 國民政府教育部社會教育司 *Minzhong xuanquan yu qingnian xunlian* 民衆宣傳與青年 訓練 (Chongqing 1938)

Guomin Zhengfu Junshi Weiyuanhui Zhengzhibu 國民政府軍事委員會政治部 *Huangpu xunlianji xuanji* 黃埔訓練集選輯 (Chongqing 1938).

Hai Yan 海燕 *Yanan Kangri Junzheng Daxue* 延安抗日軍政大學 (Hankou 1938).

Hanhanying 韓漢英 *Qi Jiguang lianjiang yaoling xinjie* 戚繼光練將要領新解 (No place, no date).

He Wenlong 何文龍 *Zhongguo tewu neimu* 中國特務內幕 (Hong Kong 1947).

He Yingqin 何應欽 *He Zongzhang Yingqin yanlun xuanji* 何總長應欽言論選集 (n. p., no date).

He Zhihao 何志浩 *Guomin junshi jiaoyu zhi mian mian guan* 國民軍事教育之 面面觀(Nanjing 1935).

Hebeisheng Zhengxie Wenshi Ziliao Yanjiu Weiyuanhui 河北省政協文史資料研究委員會 *Baoding lujun junguan xuexiao* 保定陸軍軍官學校 (Shijiazhuang 1987).

Hong Jianxiong 洪劍雄 *Guangzhou shaji tusha zhong dangli junxiao sinanzhe* 廣州沙基屠殺中黨立軍校死難者 (Guangzhou 1925).

Hong Shen 洪深 *Kangzhan shinianlai zhongguo de xiju yundong yu jiaoyu* 抗戰十年來中國的戲劇運動與教育(Shanghai 1948).

Hongjun Daxue Xunlianbu 紅軍大學訓練部 *Zhengzhi changshi tiyao* (no place, 政治常識提要1933).

Hou Wailu 侯外廬 *Kangzhan jianguo de wenhua yundong* 抗戰建國的文化運動 (Chongqing 1938).

Hu Lin 胡麟 *Yieryi de huiyi* 一二、一的回憶(Hong Kong 1949)

Huabei Xuesheng Yundong Xiaoshi Bianji Weiyuanhui 華北學生運動小史編輯委員會 *Huabei xuesheng yundong xiaoshi* 華北學生運動小史 (Beiging 1948).

Huang Meizhen, Shi Yuanhua, Zhang Yun 黃美真、石源華、張雲 *Shanghai daxue shiliao* 上海大學史料 (Shanghai 1984).

Huang Yanpei 黃炎培 *Yanan guilai* 延安歸來 (Jiaodong 1946).

Jiang Nan 江南 *Jiang Jingguo zhuan* 蔣經國傳 (Montebello 1984).

Jiang Xiaochu 蔣孝初 *Yanan zhengfeng huiyilu* 延安整風回憶錄 (Harbin 1958).

Jiang Zhongzheng 蔣中正 *Jianguo yu jianjun* 建國與建軍(Chengtu 1939).

———. *Huangpu xunlianji* 黃埔訓練集 (Huangpu 1925).

———. *Guomin jingshen zongdongyuan* 國民精神總動員 (Chongqing 1939).

―――. *Kangzhan jianguo de jiaoyu fangzhen* 抗戰建國的教育方針 (Nanning/Chongqing 1939).

―――. *Guomin jingshen zongdongyuan zhi lilun yu shishi* 國民精神總動員之理論與實施 (Chongqing, no date).

Jiaoyu Zhendishe (ed) 教育陣第社 *Kangzhan shiqi bianqu jiaoyu jianshe* 抗戰時期邊區教育建設 (Zhangjiakou 1946, 2 vols).

Jiaoyu Zazhi 教育雜志 *Tekan: kangzhan yilai de gaodeng jiaoyu* 特刊: 抗戰以來的高等教育 (Chongqing Jan. 1941).

Jiaoyubu Jiaoyu Nianjian Bianzuan Weiyuanhui 教育部教育年鑒編纂委員會 *Dierci Zhongguo jiaoyu nianjian* 第二次中國教育年鑒 (Shanghai 1948).

Jiefangshe 解放社 *Riben diguo zhuyi zai Zhongguo lunxianqu* 日本帝國主義在中國淪陷區 (Yanan 1939).

―――. *Kangri minzu tongyi zhanxian zhinan* 抗日民族統一戰指南 (Yanan 1938-40).

―――. *Zhishi fenzi yu jiaoyu wenti* 知識分子與教育問題 (Yanan, no date).

―――. *Zhengfeng Wenxian* 整風文獻 (Yanan 1944).

Jin Dongping 金束平 *Yanan jianwen lu* 延安見聞録 (Chongqing 1945).

Jin Yaoji (King, A.) 金耀基 *Zhongguo xiandaihua yu zhishi fenzi* 中國現代化與知識分子 (Taipei 1977).

―――. *Cong zhuantong dao xiandai* 從傳統到現代 (Taipei 1978).

Ju Haoran 居浩然 *Qinghua shiji biye sanshinian jinian tekan* 清華十級畢業三十年紀念特刊 (Taipei 1968).

Kang Baishi 康白石 *Chen Jiongming zhuan* 陳炯明傳 (Hong Kong 1978).

Li Chang 李昌 *Yierjiu huiyilu* 一二、九回憶録 (Beijing 1961).

Li Geng 李庚 *Huiyi 'yierjiu' shiqi Nanjing de xuesheng yundong* 回憶 一二、九時期南京的學生運動 (no place, no date, no pagination).

Li Lichu 李黎初 *Shanbei yinxiang ji* 陝北印象記 (Yanan 1937).

Li Yunhan 李雲漢 *Kangzhanqian Zhongguo zhishi fenzi de jiuquo yundong* 抗戰前中國知識分子的救國運動 (Taipei 1977).

Liang Shiqiu 梁實秋 *Tan Wen Yiduo* 談聞一多 (Taipei 1967).

―――. *Qinghua banian* 清華八年 (Taipei 1962).

Liang Shuming 梁漱溟 *Li-Wen beihai zhenxiang* 李聞被害真相 (Hong Kong 1978).

Liang Shuming and Zhou Xinmin 梁漱溟、周新民 *Li-Wen an diaocha baogaoshu* 李聞案調查報告書(Nanjing 1946).

Liang Xiong 良雄 *Dai Li zhuan* 戴笠 傳(Taipei 1982).

Lin Huanping 林煥平 *Kangzhan wenyi pinglunji* 抗戰文藝評論集 (Hong Kong 1939).

Lin Manshu 林曼叔 *Wen Yiduo yanjiu* 聞一多研究 (Kowloon 1973).

Liu Baiyu 劉白羽 *Yanan Shenghuo* 延安生活 (Xianshi Chubanshe, n.p. 1946).

Liu Jianqun 劉健群 *Fuxing Zhongguo zhi lu* 復興中國之路 (Nanjing 1933).

————. *Yinhe Yiwang* 因何遺忘 (Taipei 1966).

Liu Peichu 劉培初 *Minzhu shengdi toushi* 民主勝地透視 (No place 1947).

Liu Qun 劉群 *Xiandai xuesheng de genben wenti* 現代學生的根本問題 (Shanghai 1936).

Liu Zhi 劉崎 *Huangpu Junxiao yu Guomin Gemingjun* 黃埔軍校與國民革命軍 (No place 1947).

Liu Xuehai 劉學海 *Yinianlai xibei gongdang zhi dongtai* 一年來西北共黨之動態 (Chongqing 1942).

Liu Zhonghe 劉中銖 *Kangzhan wenhua zhendi de jianli ji qi yunyong* 抗戰文化陣地的建立及其運用 (Hong Kong 1938).

Li-Wen Er Lieshi Jinian Weiyuanhui 李聞二烈士紀念委員會 *Renmin yinglie Li Gongpu, Wen Yiduo xiansheng yuchi jishi* 人民英烈李公樸聞一多先生遇刺記實 (Kunming 1946).

Lu Ping 魯平 *Shenghuo zai Yanan* 生活在延安 (Xi'an 1938).

Lujun Junguan Xuexiao 陸軍軍官學校 *Lujun Junguan Xuexiao xiaoshi* 陸軍軍官學校校史 (Taipei 1964, 7 volumes).

Luo Ruiqing 羅瑞卿 *Kangri junduizhong de zhengzhi gongzuo* 抗日軍隊中的政治工作 (Yanan 1939).

Luo Ruiqing and Cheng Fangwu 羅瑞卿、成仿吾 *Shanbei de qingnian xuesheng shenghuo* 陝北的青年學生生活 (Shanghai 1939).

Luo Yi, Huang Jiqing 羅儀、黃志清 *Zhongguo Faxisi tewu zhenxiang* 中國法西斯特務真相 (Xinhua Shudian 1949).

Ma Guochang 馬國昌 *Yanan Qiuxue ji* 延安求學記 (Wuhan 1959).

Ma Jiling 馬季鈴 *Shanbei niaokan* 陝北鳥瞰 (Chengdu August 1940).

Man Litao 滿力濤 *Zhanshi zhishi qingnian de xiuyang yu renwu* 戰時知識青年的修養與任務 (Shanghai 1937).

Mao Sicheng 毛思誠 *Minguo shiwunian yiqian zhi Jiang Jieshi xiansheng* 民國四五年以前之蔣介石先生 (Nanjing 1937).

Mao Zedong 毛澤東 *Sixiang zhinan* 思想指南 (Hong Kong 1949).

————. *Gaizao women de xuexi* 改造我們的學習 (Shanghai 1950).

Meiri Yibaoshe 每日譯報社 Nuzhanshi Ding Ling 女戰士丁玲 (Hong Kong 1938).

Mian Zhi 勉之 *Wen Yiduo* 聞一多 (Hong Kong 1949).

Misuzu Shobo (ed) *Nitchu Senso* 日中戰爭 (Tokyo 1965).

Nankai Daxue Xiaoshi Bianxiezu 南開大學校史編寫組 *Nankai Daxue xiaoshi, 1919-1949* 南開大學校史, 1919–1949 (Tianjin 1989).

Neizhengbu Diaochaju 內政部調查局 *Gongfei zhengfeng yundong pouxi* 共匪整風運動剖析 (Taipei 1952).

Ou Yuanhuai 歐元懷 *Zhanshi jiaoyu* 戰時教育 (Chongqing 1941).

Pan Hannian 潘漢年 *Kangzhan yu minzhong yundong* 抗戰與民衆運動 (Shanghai 1938).

Qi Shijie 齊世杰 *Yanan neimu* 延安內幕 (Chongqing 1943).

Qi Wen 齊文 *Waiguo jizhe yanzhong de Yanan ji jiefangqu* 外國記者眼中的延安及解放區 (Chongqing 1946).

Qiao Jiacai 喬家才 *Haoran ji* 浩然集 (Taipei 1981).

Qiang Xiaochu 强曉初 *Yanan zhengfeng huiyi lu* 延安整風回憶錄 (Harbin 1958).

Qinghua Daxue 清華大學 *Qinghua Daxue tongxue lu* 清華大學同學録 (Beijing, 1937).

————. *Guoli Qinghua Daxue yilan* 國立清華大學一覽 (Beijing 1947).

Qinghua Daxue Xiaoshi Bianxiezu 清華大學校史編寫組 *Qinghua Daxue xiaoshi gao,* 清華大學校史稿 (Beijing 1981).

Qinghua Daxue Xiaoshi Yanjiushi 清華大學校史研究室 *Qinghua Daxue shiliao xuanbian, Vol 1, 1911- 1928,* 清華大學史料選編第一卷: 1911–1928 (Qinghua University Press, Beijing 1991).

Qinghua Daxue Xiaoshizu 清華大學校史組 *Renwu zhi* 人物志 (Beijing 1983).

Qinghua Daxue Xuesheng Zizhihui Jiuguo Weiyuanhui
清華大學學生自治會救國委員會 *Jiuwang yundong baogaoshu* 救亡運動
報告書(Beijing 1936).

Qinghua Xiaoyou Tongxunshe 清華校友通訊社 *Mei xiaozhang Yuehan xiansheng shishi sanzhounian jiniankan* 梅校長月涵先生逝世三周年紀念刊
(Taipei 1965).

Qinghua Zhoukanshe 清華周刊社 *Wen Yiduo xiansheng sinan zhounian jinian tekan* 聞一多先生死難周年紀念特刊 (Beijing 1947).

Qiu Qingquan 邱清泉 *Qiu Qingquan zhuan* 邱清泉傳 (Taipei 1968).

Qiu Zijing 邱子静 *Minzu zhanshi Qiu Qingquan* 民主戰士邱清泉 (Taipei 1959).

Ren Tianma 任天馬 *Huoyue de Fushi* 活躍的膚施(Shanghai 1938).

Renmin Chubanshe 人民出版社 *Dangshi Yanjiu* 黨史研究 (Beijing 1980).

————. *Yierjiu yundong* 一二、九運動Beijing 1954).

————. *Xiwang Zhang Bojun, Luo Longji biaoming lichang* 希望張伯鈞、羅隆基
表明立場 (Beijing 1957).

Sanmin Zhuyi Qingniantuan Zhongyang Tuanbu 三民主義青年團中央團部
Guomin jingshen zongdongyuan yundong 國民精神總動員運動
(Chongqing 1941).

Shanganning Bianqu Zhengfu 陝甘寧邊區政府 *Shanganning Bianqu Zhengfu gongzuo baogao* 陝甘寧邊區政府工作報告 (Yanan 1939-41).

————. *Shanganning bianqu zhengfu yinian gongzuo zongjie* 陝甘寧邊區政府
陝甘寧邊區政府一年工作總結 (Yanan 1944).

Shanghai Fangzhi Gongren Yundongshi Bianxiezu 上海紡織工人運動史編寫組
上海紡織工人運動史 *Shanghai Fangzhi gongrenyundonshi*
(Beijing 1991).

Shen Zui 沈醉 *Dai Li qiren*戴笠其人 (Beijing 1980).

————. *Juntong neimu* 軍統內幕 (Beijing 1985).

Shenghuo Jiaoyushe 生活教育社*Zhanshi jiaoyu lunji* 戰時教育論集
(Guangzhou 1938).

Shi Jing 史靖 *Wen Yiduo de daolu* 聞一多的道路 (Shanghai 1947).

————. *Kangzhan shiqi Kunming xuesheng yundong sanji* 抗戰時期昆明學生運動散記
(no place, no date).

————. *Wen Yiduo de gushi* 聞一多的故事 (Hong Kong 1978).

————. *Wen Yiduo* 聞一多 (Wuhan 1958).

Shi Tianxing 史天行 *Ding Ling zai Xibei* 丁玲在西北 (Hankou 1938).

Shishi Wenti Yanjiuhui 時事問題研究會 *Kangzhanzhong de Zhongguo jiaoyu yu wenhua* 抗戰中的中國教育與文化 (Chongqing 1940).

Tian Jiagu 田嘉谷 *Kangzhan jiaoyu zai Shanbei* 抗戰教育在陝北 (Hankou 1938).

Tongyi Chubanshe 統一出版社 *Zhongguo Minzhu Tongmeng gaikuang* 中國民主同盟概況 (Beijing 1949).

Wang Kang 王康 *Wen Yiduo song* 聞一多頌 (Wuhan 1978).

Wang Niankun 王念昆 *Xuesheng yundong shiyao jianghua* 學生運動史要講話 (Shanghai 1951).

Wang Tianwu, Yang Changrong 王天武, 楊長榮 *Huangpu junxiao shihua* 黃埔軍校史話 (Henan Renmin Chubanshe 1982).

Wang Wenjun, Liang Jisheng etc. (ed) 王文均, 梁至生 *Nankai Daxue Xiaoshi Ziliao Xuan 1919-1949* 南開大學校史資料選 (Tianjin 1989).

Wang Wentian 王文田 *Zhang Boling yu Nankai* 張伯苓與南開 (Taipei 1978).

Wang Yongjun 王永均 *Huangpu Junxiao sanbai mingjiang zhuan*, 黃埔軍校三百名將傳 (Nanjing 1989).

Wang Zhongming 王仲明 *Shanbei zhixing* 陝北之行 (Chongqing 1945).

Wenfeng Chubanshe 文風出版社 *Zhengdun sanfeng* 整頓三風 (Hong Kong 1946).

Wenshi Ziliao Chubanshe 文史資料出版社 *Huangpu Junxiao* 黃埔軍校 (Beijing 1984).

Wenxie Bianji Weiyuanhui 文協編輯委員會 *Wuyue de Yanan* 五月的延安, (Yanan 1938).

Wu Anjia 胡安家 *Zhonggong Yanan shiqi zhengfeng yundong zhi yanjiu* 中共延安時期整風運動之研究 (dissertation, Guoli Zhengzhi Daxue, Taipei 1973).

Wu Han 吳晗 *Shishi yu renwu* 史事與人物 (Shanghai 1948).

Wu Jian 吳建 *Zenyang kaizhan piping yu ziwo piping* 怎樣開展批評與自我批評 (Shanghai 1953).

Wu Lan 吳蘭 *Ziwo piping shili* 自我批評實例 (Hong Kong 1950).

Wu Liping and Ai Siqi 吳黎平, 艾思奇 *Sixiang fangfashang de geming* 思想方法上的革命 (Hong Kong 1949).

Wu Xiangxiang 吳相湘 *Chen Guofu de yisheng* 陳果夫的一生 (Taipei 1971).

Wuyue de Yanan Bianjihui 五月的延安編輯會 *Wuyue de Yanan* 五月的延安 (Yanan 1938).

Xia Jintao 夏進滔 *Zhanshi de jiaoyu* 戰時的教育 (Changsha 1938).

Xianggang Hongmian Chubanshe 香港紅棉出版社 *Zhengfeng wencong* 整風文叢(Hong Kong, no date).

Xianggang Huazi Ribao 香港華字日報 *Guangdong kouxie chao* 廣東扣械潮 (Hong Kong 1924).

Zhou Chengen, Yang Wenxian, et al.周承恩、楊文嫻等 *Beijing Daxue Xiaoshi 1898-1949* 北京大學校史 1898–1949 (Beijing 1988).

Xibei Yanjiushe 西北研究社 *Kangzhanzhong de Shanxi* 抗戰中的陝西 (Yanan 1940).

Xinan Lianda Chuxi Fukan 西南聯大除夕副刊 *Lianda banian* 聯大八年 (Kunming 1946).

Xinan Lianhe Daxue 西南聯合大學 *Xinan Lianhe Daxue xiaoyoulu* 西南聯合大學 校友錄 (Kunming 1946).

Xinan Lianhe Daxue xuesheng chubanshe 西南聯合大學學生出版社 *Wu ai wu shi wu you ai zhenli* 吾愛吾師, 吾尤愛真理(Kunming 1946).

Xinhua Chubanshe 新華出版社 *Jingji wenti yu caizheng wenti* 經濟問題與財政 問題 (Hong Kong 1949, 4th edition).

Xinhua Shudian Bianjibu 新華書店東北總分店編審部 *Zhengfeng xuexi wenjian* 整風學習文件 (Changchun 1950).

Xinhua Shudian 新華書店 *Zhengfeng wenxian* 整風文獻 (Canton 1950, revised edition).

Xinminzhu Chubanshe 新民主出版社 *Zhongguo xuesheng da tuanjie* 中國學生大 團結 (Hong Kong 1949).

Xu Maoyong 徐懋庸 *Xu Maoyong huiyilu* 徐懋庸回憶錄 (Beijing 1982).

Xu Shihua 許世華 *Wusan yundong* 五卅運動 (Beijing 1956).

Xu Shuhuai 許舒懷 *Kangda guilai* 抗大歸來 (Hankou 1939).

Xu Zhongyu 徐中玉 *Kangzhanzhong de wenxue* 抗戰中的文學 (Chongqing 1941).

Yanan Geming Jinianguan 延安革命紀念館 *Yanan geming jinian jianzhu* 延安革命紀念建築 (Beijing 1953).

Yanan Shishi Wenti Yanjiuhui 延安時事問題研究會 *Kangzhanzhong de Zhong-guo zhengzhi* 抗戰中的中國政治 (Yanan 1940).

Yang Shu 楊述 *Ji yierjiu* 記一二、九 (Beijing 1960).

Yao Shufeng 姚蘇鳳 *Kangzhan yu dianying* 抗戰與電影 (Changsha 1938).

Ye Zhou 葉舟 *Ding Ling: Xinzhongguo de nuzhanshi* 丁玲: 新中國的女戰士 (Shanghai 1936).

Yin Yanjun 尹衍鈞 *Zhanshi jiaoyu lun* 戰時教育論 (Chongqing 1938).

You Yang 游揚 *Junxiao shenghuo de huiyi* 軍校生活的回憶 (Kowloon 1950).

Yu Zai xiansheng jinian weiyuanhui 于再先生紀念委員會 *Yieryi minzhu yundong jinianji* 一二、一民主運動紀念集 (Shanghai 1946).

Yuan Jingxin 原景信 *Shanbei Jianying* 陝北剪影 (Wuhan 1938).

Yuan Zhe 袁哲 *Kangzhan yu jiaoyu* 抗戰與教育 (Wuhan 1938).

Zhang Aiping and Xiao Hua 張愛萍、肖華 *Qingnian yundong huiyilu diyiji* 青年運動回憶錄第一集 (Beijing 1978).

Zhang Fakui 張發奎 *Disijun jishi* 第四軍紀實 (no place, 1948).

Zhang Anguo 張安國 *Jiaoyu gaizao de xin tujing* 教育改造的新途徑 (Chongqing 1942).

Zhang Zhiyi 張執一 *Kangzhanzhong de zhengdang he paibie* 抗戰中的政黨和派別 (Chongqing 1939).

Zhao Chaogou 趙超構 *Yanan yiyue* 延安一月 (Chongqing 1944).

Zhao Qinghe 趙清閣 *Kangzhan xiju gailun* 抗戰戲劇概論 (Chongqing 1938).

Zhao Qixiang 趙啓祥 *Kangzhanqian Zhongguo daxue jiaoyu de xin fangxiang* 抗戰前中國大學教育的新方向 (Taipei 1973).

Zhonggong Beijing Shiwei Dangshi Yanjiushi and Zhonggong Tianjin Shiwei Dangshi Ziliao Zhengji Weiyuanhui 中共北京市委黨史研究室中共天津市委黨史資料徵集委員會 *Beifang zuoyi wenhua yundong ziliao huibian* 北方左翼文化運動資料匯編 (Beijing 1991).

Zhonggongdang Shenyang Shiweihui Xuanquanbu 中共黨沈陽市委會宣傳部 *Dangyuan zhengfeng duben* 黨員整風讀本 (Shenyang 1958).

Zhonggong Shanghai Shiwei Dangshi Ziliao Zhengji Weiyuanhui 中共上海市委黨史資料徵集委員會 *Kangri zhanzheng shiqi Shanghai xuesheng yundong shi*, 抗日戰爭時期上海學生運動史 (Shanghai 1991).

Zhongguo Guomindang Zhongyang Weiyuanhui Diliu Zu 中國國民黨中央委員會第六組 *Gongfei lici wenyi zhengfeng zhenxiang* 共匪歷次文藝整風真相 (Taipei 1970).

Zhongguo Guomindang Zhongyang Xuanquanbu 中國國民黨中央宣傳部 *Kangzhan liunianlai zhi xuanquan zhan* 抗戰六年來之宣傳戰 (Chongqing 1943).

Zhongguo Guomindang Zhongyang Zhixing Weiyuanhui Xuanquanbu 中國國民黨中央執行委員會宣傳部 *Kangzhan liunianlai zhi jiaoyu* 抗戰六年來之教育 (Chongqing 1946).

Zhongguo Minzhu Tongmeng Nanfang Zongzhibu 中國民主同盟南方總支部 *Zhishi fenzu de sixiang gaizao wenti* 知識分子的思想改造問題 (n. p. 1952).

―――. *Chi Zhongyangshe suowei ' minmeng canjia panluan zhenxiang* 斥中央社所謂"民盟參加叛亂真相" (no place 1949).

Zhongguo Minzhu Tongmeng Zongbu 中國民主同盟總部 *Zhongguo Minzhu Tongmeng erzhongquan zhengzhi baogao* 中國民主同盟二中全政治報告 (Shanghai 1947).

Zhongguo Renmin Zhengzhi Xieshang Huiyi and Xinan Diqu Wenshi Ziliao Xiezuo Huiyi 中國人民政治協商會議西南地區文史資料寫作會議 *Kangzhan shiqi xinan de wenhua shiye,* 抗戰時期西南的文化事業 (Chengdu 1990).

Zhongyang Dangshi Shiliao Bianzuan Weiyuanhui 中央黨史史料編纂委員會 *Huangpu jianjun zhi sanshinian gaishu* 黃埔建軍之三十年概述 (Taipei 1954).

Zhongyang Junshi Zhengzhi Xuexiao 中央軍事政治學校 *Guomin Gemingjun Zhongyang Junshi Zhengzhi Xuexiao diwu qi tongxue hui* 國民革命軍中央軍事政治學校第五期 同學會 (Nanjing 1927).

―――. *Diyi Fenxiao tongxue lu* 第一分校同學録 (Guilin 1928).

―――. *Zhongyang Lujun Junguan Xuexiao diyi qi tongxue lu* 中央陸軍軍官學校第一期同學録 (Huangpu 1925).

―――. *Xueyu ansheng xiaozu huiyi taolun ji* 學員生小組會議討論集 (Nanjing 1930).

―――. *Xiaozu huiyi xuzhi* 小組會議須知 Canton, n.d.).

―――. *Zhongyang Lujun Junguan Xuexiao diqi qi tongxuelu* 中央陸軍軍官學校第七期同學録 (Nanjing 1927).

―――. *Zhongyang Lujun Junguan Xuexiao shigao* 中央陸軍軍官學校史稿 (Nanjing 1936).

―――. *Zhongyang Lujun Junguan Xuexiao Zhengzhi Yanjiuban jiangyi hedingben* 中央陸軍軍官學校政治研究班講義合訂本 (n.p., no date).

————. *Zhonggong pohuai kangzhan jianguo zhi bufa xingwei* 中共破壞抗戰建國之不法行爲 (Chongqing 1940).

Zhongyuan Chubanshe 中原出版社 *Wo suo zhidao de Juntong neimu* 我所知道的軍統内幕 (Hong Kong 1985).

Zhou Enrun 鄒恩潤 *Kangzhan yilai* 抗戰以來 Shanghai 1947).

Zhou Leshan 周樂山 *Kangri zhanzheng yihua* 抗日戰爭逸話 (Shanghai 1932).

Zhu Ziqing 朱自淸 *Lun ya xu gongshang* 論雅俗共賞 (Shanghai 1948).

Zhuang Zexuan 莊澤宣 *Kangzhan shinianlai Zhongguo jiaoyu zong jiantao* 抗戰十年來中國教育總檢討 (Shanghai 1947).

Zi Fang 子方 *Ji Yierjiu* 記一二、九 (Beijing 1955).

Zuo Shen, Hu Ruguang 左森、胡如光 *Beiyang Daxue renwu zhi* 北洋大學人物志 (Tianjin 1990).

Zhongyang Yanjiuyuan Jindaishi Yanjiusuo 中央研究院近代史研究所 *Kangzhan jianguoshi yantaohui lunwenji 1937–1945* 抗戰建國史研討會論文集 1937–1945 (上册) (台北 1985) (Taipei 1985).

Articles in Chinese/Japanese

Amako Satoshi 天兒慧 "Chukoku no seiji shido shisutemu to kizo kanbu—toku ni 1940 nendai o chusin toshite," *Ajia Kenyu*, vol. 29, No 2, July 1982, pp. 34–71

Cai Mengjian 蔡孟堅 "Yu He furen tan He Zhonghan xiansheng shengping," 與賀夫人談賀衷寒先生生平 *Zhuanji* Wenxue, vol. 40, no. 3, pp. 55–60

———. "Zuinian Hu Zongnan jiangjun," 追念胡宗南將軍 *Zhuanji Wenxue*, vol. 46, no. 2, pp. 28–39

———. "Yi Gui Yongqing jiangjun," 憶桂永清將軍 *Zhuanji Wenxue*, vol. 19, no. 6

Cha Liangzhao 查良釗 "Kunming huban—shisannianqian de yiduan huiyi," 昆明湖畔----十三年前的一段回憶, 傳記文學 *Zhuanji Wenxue*, vol. 1, no. 2, pp. 29–30

Chen Dunzheng 陳敦正 "Kang Ze de shengping," 康澤的生平, 中外雜志 *Zhongwai Zazhi*, vol. 31, no. 6, pp. 70–75

Cheng Fangwu 成仿吾 "Xie shenmo?," 寫什么? *Jiefang* (Zhoukan), no. 3, May 1937, pp. 27–28

Cheng Fangwu 成仿吾 "Bannianlai de Shanbei Gongxue," 半年來的陝北公學, 解放周刊 in *Jiefang* (Zhoukan), no. 38, May 15, 1938, pp. 23–24

———. "Shanbei Gongxue de xin jieduan," 陝北公學的新階段, 解放周刊 in *Jiefang* (Zhoukan), no. 72, May 31, 1939, p.17

Deng Wenyi 鄧文儀 "Fuxingshe chuangjian jingguo ji qi gongxian," 復興社創建經過及其貢獻 *Yiwen Zhi*, no. 225, pp. 18–22

———. "Wo yu tongzhi haoyou Dai Li," 我與同志好友戴笠 in Tianyi Chubanshe, *Dai Li Zhuanji Ziliao* (Taipei, n.d.)

Deng Yuanzhong 鄧元忠 "Sanmin Zhuyi Lixingshe shi chugao," 三民主義力行社史初稿 *Zhuanji Wenxue*, (1) vol. 39, no. 4, (2) vol. 39 no. 6, (3) vol. 40, no. 1, and (4) vol. 49, no. 6

Ding Lijin 丁履進 "Nankai xiansheng' Zhang Boling," 南開先生張伯苓 *Zhuanji Wenxue*, vol. 26, no. 4, pp. 70–72

Du Xinyuan 杜心源 "Jin xibei zhengquan xitong jingbing jianzheng de chubu jiancha," 近西北政權系統精兵簡政的初步檢查 in *Jiefang Ribao*, Feb. 26, 1943, p. 4.

Fei Bai 非白 "yinianlai Beiping xuesheng yundong de huigu," 一年來北平學生運動的回顧 *Jiefang*, no. 4, May 1937, pp. 21–23.

Feng Wenbin 馮文彬 "Zhongguo qingnian de dangqian renwu," 中國青年的當前任務 *Jiefang*, Nos. 106/107, May 1940, pp. 23–27

Gan Guoxun 干國勛 "Lixingshe yu Juntongju," 力行社與軍統局　*Zhongwai Zazhi*, no. 179,　　　　　January 1982

———. "Annei rangwai tongyi yuwu (Lixingshe, Fuxingshe shihua)," 安内攘外統一禦侮(力行社、復興社史話)　*Zhongwai Zazhi*, vol. 16, no. 6, 1974.

———. "Minzu fuxing yundong ji: Lixingshe, Fuxingshe shihua," 民主復興運動記---力行社、復興社史話　*Zhongwai Zazhi*, vol. 16, no. 1, July 1974.

———. "Kangzhan qianxi de Huabei fengyun," 抗戰前夕的華北風雲 *Zhongwai Zazhi*, vol. 16, no. 4, October 1974

———. "Kangzhan qianxi de tongyi yundong," 抗戰前夕的統一運動 (shang), *Zhongwai Zazhi*, vol. 16, no. 5, November 1974

———. "Dai Li, Teng Jie, Liu Jianqun," 戴笠、滕杰、劉健群 *Zhongwai Zazhi*, vol. 16, no. 3, September 1974

He Dongfang 何東方 "Dongbei xiangong yi dongnian," 東北陷共憶當年 *Yiwen Zhi*, Nos. 132 and 133.

Japanese Intelligence Report "Ran'isha no hokushi ni okeru saikin no doko," in *Joho*, no. 8, Dec. 15, 1939, pp. 71–86. "Kanan Ran'isha ni kansuru chosa," in Joho, no. 18, May 15, 1940, pp. 59–65.

Kai Feng 凱灃 "Lun muqian Zhongguo qingnian yundong de renwu," 論目前中國青年運動的任務 *Jiefang*, no. 36, April 1938, pp. 17–27

Le Shuren 樂恕人 "Kangzhan zhanyou Sun Liren," 抗戰戰友孫立人 *Zhongwai Zazhi*, vol. 38, no. 1, pp. 134–37

Li Ping 黎平　"Ba kangzhan shiye jiaoyu qian qian wan wan minzhong," 把抗戰事業教育千千萬萬民衆 in *Jiefang* (Zhoukan), no. 19, Oct. 10 1937, pp. 11–15

Li Tingqing "Qinghua xuechao qianhou," 清華學潮始末 in *Xiao Xia Zhoukan*, no. 6, Jan. 9, 1930

Li Zhongxiang 李鐘湘 "Guoli Xinan Lianhe Daxue shimo ji," 國立西南聯合大學始末記 *Zhuanji Wenxue* (shang) no. 231, pp. 72–78; (zhong) no. 232, pp. 63–66; and (xia) no. 233, pp. 82–88

Liang Xiong 良雄 "Dai Li yu Lixingshe," 戴笠與力行社　*Zhuanji Wenxue*, vol. 36, no. 2, pp. 98–102

Liang Yangping 梁仰平 "Huabei xuesheng zhanshi xinanxing," 華北學生戰時西南行 *Zhongwai Zazhi*, vol. 30, no. 4, pp. 98–103

Lin Biao 林彪 "Lun Huabei zhengguizhan de jiben jiaoxun yu youji de fazhan tiaojian," 論華北正規戰的基本教訓與游擊的發展條件 *Jiefang*, nos. 43/44, July 1 1938, pp. 54–59

Liu Gong 劉恭 "Wu suo zhidao de Zhongtong," 我所知道的中統 Hunan *Wen-shi Ziliao Xuanji*, vol. 2, (Changsha 1981)

Liu Jianqun 劉健群 "Huabei xuanchuan huiyi," 華北宣傳回憶, 藝文志 *Yiwen Zhi*, vol. 13, pp. 25–27

———. "Lianggenanwang de hao tongzhi—Gui Yongqing yu Zheng Jiemin," 兩個難忘的好同志－桂永清與鄭介民 *Zhuanji Wenxue*, vol. 6, nos. 1 and 2

———. "Beifa qianhou gurenqun," 北伐前后故人群 *Zhuanji Wenxue*, vol. 8, nos. 2, 3, and 4

———. "Kuice Xi'an shibian de qianyin houguo," 窺測西安事變的前因后果 *Zhuanji Wenxue*, vol. 9, Nos 3 and 4

———. "Xuechao huiyi yougan," 學潮回憶有感 *Zhuanji Wenxue*, vol. 4, no. 6, pp. 35–42

Liu Shaoqi 劉少奇 "Jianzhi Huabei kangzhanzhong de wuzhuang budui," 堅持華北抗戰中的武裝部隊 *Jiefang*, nos. 43/44, July 1938, pp. 49–53.

Liu Zhi 劉峙 "Huangpu Junxiao yu Guomin Gemingjun," 黃埔軍校與國民革命軍 *Huangpu Jikan*, vol. 3, no. 1, January 1939

Liu Zhenghong 劉征鴻 "Kang Ze ban Zhongguo Ribao," 康澤辦中國日報 *Yiwen Zhi*, July 1973, no. 94, pp. 27–28

Luo Fu 洛甫 "Lun qingnian de xiuyang," 論青年的修養 in *Jiefang*, no. 37, May 22, 1938

Luo Mai 羅邁 "Shanbei Gongxue de chengjiu," 陝北公學的成就 in *Jiefang*, no. 54, Oct. 15, 1938

Luo Ruiqing 羅瑞卿 "Kangda de guoqu yu xianzai," 抗大的過去與現在 *Jiefang*, no. 48, August 1938, pp. 17–22

Luo Ruiqing 羅瑞卿 "Gonggu budui de zhengzhi gongzuo," 鞏固部隊的政治工作 in *Jiefang*, no. 46, July 23, 1938, pp. 16–21 and no. 47, August 1, 1938, pp. 15–19

———. "Cong guoqu Balujun zhengzhi gongzuo de jingyan shuodao jintian kangzhan junduizhong de zhengzhi gongzuo," 從過去八路軍政治工作的經驗說到今天抗戰軍隊中的政治工作 *Jiefang*, no. 3, February 8 1938, pp. 15–22

———. "Dongyuanshi de zhengzhi gongzuo," 動員時的政治工作 *Jiefang*, no. 34, April 1938, pp. 10–13

Ma Wu xiansheng 馬五先生 "Hu Zongnan yinhen beitan ji," 胡宗南飲恨被彈記 *Yiwen Zhi*, no. 148, 1978, pp. 10–13.

Mao Zedong 毛澤東 "Zai Yanan wenyi zuotanhuishang de jianghua," 在延安文藝座談會上的講話 in *Jiefang Ribao*, Oct. 19, 1943, pp. 1–2 and 4

Ou Weiwen 區偉聞 "Lanyishe yu Zhongguo Guomindang," 藍衣社與中國國民黨 *Nanfang Zazhi*, no. 6, September 1933

Qiao Jiacai 喬家才 "Sanmin Zhuyi Lixingshe yu Zhongguo Guomindang," 三民主義力行社與中國國民黨 *Zhongwai Zazhi*, no. 191 and no. 192, January and February 1983

———. "Gan Guoxun yu Lixingshe," 干國勛與力行社 *Zhongwai Zazhi*, vol. 34, no. 1, pp. 26–29

Shao Shiping 邵式平 "Shanbei Gongxue shishi guofang jiaoyu de jingyan yu jiaoxun," 陝北公學實施國防教育的經驗教訓 *Jiefang*, no. 36, May 1938, pp. 11–13

———. "Shanbei Gongxue yinianlai jiaoxue de diandi jingyan," 陝北公學一年來教學的點滴經驗 in *Jiefang* (Zhoukan), nos. 63/64, Feb. 16, 1939, pp. 31–35

Shen Zui 沈醉 "Wo suo zhidao de Dai Li," 我所知道的戴笠 in *Wenshi Ziliao Xuanji*, vol. 22, pp. 61–66

Tan Zheng 譚政 "Guanyu jundui zhengzhi gongzuo wenti," 關于軍隊政治工作問題 in *Jiefang Ribao*, April 4, 1944, pp. 1, 3–4

Teng Jie 藤 傑 Liunian zhunbei banian kangzhan," 六年准備八年抗戰 *Zhongwai Zazhi*, vol. 34, no. 1, pp. 14–19

Wan Zilin 萬子霖 "Dao Kang Ze jiangjun," 悼康澤將軍 *Zhongwai Zazhi*, vol. 14, no. 6, pp. 67–72

Wang Boling 王柏齡 "Huangpu chuangshi zhi huiyi," 黃埔創始之回憶 *Huangpu Jikan*, vol. 1, no. 1, January 1939, and no. 2, April 1939

Wang Yuting 王禹廷 "Huabei zhi shoufu yu xianluo," 華北之收復與陷落 *Zhuanji Wenxue*, vol. 38, no. 3, pp. 78–80; no. 5, pp. 120–28

Wei Daming 魏大銘 "Pingshu Dai Yunong xiansheng de shigong," 評述戴雨農先生的事功 *Zhuanji Wenxue*, (shang), vol. 38, no. 2, (zhong), vol. 38 no. 3, (xia) vol. 38 no. 4

Xu Bing 徐冰 "Zenyang jinxing shuqi gongzuo," 怎樣進行暑期工作 *Jiefang*, no. 5, May 31, 1937, pp. 15–17

———. "Kangzhanzhong de qingnian xuesheng," 抗戰中的青年學生 in *Jiefang* (Zhoukan), no. 16, September 15, 1937, pp. 30–41

Xu Guangda 許光達 "Kangda zuijin de dongxiang," 抗大最近的動向 *Balujun Junzheng Zazhi*, no. 2, February 15, 1939, pp. 26–31

Xu Jiling 許紀霖 "Zhongguo ziyouzhuyi zhishifenzi de canzheng, 1945–1949," "中國自由主義知識分子的參政1945–1949" *Ershiyi Shiji* [Twenty–first century], 1991 (6), pp. 37–46

Xuan Jiexi 宣介溪 "Riben xianbing Beiping `bu' wo ji," 日本憲兵北兵捕我記 *Zhuanji Wenxue*, vol. 38, no. 5, pp. 55–60

———. "Lanyishe zhi lailong qumai," 藍衣社之來龍去脈 *Zhuanji Wenxue*, vol. 41, no. 5, pp. 47–56

Yang Ximeng 楊西孟 "Jiunianlai Kunming daxue jiaoshou de xinjin ji xinjin shizhi," 九年來昆明大學教授的薪津及薪津實值 *Guancha*, vol. 1, no. 3, September 1946

Ye Dao 葉島 "Huangpu jiaoyu zhi shide yanjiu," 黃埔教育之史的研究 *Huangpu Jikan*, vol. 1, no. 3, 1939

Yu Zidao and Xu Youwei 余子道、徐有 "Lixingshe shulun," 力行社述論 in *Jindaishi Yanjiu*, no. 6, 1989

Zhang Gongping 張贛萍 "Guan Linzheng jiangjun zhuanji," 關麟徵將軍傳記 *Yiwen Zhi*, no. 187, April 1981, pp. 32–37; no. 188, May 1981, pp. 26–31; no. 189, June 1981, pp. 35–42; No. 190, July 1981, pp. 37–43

Zhu De 朱德 "Yinian yilai de Huabei kangzhan," 一年以來的華中抗戰 *Jiefang*, no. 53, September 1938, pp. 11–15

Zhu Wenchang 朱文長 "Wen Yiduo shi ruhe chengwei 'minzhu doushi de?'," 聞一多是如何成爲"民主鬥士"的? *Zhuanji Wenxue*, vol. 38, no. 5, pp. 20–26

Works in English

Anderson, B. *Imagined Communities*. London 1984.

Ayers, W. *Chang Chih–tung and Educational Reform in China*. Cambridge, Mass., 1971.

Bennett, G. *Yundong: Mass Campaigns in Chinese Communist Leadership*. Berkeley, 1976.

Bertram, J. *First Act in China: The Story of the Sian Mutiny*. New York, 1938.

Bing, Dov. "Sneevliet and the early years of the CCP." *China Quarterly*, no. 48, Oct./Dec. 1971, pp. 677–97.

Borodin, N.M. *One Man in His Time*. London 1955.

Braun, Otto. *A Comintern Agent in China 1932–1939*. St Lucia, 1982.

Cameron, M. E. *The Reform Movement in China, 1898–1912*. Stanford, 1931.

Chan, Gilbert. "A Chinese Revolutionary: the career of Liao Zhongkai 1878–1925", doctoral dissertation. Columbia, 1975.

Chan, Gilbert, and Etzold, T.H. *China in the 1920s: Nationalism and Revolution*. New York, 1976.

Chang Chih–tung. *China's Only Hope*. New York reprint, 1975.

Chang, Maria Hsia. "'Fascism' and Modern China." *China Quarterly*, September 1979.

Cheng Chu–yuan. *Behind the Tiananmen Massacre*, Boulder, 1990.

Chesneaux, J. *The Chinese Labor Movement, 1917–1927* Stanford, 1968.

Ch'i Hsi–sheng. *Nationalist China at War*. Ann Arbor, 1982.

Chow Tse–tsung. *The May Fourth Movement*. Stanford, 1967.

Clark, Elmer T. *The Chiangs of China*. New York, 1933.

Clubb, O.E. *China and Russia: the "Great Change."* New York, 1971.

Cobles, Parks M. "The Shanghai capitalist class and the Nationalist government, 1927–1937." Doctoral dissertation, University of Illinois, Urbana–Champaign, 1975.

Compton, Boyd. *Mao's China: Party Reform Documents, 1942–1944*. Seattle, 1952.

Duus, P., R.H. Myers, M.R. Peattie (eds.). *The Japanese Informal Empire in China 1895–1937*. Princeton, 1984.

Eastman, Lloyd E. *Seeds of Destruction: Nationalist China in War and Revolution, 1937–1949*. Stanford, 1984.

———. *The Abortive Revolution: China under Nationalist Rule, 1927–1937*. Cambridge, Mass., 1974.

Elkins, W.F. "'Fascism' in China: the Blue Shirt Society 1932–1937." *Science and Society* vol. 33, no. 4, 1969, pp. 426–433.

Epstein, Israel. *The People's War*. London, 1939.

Eudin, Xenia J., and North, R.C. *Soviet Russia and the East, 1920–1927: A Documentary Survey*. Stanford, 1957

Feuerwerker, A. (ed.). *History in Communist China*.(Cambridge, Mass., 1968.

Fischer, Louis. *The Soviets in World Affairs*. New York, 1930.

Foreign Language Press. *Selected Works of Mao Zedong*. Beijing, 1975.

Fung, Edmund *The Military Dimension of the Chinese Revolution*. Canberra, 1980.

Furth, Charlotte (ed.). *The Limits of Change*. Cambridge, Mass., 1976.

Gillespie, R. E. "Whampoa and the Nanking Decade 1924–1936." Doctoral dissertation, American University, 1971.

Godley, M. R. "Lessons from an Italian Connection," in D. Pong and E. Fung (ed.), *Ideal and Reality*. Lanham, 1985.

Gourlay, W. E. "The Kuomintang and the Rise of Chiang Kai-shek." Doctoral dissertation, Harvard 1966.

Greene, Nathan. *Fascism an anthology*. New York, 1968.

Grieder, Jerome. *Intellectuals and the State*. New York, 1981.

Hao Chang. *Liang Ch'i-ch'ao and Intellectual Transition in China 1890–1907*. Cambridge, Mass., 1971.

Holybnychy, Lydia. *Borodin and the Chinese Revolution 1923–1925*. New York, 1979).

Hsu, Leonard S.L. *Sun Yat-sen, His Political and Social Ideals*. Los Angeles, 1933).

Huang, Jianli. "The Guomindang Youth Corps: Policy on the Recruitment of Students, 1938–1940," a paper delivered at the Fifth

National Conference of the Asian Studies Association of Australia. Adelaide, May 1984.

Isaacs, H. R. *The Tragedy of the Chinese Revolution.* Stanford, 1961.

Israel, John. *Student Nationalism in China, 1927–1937.* Stanford, 1966.

————. "The fate of Liberal Education in China," in Ronald Moore (ed), *China: the Limits of Reform.* Boulder: Westview, 1982.

————. "Southwest Associated University: Preservation as an Ultimate Value," in Paul K.T. Sih (ed), *Nationalist China during the Sino-Japanese War, 1937–1945.* Hicksville: Exposition Press, 1977.

————. "Chungking and Kunming: Hsinan Lienta's Response to Government Educational Policy and Party Control," in Zhongyang Yanjiuyuan Jindaishi Yanjiusuo Bian, *Kangzhan Jianguoshi Yantaohui Lunwenji 1937–1945.* Taipei, 1985, volume 1, pp. 343–79.

Jacobs, Dan N. *Borodin, Stalin's Man in China.* Cambridge, Mass., 1981.

Jacobs, Dan N. "Recent Russian material on Soviet advisors in China: 1923–1927," *China Quarterly,* no. 41, January–March 1970.

Jansen, M.B. *Japan and China: from War to Peace 1894–1972.* Chicago, 1975.

Johnson, C.A. *Peasant Nationalism and Communist Power.* (Stanford, 1962.

Johnson, N.T. *Nelson T. Johnson Papers,* Memorandum on conversation with G. W. Shepard. Nanjing, May 17, 1937.

Jordan, D.A. *The Northern Expedition: China's revolution of 1923–28.* Cambridge, 1983.

————. *Chinese Boycotts versus Japanese Bombs: The Failure of China's "Revolutionary Diplomacy," 1931–1932.* Ann Arbor, University of Michigan Press, 1991.

Klein, D.W., and Clark, A.B. *Biographical Dictionary of Chinese Communism.* Cambridge, Mass., 1971.

Landis, Richard Brian. "Institutional trends at the Whampoa Military School," doctoral dissertation, University of Washington, 1969.

Lary, Dianne. *Region and Nation.* Cambridge, 1974.

League of Nations. *Report of the Commission of Enquiry of the League of Nations signed at Peip'ing, 4th September 1932*. Shanghai, 1932.

Li, L. *The Japanese Army in North China 1937–1941*. Tokyo, 1975.

————. *Japan over Manchuria 1931–36*. Hong Kong, August, 1992.

Lin Yu–sheng. *The Crisis of Chinese Consciousness, Radical Antitraditionalism in the May Fourth Era*. Madison, 1979.

Liu, F.F. *A Military History of Modern China*. Princeton, 1956.

Loh, Pichon. *The Early Chiang Kai-shek*. New York, 1971.

MacFarquhar, R.L. "The Whampoa Military Academy." *Papers on China*, no. 9. Cambridge, Mass., 1955.

McNelly, T. (ed.). *Sources in Modern East Asian History and Politics*. New York, 1967.

Myers, R.H., and Peattie, M.R. (eds.). *The Japanese Colonial Empire 1895–1945*. Princeton 1984.

North, R.C. *Moscow and Chinese Communists*. Stanford, 1965.

Ogata, S.N. *Defiance in Manchuria*. Berkeley, 1964.

Palmer, Norman D. *Sun Yat-sen and Communism*. New York, 1960.

Peck, Graham. *Two Kinds of Time*. Boston, 1967, 2nd revised edition.

Peking Metropolitan Police Headquarters. *Soviet Plot in China*. Peiping, 1927, documents siezed from the Soviet Embassy.

Pepper, Suzanne. *Civil War in China*. Berkeley 1978.

Pickowicz, P. G. *Marxist Literary Thought in China: the influence of Ch'u Ch'iu-pai*. Berkeley, 1981.

Price, Jane. *Cadres, Commanders, and Commissars*. New York, 1976.

Rigby, R.W. *The May 30th Movement: Events and Themes*. Canberra, 1980.

Roy, M.N. *Revolution and Counter Revolution in China*. Calcutta, 1946.

Selle, E.A. *Donald of China*. New York 1948.

Seybolt, Peter J. "The Yenan Revolution in Mass Education," *China Quarterly*, no. 48, 1971.

Shirley, J. R. "Control of the KMT after Sun Yat-sen's death," *Journal of Asian Studies*, vol. 25, no. 1, November 1965.

————. "Factionalism and the Left KMT." *Studies on Asia*, vol. 5, 1965.

Sih, Paul T.K. *Nationalist China during the Sino-Japanese War, 1937–1945.* Nw York, 1977.

So Wai-chor. "Organization and power base of the Kuomintang Left 1928–1931." A paper delivered at the Fifth National Conference of the Asian Studies Association of Australia. Adelaide, May 1984.

Strand, David. *Rickshaw Beijing, City People and Politics in the 1920's.* Berkeley 1989.

Thaxton, Ralph. *China Turned Rightside Up.* New Haven, 1983.

Tien Hung-mou. *Government and Politics in Kuomintang China, 1927–1937.* Stanford, 1972.

Townsend, J.R. *Politics in China.* New York, 1974.

Van Vleck, B.G. "Michael Borodin: Soviet Adviser to Sun Yat-sen. M.A. thesis, Florida Atlantic University, June, 1977.

Vishnyakova-Akimova, V.V. *Two Years in Revolutionary China, 1925–1927.* Cambridge, Mass., 1971.

Wang, Y.C. *Chinese Intellectuals and the West.* Chapel Hill, 1966.

Wasserstrom, J.N. *Student Protests in Twentieth-century China: the view from Shanghai.* Stanford, 1991.

West, Philip. *Yenching University and Sino-Western Relations 1916–1952.* Cambridge, Mass., 1976.

White, T., and Jacoby, A. *Thunder out of China.* New York, 1946.

Whiting, Allen S. *Soviet Policies in China 1917–1924.* Stanford, 1968.

Wilbur, C. Martin. *Sun Yat-sen, Frustrated Patriot.* New York, 1976.

Williamson, T. M. "Political training and work at the Whampoa Military Academy prior to the Northern Expedition." Doctoral dissertation, Duke University, 1976.

Yi Mu, and Mark V. Thompson. *Crisis at Tiananmen.* San Francisco 1990.

Young, Arthur N. *China's Nation Building Effort.*(Stanford, 1971.

Young, Arthur N. *China's Wartime Finance and Inflation 1937–1945.* Cambridge, Mass., 1965.

Index